# SIBERIAN DREAMS

# SIBERIAN DREAMS

Andy Home

Siberian Dreams
1st Edition
Date 2007

Published by Eye Books Ltd
8 Peacock Yard
London
SE17 3LH
Tel: +44 (0) 845 450 8870
website: www.eye-books.com


ISBN 10:   1 903070 51 1
ISBN 13:   978 1 903070 51 2

British Library Cataloguing in Publication Data
A catalogue record for this book is available from the British Library


Set in Frutiger, ITC Garamond and Helvetica Inserat
Cover design by Peter Scott

Printed and bound in Denmark by Nørhaven Paperback A/S

# SIBERIAN DREAMS

Andy Home

Published by Eye Books

# Dedication

To John Pilkington, founder of the Journey of a Lifetime Award, and the Royal Geographical Society, for believing that the world must always be re-discovered.

# CONTENTS

# CONTENTS

# INTRODUCTION

I first heard about the *Journey of a Lifetime* award from a friend.

Fifteen years of comfortable middle-class life in a leafy suburb of London had recently dissolved into bankruptcy and redundancy, both of my employer and my personal relationship. Forcing myself to focus on the dwindling positives in my life – free time, no commitments, and a hard-fought-for but ultimately generous pay-off – I'd decided to take a year out of the rat race and fulfil some long-cherished travel schemes.

That year had passed wonderfully but all too quickly and I'd returned from my journeying to try and figure out what to do with the second part of my life. I was contemplating my long-out-of-date CV when the phone rang.

My friend Pete had just heard about the *Journey of a Lifetime* award on Radio 4. A joint annual initiative between the BBC and the Royal Geographical Society, the deal is deceptively simple. You write in with the details of the journey you'd most like to make, and if they like your idea more than anyone else's, you get £4,000 to undertake it and make a radio programme for the BBC about your experiences.

'You could go to that place in Russia you're always banging on about,' Pete said.

It's not every day you get offered money to take your trip of a lifetime. It seemed ridiculous NOT to write in, particularly since I was struggling to think of how exactly I was going to pick up the pieces of my shattered life. My 'journey of a lifetime' might be bizarre enough to at least catch someone's eye in the hundreds of application letters that would flood in to the Royal Geographical Society.

What Pete said was true. I had been banging on about the place for years. What had started as a joke among work colleagues – 'Behave, or I'll send you on a fact-finding mission to Norilsk!' – had slipped unnoticed into my sub-conscious over the course of time. Not strong enough to be called accurately an obsession, it had nevertheless become a familiar part of my mental furniture, a curiosity to be trotted out occasionally during late-night ramblings with friends about weird travel destinations.

I admit I was unusual in even knowing of the existence of this mining city in Russia's frozen Siberian expanses. I only did so thanks to my career as a financial journalist. I'd written about commodity markets and then I'd progressed to managing other people who wrote about commodity markets. Oil, gas, grain, sugar, coffee, cocoa and rubber – most of us take them for granted, and most of us are blissfully unaware of the powerful forces that make these building blocks of life some of the most volatile markets in the ever-expanding world of global trading.

My area of special expertise encompassed the markets for industrial metals such as copper, aluminium, nickel and zinc, the raw materials that invisibly facilitate much of our modern, day-to-day life.

Norilsk is a massive producer of metals. Inside the Arctic Circle, literally in the middle of nowhere, some 200,000 inhabitants live and work around its sprawling network of mines and metallurgical factories. Winter lasts eight months. Temperatures drop to levels I find impossible to get my head round. It has periods of both twenty-four-hour night and, during the brief summer, twenty-four-hour daylight. It's the biggest single source of industrial pollution in Russia, which means it's off the scale of any other developed country.

The more I'd written about the metals that spewed out of this Siberian giant, the more I'd wondered about the people who lived there. My career as a financial journalist had not been planned. It had resulted from a couple of fortuitous turns in an otherwise directionless path. Was that also how you ended up working in a polluting metals plant in what must be a strong candidate for the world's grimmest city? And if a couple of life's rolls of the dice had brought you there, why on earth would you stay?

With my growing curiosity about life in this alien city had come a different set of questions. Questions about Russia. Norilsk's history is as alien as its climate, but it is one that has melded the place into a refracted Siberian reflection of Russia's uniquely weird development over the second half of the twentieth century.

From a gleam in Josef Stalin's eye in the 1930s, Norilsk was born as a prison camp in the Soviet gulag system and remained so until after his death in the 1950s. Then, like many other camps, it metamorphosed into a closed city, part of the Soviet Union's huge military-industrial complex, near invisible to outside eyes. Only with the fall of the Berlin Wall in 1989, and the resulting tidal wave of change that swept eastwards, did Norilsk emerge into at least partial daylight.

Its only customer, the Soviet military, had just gone out of business and it survived in the only way it could, by exporting its metals to the West, to us. It was still touch and go as to whether it would survive, though. There were times in the 1990s when the miners weren't paid for months, the power stations were failing and the company which ran the whole place, Norilsk Nickel, was technically bankrupt. And to rub salt into the wound, most Russians had just seen their savings wiped out, which meant that no one had any money to leave Norilsk, whether they wanted to or not.

Since then, though, it had hauled its way back into profitability thanks to the intervention of the enigmatic Interros Group, the corporate embodiment of one of Russia's new oligarchs.

The multiple personality changes of this far-flung city made me come to view Norilsk as an Arctic palimpsest of all the drunken lurches in Russia's stagger to the new millennium.

I had never been to Russia. I consider myself both a moderately literate and well-travelled man, but Russia in any living sense was a void to me. Beyond a schoolboy knowledge of its history and a lot of dry financial facts and figures, my visualisation of the place didn't extend much beyond a random collage of parts of the film *Doctor Zhivago*, a few of the James Bond series, and footage of the May Day parades in Red Square with all those missile launchers rolling past.

That last bit, of course, was also the main reason for my almost complete lack of knowledge about the country. It's easy now to forget how long the Soviet Union was our enemy, that swathe of red sprawling across the pages of the atlas, making Western Europe look like a small, messy disintegration of land into the sea. Generations of us lived under the threat of nuclear obliteration by this menacing eastern giant. What else were those May Day parades about, if not a blunt way of saying, 'Look how many tanks and missile launchers we have'?

When the Soviet Union finally collapsed under its own inert weight in the early 1990s, Russia was welcomed back by the rest of the world as a long-lost relative. I happened to be in Rome when President Gorbachev visited the city. Hundreds of thousands of people lined the streets to hail this liberator of the East.

But the public interest didn't last more than a handful of years of curiosity – 'So, how have you been all this time?' – before it shifted elsewhere. The typically Russian shambles of a coup attempt in 1991 seemed to reassure the rest of the world that the country could safely be left to shuffle along in its own chaotic way without too much scrutiny.

Friends went on weekend city-breaks to Moscow and more so to St Petersburg. Everyone told me I should go and see the Hermitage museum. But I didn't want to go and see the pre-Revolution palaces of the Tsars. These buildings, however impressive their façades and however delightful their interiors, would not help me find out about the Russians. Who the hell were these people who had been my enemy for half a century? And what were they up to now? Was life good? Was it better than it had been?

If I was going to get any insight at all into this country of 200 million people which Winston Churchill described as 'a riddle wrapped in a mystery inside an enigma', I would have to go to somewhere I could peek up Mother Russia's skirts.

Norilsk, I reckoned, was the perfect vantage spot – half a

continent distant from Moscow but with a history completely intertwined with the arrhythmic heartbeat of the Kremlin. The hardy souls of Norilsk could tell me a bit about what life was like as a Russian. Norilsk was my dream 'journey of a lifetime'. I wanted to go to Norilsk and ask people there what their dreams were.

There was a practical problem, however, which was my almost total lack of Russian. So I asked a Russian friend and former colleague to apply with me. Grigori liked the idea a lot. He had his own reasons for wanting to go back to see what Russia was like.

The Royal Geographical Society and the BBC liked the idea a lot as well. Frankly, I'm fairly confident that among the 600 or so applicants for the 2003 award they received only one letter asking to go to a Siberian industrial mining city. I suspect they hadn't received one before and they haven't since.

My girlfriend told me I was 'off my rocker' when I explained to her what I was going to do. I didn't begrudge her the reaction. I heard it in various forms in the time between being told we'd won the *Journey of a Lifetime* award and actually setting off in May 2003. 'But you could have gone anywhere!' wailed another friend in disappointed disbelief.

Grigori and I went on a training day at the BBC and were given a crash course in recording for radio. Within a few days I'd forgotten most of what they'd told us and was only left with the memory of how many times both of us had messed things up in our practice sessions.

The following is an account of what happened to us on the journey. I have taken some minor liberties with the time sequencing for dramatic effect and have edited the transcript both for reasons of comprehensibility and to excise moments of stupidity and/or inarticulacy. Otherwise, it is a truthful account of our experiences.

# GETTING THERE
## The Man in the Ministry

We are sitting nervously in a small anteroom next to the office of one of the most powerful men in Russia and he is keeping us waiting. 'We' are myself, Grigori and Sergey and 'he' is Dmitry Zelenin, the man who will decide whether we get to go to Norilsk.

Grigori is my co-traveller on this trip. Born in Moscow, he has twice left his native Russia, first as an émigré Jew in the 1970s and then at the end of the 1990s after several years of growing disillusionment with the new, post-Berlin Wall Russia.

If I have the role of 'stupid white man' on this journey, Grigori plays the part of 'wise native guide'. This will suit him, because somewhere in his kaleidoscopic life, with stints in two different armies, three marriages, books of poetry in Russian and English, a job as a street cleaner and, perhaps most bizarrely, a sideline in playing trumpet in a 1960s Soviet jazz band, there was also, I'm pretty sure, some acting involved. I can't say for certain. I find it hard to remember all Grigori's life-stages.

In many ways, he has been my guide to Russia since our paths first crossed in the early 1990s. I was then a reporter for a now-deceased financial news-wire. As our Moscow Correspondent, he had been a willing and concise teacher of how in Russia nothing was ever quite what it seemed. In his country, the 'news', particularly political and financial news, was little more than 'noise', a distraction from any useful analysis, he used to explain. Day-to-day events were merely a hall-of-mirrors distortion of deeper-lying realities. But looked at from the right angle, they could also be a prism through which to see a constantly shifting game of power, politics and money.

Grigori is on this trip to test his own ambivalent feelings

about his mother country. For me, it's precisely his combustible mixture of pride, fear and loathing of Russia that makes him such an invaluable guide.

I also need someone who speaks Russian because I'm not sure how far I'll get in this vast country with only four words – 'yes', 'no', 'vodka' and 'cheers'. As well as his mother tongue, Grigori is fluent in English, although sometimes his dilettantish past means he has a tendency towards the poetic, which is often amusingly juxtaposed to what he is actually saying. I regret that my almost complete lack of Russian prevents me from knowing whether he talks this way in both languages or just in English.

But Grigori, like a lot of Russians, has not been to Siberia. And that's why Sergey is the third man on our expedition.

Sergey comes from Irkutsk in eastern Siberia. He'd been a photographer for the official Soviet Tass news agency before he moved to Moscow and started working with Grigori as a journalist. He's been at least twice to the North Pole, and he's been to Norilsk a couple of times as well, which should come in handy.

Grigori has told me that Sergey smashed his skull in a climbing accident and has a large metal plate in his head, sitting beneath his mini bearskin of dark hair. Sometimes it makes him 'a bit funny', Grigori added conspiratorially.

Grigori also frequently tells Sergey he looks like 'a Georgian' because of his bushy moustache. This makes them both laugh a lot. It's a Russian thing.

The last time they met was a couple of years ago, when they cycled the length of the UK from Land's End to John O' Groats in eight days. Cycling is Sergey's *big thing*. When we were all working together back in the 1990s, I was once taken aback to learn that Sergey was going to use his two-week holiday to go for a cycling trip in Mongolia. Now, *that* is a Siberian thing.

## Closed City

Sergey is our Mr Fix-It on this journey. And his first task is to help us get some permits to go to Norilsk.

The city of Norilsk is not only absurdly remote, even by

Russian standards, but it and the port of Dudinka nearby are now also 'closed to foreigners', part of a discreet closing of the curtains that is creeping across Russia.

'Closed' cities are supposed to be a thing of the past. Pre-1989 they were dotted throughout the then Soviet Union, coming together in occasional clusters in particularly remote regions of the red empire. In Russia itself, they included really big cities such as Krasnoyarsk, Vladivostok and Perm. Access was denied to anyone carrying a foreign passport. In most cases access to Russians was also denied.

Norilsk had been one of these cities. Controlled by the Ministry of Defence, the metals from its labyrinth of underground mines in the Arctic Circle were channelled through a secret grid of other closed cities to be used in the Soviet Union's voracious arms industry.

All that changed after 1989. The 'closed' cities were opened, an internal blossoming to match the sudden unveiling of Russia itself. Article 27 of Russia's new constitution guaranteed complete freedom of movement to 'everyone legally present in the Russian Federation', regardless of citizenship.

The new openness didn't last very long, because in 1992 the then prime minister, Yegor Gaidar, signed Decree No. 450, limiting access once again to some 'sensitive' areas, those close to key borders or near military facilities. The decree was updated every couple of years throughout the 1990s, each revision adding a few more names to the list of no-go zones.

The Atomic Energy Ministry and the Defence Ministry also reserved the right to close off key installations and the towns around them. The Atomic Energy Ministry has published details of ten such places. The Defence Ministry says its information is a state secret and won't say how many it has re-closed.

The thing about Norilsk, though, is that it asked to be re-closed. The company that controls the city, Norilsk Nickel, applied to Moscow in 2001 to have itself locked away again from the outside world. It cited the recent influx of 'foreigners', economic migrants from former Soviet republics far away in the South – Azerbaijan in particular. Mostly unable to find long-term employment in the company's mines and factories, they

3

formed a sub-class of vagrants and criminals, the company and the city officials told Moscow. Heroin, a commodity previously unknown in the Arctic North, had insidiously crawled its way into the community, they said. Crime, also a rarity in the old days, had grown at alarming rates, they said.

At least 40,000 local people agreed with them. That's how many apparently[i] signed a petition asking for the ban on 'foreigners'. That's just over one in five people living in Norilsk and its satellite towns.

The Russian government agreed, and within months old-style travel restrictions were put back in place and the city started disappearing from view back into the Arctic snow whence it had briefly emerged. To get there now you need a special permit. There are only two ways to get a permit: be related to someone in the city, or get an official invitation from Norilsk Nickel itself.

And although the travel ban applies to all 'foreigners', there's 'foreigners' and then there's *foreigners*. In the case of Norilsk, this is not a simple return to the days when 'closed' cities were sealed off to keep away prying Western eyes. 'Foreigners' from Europe, North America and Japan are welcome in Norilsk, particularly if they are bankers, equipment suppliers, technical consultants or, best of all, buyers of the company's metals. The ban really only applies to *foreigners*, those from the periphery of Russia's once sprawling empire.

But you still need a permit. Or that is, I need a permit. So does Grigori, and so does Sergey.

The issue of the permits has loomed ever larger in our planning of this journey, a black dot on the horizon that has grown steadily over the preceding year to assume truly monstrous proportions.

'What about the permits?' I asked Grigori when we first sat down and talked about the idea of travelling to Norilsk as a journey of a lifetime. He told me enquiries would be made via Sergey.

A few weeks later, he told me the company was keen to invite us 'to make a programme for the BBC' and getting the permits would be no problem.

The issue naturally arose in our interview with the Royal

Geographical Society and the BBC on the hallowed ground of the Society's Victorian brick headquarters on Kensington Gore in the heart of London. Grigori told them what he'd told me. I nodded in what I hoped was a reassuringly confident way.

Three months later and one month before our flight to Moscow, still no permits. Grigori told me there had been 'a little problem', three words which caused my stomach to start tightening.

The 'little problem' was a very Russian problem. Norilsk Nickel was only too happy to give us the permits, but the Duma, Russia's parliament, had passed a new law on travel restrictions to closed cities which in turn meant new paperwork. But President Vladimir Putin hadn't signed the law, meaning it could not officially be enacted. The company didn't want to issue us with the old permits in case they were rendered obsolete by the new permits.

'When's Putin expected to sign the law?' I asked Grigori. He shrugged. 'Who knows? It's already been waiting several months for him to sign.'

It was not the answer I wanted to hear.

On 18 May 2003 we left for Moscow. We did not have the special permits for travel to Norilsk. I heard the beating black wings of suppressed panic following me up the steps onto the plane. Our budget for the trip was £4,000. An eighth of that was already spent on the flights to Moscow. I didn't relish going back to the BBC and telling them we'd need some more money because we didn't get our permits.

Grigori was all breezy confidence, telling me everything would work out. 'You'll see!' Anyway, he said, Moscow would be good acclimatisation for me before I went to Norilsk. 'So you can see the place like a Russian!'

Maybe...

## Moscow

You don't so much drive in from Moscow airport to the city, rather it races out to meet you. The commercial sprawl seems to be dashing to break free into the birch forests that surround the Russian capital. Some of it is still half-built. Through the

5

steel skeleton of what will be a space-age superstore, I catch glimpses of fields and small clusters of dismal-looking tower blocks.

A massive, shiny-new Ikea with a giant banner proclaiming 'WE'RE GOING TO THE DACHA!' is still surrounded by half-waterlogged fields. Assorted cows stand chewing the cud and contemplating this wondrous addition to their landscape.

A few miles from the airport Grigori points out the famous tank-traps set in the road, marking the point just ten miles outside Moscow where the German army ground to a halt in the Second World War. A couple of hundred yards further on a gleaming McDonald's beams down ironically on this memorial to Soviet sacrifice.

It's only a few minutes after this new landmark of consumer capitalism that we hit the first of a series of seemingly interminable traffic jams. As our progress slows to a near standstill, Sergey entertains us with the story that has gripped Moscow for the last few days. Grigori translates for me.

The 8 May Victory Day Celebrations had been thrown into chaos by a homesick soldier going AWOL in possession of an army oil tanker. He had taken a wrong turning on the ring-road trip to his mother's apartment and had started heading for the centre of town and the official celebrations. In a city that has seen Chechen rebels take hostage an entire cinema, this had understandably caused something of a panic and had led to a spectacular televised car chase with the police shooting out the tanker's tyres, only for them to automatically inflate as apparently they are designed to do.

'Good Russian technology,' Sergey and Grigori nod in agreement at this stage.

Anyway, the speeding reservist had only been stopped when the police had set up a roadblock improvised from bulldozers.

'And just because he missed his mother,' Grigori translates the punch line.

The Russians in the car, including the driver, think this is just the funniest thing they've heard. There's a lot of laughing.

'Didn't the guy think it was strange that he was being shot

at?' I ask 'He was probably drunk, maybe something more… anyway, he's a soldier, he's used to being shot at,' Grigori manages to reply through splutters of laughter.

It's the first example of Russian humour I've encountered in the raw. As I realise over my ensuing time in the country, Russian jokes always seem to be tinged with a darkness that adds a new dimension to what we Brits like to boast is our own black sense of comedy.

Moscow is huge. Or maybe it just feels that way if you're stuck in a traffic jam most of the time. It's obvious the last few years have been good for the advertising industry since large parts of the city are dripping with billboards and neon signs. Behind this recently acquired glitz, though, the city is still largely a vision of Soviet planning – an endless jigsaw of grey, utilitarian, concrete buildings.

After an hour and a half of inching through traffic, we reach a purely residential area which is where Sergey lives and where we'll live until we get our permits for Norilsk. *If* we get our permits for Norilsk…

The vista is one of countless apartment blocks stretching down wide roads that disappear over the horizon in canyons of brick and glass.

The car finally stops in front of a couple of particularly kicked-in looking buildings. After unloading ourselves and our luggage, we stand on the walk-way leading up to the front entrance and decide to have a go at recording our first impressions of our new temporary home.

Grigori and I have an abiding mistrust of the equipment we've been given, having managed to accidentally erase whole tracks during our practice day with the BBC. At this stage our comments to the mike are interspersed with panicky exclamations such as, 'Is it still on?' and 'Why's it blinking like that?' Nor have we got used to each other's speaking rhythms. The recordings are full of long breaks when one of us has stopped talking and the other one is respectfully waiting for the flow of words to continue before realising it's his turn. Over the first few days of our trip we evolve our own non-verbal system of meaningful glances and nods to indicate the recording baton is about to be passed back.

---

*Transcript.*
*Moscow.*
*Arrival at Sergey's flat.*

Grigori: *We've arrived at an apartment block about forty minutes from central Moscow. We're very near the edge of Moscow. It's where ordinary Muscovites live. I can assure you no tourists or Western businessmen come here.*

Andy: *I guess I'd describe the building as a medium high-rise, about twelve stories high. It looks as if it's seen a little bit better days.*

Grigori: *It's Brezhnev style, 1980s, so they really look pretty awful.*

Andy: *They look as if someone's just kicked the crap out of them.*

Grigori: *A similar area in London would be working class but here it isn't the case. There are hardly any working-class people left in the city, it's intelligentsia and middle class in these areas.*

Andy: *There are people I would regard as looking very poor, they're in tracksuit bottoms and such. Frankly, they look like muggers. But they're standing next to people looking very posh. Everyone's mixed together. I couldn't say whether they're working class or middle class. And all sorts of nationalities, that's something I've really noticed here.*

Grigori: *Just people hanging out. It's all very sociable.*

Andy: *On the other side of that road over there? Are those ponds and lakes?*

Grigori: *There is a park and the remains of a village built by Catherine the Great for one of her lovers. The story is, she and her lover fell out and she ordered it to be destroyed but she died before she could do so. It's eighteenth century. Most buildings built by Khrushchev and Stalin have already collapsed but those from Catherine the Great's time are still standing.*

Andy to Sergey: *Is this a safe place to live?*

Sergey via Grigori: *It's perfectly safe. There is no crime here. Okay, if you get involved with some market-place traders, like shaking them down or something, you may get killed or whatever. But if you're just a normal citizen living here, you're much safer than in most European towns.*

Andy to Sergey: *How much does it cost to live here?*

Sergey via Grigori: *$350 per month. (Sergey shrugs his shoulders philosophically). It's okay. It's medium.*

Andy: *If you were standing in a place like this in the UK, you'd see graffiti, you'd have vandalism, you'd be running away from the kids, you'd...*

Grigori: *... you'd be standing without your trousers.*

Sergey's ground-floor flat is cosy enough inside. One bedroom, one lounge (our bedroom), a small bathroom and a kitchen. In the hallway are three bicycles.

Grigori laughs at me for taking off my shoes and producing a pair of slippers from my travel bag. Then Sergey tells him to take his shoes off whenever he comes into the flat. I grin. A small one for the Stupid White Man!

We celebrate our arrival in Russian style. Sergey produces a roast chicken, a range of smoked fish, cold meats, salads and fresh black bread and lays it on the small table. He takes a bottle of vodka out of the freezer, provoking a long and detailed conversation in Russian between him and Grigori.

Grigori finally turns to me and says the vodka is a new brand which has just been launched and is apparently very good. It is called 'Stalin'. It is made to Uncle Joe's favourite recipe. What would the great leader have made of his name being used as a marketing brand, I wonder. For that matter, what do I make of drinking a vodka named after a psychotic mass murderer?

The vodka is very good, though. Crystal clear and clean tasting. It goes well with the food. The shots, which apparently always require a toast, build to a warming sensation of well-being that gradually spreads up from the pit of my stomach to my head. The three of us finish two 500ml bottles before Grigori and I get into our makeshift sleeping accommodation in Sergey's front room.

The kitchen becomes the communal meeting room over the next couple of days as Sergey works away at his contacts to get us our permits. He's also trying to fix up an interview with one of the former Soviet-era managers of Norilsk who is now based in Moscow. This all means a certain amount of pottering time for Grigori and me as we adjust to life in our new surroundings… a Brezhnev-era tower block on the edges of Moscow.

I'm immensely frustrated by this hanging around and only just managing to keep at bay a growing anguish that we're not going to get the permits. We've booked return tickets to London in two weeks' time. Every hour spent here is an hour not spent where we're supposed to be… in Norilsk itself.

I drink black tea with Grigori at the kitchen table. I try and concentrate on reading the books about Siberia I've brought with me. I begin the audio journal I've agreed to keep during our *journey of a lifetime'*.

But as idle hour follows idle hour, I also start to realise that Grigori was right in what he said about acclimatisation. I don't notice it to begin with, but this highly unusual first experience of Russia is starting to prise away layers of preconception and misperception.

In addition to the shoes rule, Sergey insists that any cigarettes be smoked outside. For me this involves regular trips to one of the communal porches that project from the front wall by every entrance to the block. This becomes my vantage point for starting to learn how they live here in Moscow.

The porches themselves look a bit like rural bus shelters, a wooden bench running down one of the concrete sides, the other side open to the pathway. They prove to be hives of sociability for residents of the tower block. The complexion of the occupants changes over the course of the day. From Babushka grandmothers in the morning to guys watching guys mending their cars in the afternoon to kids in the early evening to their parents in the late evening.

The whole length of the block of flats is punctuated by these regularly spaced social gathering places. The next block is the same. All the blocks seem to have their own shifting pattern of porch socialites.

Opposite the flat, mothers supervise their children in a communal playground. Shoppers trudge down the street with bulging carrier bags. People walk their dogs. There are many breeds I've never seen before.

Sergey's street, like many running through this Soviet skyline of rectangles, is lined with lilac trees. It's spring in Moscow, the temperature's getting into the high twenties and the still faint smell of lilac drifts on the occasional breeze.

Far from being the bleak, wind-swept housing estate I'd expected on first sight, the place teems with life at just about every hour of the day. There is no graffiti. There are no broken windows. There are no menacing groups of hooded teenagers like those who instil a sense of watchful foreboding in any visitor to much of the UK's communal living space.

Evenings bring what looks like an ice-cream van to the end of the road. It is in fact selling alcohol and is crammed with bottles of beer, wine, vodka and alcopops. It is soon surrounded by a throng of people of all ages and all types – couples, families, groups of teenage girls, muscled men of conscription age.

It's as if someone has managed to remove the pub building, while leaving the customers doing exactly what they were doing. Everyone's just standing around chatting, drinking and smoking cigarettes. Beer seems to be the most popular drink, even with the women. Grigori tells me that it was strictly forbidden to drink alcohol in public under Soviet laws, so there's an element of lingering defiance about these open-air gatherings.

In fact, they're a hallmark of Moscow, as I find out the next day when Grigori takes me on a whistle-stop tour of the city centre. As well as the numerous bars and restaurants in the centre of town, Moscow is sprinkled with groups of outdoor drinkers standing around alcohol kiosks or one of the vans. I never witness any trouble among any of these groups, even late at night, which is only surprising if you come from England.

From Sergey's apartment on the very outskirts to the centre of Moscow is a forty-minute journey on the underground system. To someone who lives in London the Moscow tube system is a wondrous revelation. A Stalinist showpiece, the stations are lined with marble columns and the trains run with almost unbelievable regularity. Every platform has a small electronic display at one end, counting down the minutes and seconds to the next arrival. I become fixated by these ticking numbers as we criss-cross the central underground system. I never see any of them start from over two minutes.

The centre of the city is bustling with activity. The pavements are heaving with well-dressed men and women and the streets are filled with cars locked in the ebb and flow of what appears to be semi-permanent traffic gridlock.

Grigori shows me the tourist sights, which in Moscow largely means the Bolshoi Theatre, Red Square and the Lubyanka.

The Bolshoi Theatre is a rare burst of neoclassical architecture in the sprawl of Soviet greyness. Its columned portico and geometrically perfect, tree-lined square and fountains are a distant echo of cities closer to home at the western end of our shared continent. But here in this city, the Mediterranean grandiosity of the design simply makes the Theatre look out of place and out of time, as if it's been thoughtlessly transplanted from somewhere completely different.

Red Square looks drab next to the pulsating streets around it. It doesn't help that St Basil's Cathedral is partially draped with green netting for renovation work. Nor that one end of the Square is dominated by a huge stage being put up for a concert by Paul McCartney. I wait for a sense of history to surge up in me. It doesn't.

Grigori tells me the folkloric history of St Basil's Cathedral. Apparently it was built on the instructions of Ivan the Terrible who was so pleased with it that he had the architect blinded so he couldn't ever repeat his success.

I'm faintly shocked by the story. Upon reflection, I realise that it is not so much the cruel act itself that disconcerts me as the fact that this is still the conventional tourist commentary on the building. London's history is equally laden with its own historical horrors but the city has taken care to overlay them with a gaudy veneer of union jack T-shirts and plastic policemen's helmets in a very twentieth-century display of prurience.

Moscow has no such embarrassment about its blood-soaked past, which is why the Lubyanka is also one of the top tourist spots in the Russian capital.

The Lubyanka, the dreaded headquarters and prison of the KGB, the former secret police, is now everyone's favourite photo opportunity. The building is imposing enough with its carefully planned symmetry of windows and lines, but the jaunty yellow paintwork jars with the knowledge of what terrors it has witnessed over the years.

Grigori insists on taking a photograph of me in front of it. Passers-by laugh and smile appreciatively. 'Everyone does this... that's why they're laughing,' says Grigori.

No one seems to mind that the KGB's successor, the Federal Security Service Directorate (FSB) still uses it as its headquarters.

Moscow is evidently going through something of a boom time. It has the vibrancy that comes with money being made and lots of it.

I guess I expected a dour post-Soviet city of downtrodden workers and streets empty of life apart from the odd wheezing Soviet-designed car. What I get is designer shops, conspicuous wealth and sports utility vehicles.

My discomfort in just how wrong I have been about this place is partly lifted by the fact that Grigori seems even more surprised at what Moscow has become.

The last time he lived here was in the early 1990s in the days following the disintegration of the former system. Russia's new leadership proved completely unprepared for the cataclysm that had befallen it.

Gorbachev, after all, had only meant to prise open the door a little to let in some fresh air. The resulting whirlwind had flung him and the rest of the party apparatus to the other side of the room.

The subsequent economic collapse and 'shock therapy'[ii] managed to wipe out just about everyone's savings, stop pensioners being paid and bring large parts of the country's industry to a grinding halt due to a massive collective liquidity freeze.

In return for Soviet-era security, Moscow's citizens got 'Wild East Capitalism'. Gun-battles raged through the city as the financial carve-up of the former Soviet Union was fought out. Conflict on the street between black-market gangs over drugs territory was mirrored by pent-house assassinations among the big money men trying to get their hands on the still-huge Soviet raw materials industries.

Most businesses, including those set up by Western companies, were expected to pay protection money. One of the first commodity trading companies to set up business in Moscow at the time was subjected to a terrifying attack by hooded armed men, who viciously beat up several staff members. It was said they hadn't paid. Or maybe they'd just crossed someone they shouldn't have crossed.

Even a taxi ride from the airport to the city centre amounted to a flirt with real danger. The bodies of several unsuspecting Western businessmen had been found at quiet spots just outside the city's perimeter. Everyone got a friend or hired car to meet them at the terminal building, which is exactly what we had done of course.

It wasn't too safe for financial journalists back then either. Grigori had the good sense to locate our Moscow news bureau in the grounds of a Central Asian embassy building – security included.

Grigori takes me for a beer at the five-star Meridian hotel and we sit in a cool marble-floored bar, listening to an assortment of ring tones from the mobiles clutched by the businessmen at the tables around us.

As we leave the hotel, Grigori stops in the lobby – 'the most dangerous place to be in Moscow back then,' he tells me with wide eyes and then a characteristic grin. This was a favourite spot for Russia's jostling would-be tycoons to be assassinated.

As we wind our way through a series of drinking holes

that evening, Grigori tells me repeatedly he can't believe the changes since he was last here. 'Everyone looks so content. Everyone looks so well off. Everything feels so safe.'

We put the last part to the test when we come out of the underground station back in Sergey's district later that night.

As we emerge from the stairs into the fresh night air, we come to a stop and look around us. We are faced with an endless mosaic of tower blocks of varied size and age. As far as the eye can see they stretch in every direction. Both of us scour the horizon for any landmarks.

We realise we haven't a clue how to navigate the intricate web of paths and small roads that criss-cross the blocks to find our way back to Sergey's.

The streets out here are much quieter now. There are no pedestrians and just the occasional car. The only people in sight are three particularly dishevelled-looking drunks sitting at the entrance to the tube station. Grigori is reluctant to engage them in conversation. He tells me he thinks they're from the Caucasus. I'm already learning that this is Russian shorthand for being a dangerous, drug-peddling terrorist.

But lacking any other obvious choice, Grigori reluctantly walks over to them and asks for directions. After several confirmations of the details, one of them staggers to his feet and accompanies us to the start of three footpaths leading into the maze. Although swaying gently in the night breeze, he gives us a coherent explanation of the complex route we have to follow, pausing occasionally to make sure Grigori has taken it all in. Waving us off, he wishes us good luck and returns to his two friends for a resumption of the animated conversation we had interrupted. Within ten minutes we've found our way home.

Jeez, even the drunks are helpful in this reborn city.

The next morning Sergey tells Grigori and me it is our turn to do the shopping while he finalises the deal that will see us get our permits issued. The supermarket is a five-minute walk away and in daylight we're confident of finding it. It proves to be an illumination to match anything I have yet experienced.

What was I expecting? Sheepishly, I have to admit my image of a Russian supermarket had got stuck in a bygone age sometime before 1989, when the vegetable section sold week-old cabbages, the meat section sold summer sandals and the fish section was permanently empty.

This, however, is of a size and splendour to match anything back home. The fresh fish section is selling fresh fish, the meat section is selling fresh meat and the delicatessen section is selling an intimidating selection of cold meats and cheeses.

The only noticeable difference from my local Waitrose is the inversion of space in the alcohol section. Where the wine should be – under small blackboard signs denoting country of origin – is the vodka section, stretching down the side of a whole aisle. The wines are limited to a few shelves tucked away at one end, just as the spirits section would be back home. We spend an inordinate amount of time trying to choose a vodka. In the end we decide on the Stalin brand. 'I tell you something about Stalin… he really knew his vodka,' Grigori tells me for the tenth time since we opened the first bottle.

We arrive back laden with food and elated by the unexpected cornucopia of a suburban Muscovite superstore.

Sergey adds to our good humour. The deal is on. Dmitry Zelenin will get us our permits. We get to interview Dmitry Zelenin in return.

### The Man in the Ministry

Zelenin is very rich. Not a billionaire but a multi-millionaire. He was president of finance at Norilsk Nickel between 1996 and 2001. He was part of a team of young technocrats brought in to manage the place when it was bought by the Interros Group. He's also a senior manager in Interros[iii], one of the mammoth financial and commercial groups that now control large swathes of the country's economy. Its interests range from industrial metals to insurance companies, from power plants to newspapers, from banking to ski resorts. Like most of these groups, ultimate power rests in the hands of one man at the very top, the oligarch Vladimir Potanin.

Zelenin is now vice-chairman of the Russian Sports Commission. Sergey works for him in a newly-launched marketing and publicity department. Zelenin is a very important man.

Will we be interviewing Zelenin or will he be interviewing us, I wonder?

But that's why the three of us are sitting in the anteroom to his office in the Ministry of Sports.

The ministry is located in the grounds of a nineteenth-century building that once belonged to a Russian count. The inside of the main building is entirely perfunctory and the whole ministry gives the impression that it has just requisitioned this place for a brief stay and will be moving somewhere else just as soon as it can. In fact, the only give-away that we are in the Sports Ministry at all is the huge amount of very conspicuous security.

Not wanting to be late for such an important meeting, we had over-compensated by arriving half an hour early. We killed time by strolling around the slightly ramshackle complex of courtyards and gardens. There's some half-hearted renovation work going on, which means that parts of the rambling compound look a bit dilapidated and mournful.

Our leisurely progress was monitored by a combination of green-uniformed guards and a variety of very hard-looking plain-clothes guys. The latter seemed to be everywhere, peering through windows, lurking around corners or standing like statues in the middle of one of the colonnaded mini-courtyards scattered through the grounds. They stared at us through plumes of smoke that trailed from the cigarettes they always seemed to be holding – as much a part of the equipment as the guns bulging in the breasts of their suits.

In the middle of the main courtyard, a dozen men in blue army camouflage were guarding and loading a twenty-tonne articulated truck. Grigori translated the Cyrillic lettering on the side. *'Extraordinary Situations Ministry – For the Serbs of Kosovo.'*

The translation brought a swell of further questions to my lips, but our curiosity was deterred by one of the guys in the snazzy blue camouflage gear turning round and scowling at us in a very meaningful way. We continued our stroll in a different direction.

The contrast with the rest of what I'd seen in Moscow could

not be sharper. Yes, most of the banks and money change places have an armed guard at the door. But their presence now has a somewhat token feel to it like the security desks in offices back home, and the pervasive criminal violence of the 1990s seems to have passed. The police spend most of their time trawling the streets in search of the new enemy. Several times already I've seen a hapless Armenian or Azerbaijani being led away protesting to the back of a van.

But here in the Ministry it feels like I'm on the set of a James Bond film. It's a Russian trait I'll come to know well during my stay here. Just when I start to readjust my perception of the place, it springs back with a rabbit punch!

Waiting for Zelenin to see us, Grigori and I fiddle nervously with our recording equipment which comprises a MiniDisc player and a couple of mikes. Designed for kids to listen to their favourite pop tracks, the technology has taunted and occasionally baffled two grown men.

We're all dressed in our Sunday best. I'm wearing the only suit and tie I've brought with me for the trip. Ditto Grigori. Sergey is outdoing us with an expensive-looking suit and a genuine Italian designer tie. Everyone in the Ministry is wearing Italian designer ties. That's because Dmitri Zelenin wears Italian designer ties.

Apparently Zelenin can tell a man's long-term prospects by what he's wearing. That's what he told the glossy magazine *Mercury* anyway. There was a big profile of Zelenin in an issue lying in Sergey's flat. Lots of pictures of him dressed in expensive-looking clothes, sitting inside one or another of his prized collection of antique cars. He was the first Russian to own a Bentley, apparently. He also collects horses – he's a fine judge of them, according to the Russian equivalent of *Hello*. Every morning when he gets up, he doesn't like to spend too much time thinking what to wear, so normally he chooses all his clothing each day from one designer – Armani one day, Gucci the next.

A bit like me then… but without the Italian brands. Also, like me, he's forty years old. But that, sadly, is the end of what we've got in common. Unlike me, he's already overseen the turnaround of two major Russian companies, dragging both from the brink of bankruptcy to profitability. The first was the old Soviet car company ZIL and the second was Norilsk Nickel.

Also unlike me, he appears to be running a government ministry, although why he wouldn't want to spend more time driving his cars and riding his horses is something of a mystery to me. Grigori's response is that Zelenin is being groomed by the Interros Group for something very special – a governorship of a territory, maybe even (Grigori's eyes widen at this point) prime minister!

After what seems ages but is probably only five minutes, a tall muscular woman with peroxide hair abruptly opens the door to let us into Zelenin's office.

The room is dominated by a large board table, or maybe that should be committee table, with enough space to sit twenty people. The walls are whitewashed and there is little excess furniture, reinforcing the impression that there's a certain impermanence to the Ministry's stay here.

After brief introductions and an exchange of cards...

*Dmitry V. Zelenin*
*Deputy Chairman*
*The State Committee of Russian Federation*
*for Physical Culture and Sport*

... Zelenin sits on one side with the powerfully-built blonde – his PA as it turns out – with the three of us sitting opposite him on the other side.

Zelenin looks younger than his age. He has film-star good looks, a square jaw and dark intelligent eyes. He's very smartly dressed but in a calculatedly understated way. You know his suit costs a lot of money but there's nothing flash about it. Same with the tie. It's as if someone very rich is trying to dress down.

He's an immediately likeable man. Also, unlike many senior Russian officials, he's a very approachable man. The interview is not pre-arranged, with the submission of written questions,

19

as is still often the norm for talking with high-ranking bigwigs in just about any walk of Russian life. He listens to the questions very closely, pauses to collect his thoughts before answering and replies in a very precise way.

My first strong impression is of a Russian chess grandmaster. Zelenin always seems to be working out the answer to the question you're going to ask next... planning... but that's what he's supposedly good at.

Just occasionally, something of a younger, slightly mischievous Dmitry makes a brief appearance... a wry smile or an occasional wink to imply some irony in what he's saying. But it's always quickly pulled back in again.

We start the interview in English, Zelenin speaking almost fluently, but on the first occasion he struggles to find the words to explain his thoughts, he asks to switch to Russian, which Grigori then translates.

And if you want to know how to be a multi-millionaire in Russia by the age of forty, the answer is it helps if you're a rocket scientist. Zelenin came from a family of engineers and studied applied mathematics at the Moscow Institute of Physics and Technology (the equivalent of MIT in the US) before working at the Scientific Research Institute of Aviation Systems. Which sounds damn close to being a rocket scientist to me!

Even as a research worker, he had been supplementing his income with a range of extra-curricular activities from mini-cabbing to tulip growing. When the Soviet Union's bankrupt economic system crumbled in on itself, Zelenin set up his own computer company. That somehow metamorphosed into a stake in two Russian banks, which somehow metamorphosed into the ZIL car company.

In 1996 his 'friend' Potanin asked him to become financial director of the Interros Group. Later that year Interros made its move on Norilsk Nickel and Zelenin was brought in as vice president finance. That's where he stayed, although, with a slightly dismissive gesture of the hand, he 'ran some other departments at various times'.

Newspaper and magazine articles about Interros' move on Norilsk Nickel, one of the undoubted jewels in the Soviet

Union's tatty industrial crown, almost always contain the word 'controversial'.

The original stake had been won through the 'controversial' loans-for-shares scheme. The idea had been sold to the then president, Boris Yeltsin, by young free-market visionaries, including among others a certain Vladimir Potanin, as a way out of the government's rolling financial crisis of the first half of the 1990s.

Fresh loans to the state were guaranteed against government holdings in key industrial enterprises. UNEXIMBANK, part of the Interrros Group, got thirty-eight per cent of Norilsk Nickel as surety against a $170m loan to the government. The loan was not repaid and the stake was sold at an auction in 1997, which is where things got a bit… well… controversial.

The auction was won by a company called Svift, which turned out to be a subsidiary of UNEXIMBANK. An audit committee of the Duma several years later said Norilsk Nickel had been sold for less than half of its value and questioned the relationship between Svift and the company, MFK Moscow Partners, which handled the auction and took the $500m deposit. MFK, like UNEXIMBANK, was part of the Interros Group, giving the unfortunate impression that the deposit had been lent from one arm of the company to another arm to support the winning bid of a third arm.

That's why the words 'loans-for-shares" are always accompanied by the word 'controversial'. Potanin and his Interros Group survived several investigations by Russia's prosecutor's office in the late 1990s.

But at least they seemed to know something about managing big enterprises. The previous management had reduced Norilsk Nickel to the point of near financial collapse.

In Russia's first panicked rush to privatisation, companies had been placed on a private footing whilst leaving the old Soviet-era management in charge. The so-called 'Red Directors' had zero experience of existence outside the controlled economy.

## Transcript.
## Interview Zelenin

Andy: *How can a company be reduced almost to a state of bankruptcy when it's sitting on such a gold mine of raw materials?*

Zelenin via Grigori: *If the management skims a certain part of capital, wasting it on projects not calculated properly, wasting it in other regions of Russia, things that have nothing to do with Norilsk Nickel, and these new projects demand more and more money and there is no money left so they cannot buy equipment and raw materials. Then along comes a little dip in the market price (for the metals) and they suddenly have no money to pay their workforce. The previous management had been used to the idea that no matter what happened, the state would bail them out. Most of them had worked in the Soviet times.*

*They also had the wrong export policy. They had a large number of sales agents. There was no consistent and consolidated sales policy. So the debts to banks, to suppliers and to the workforce became catastrophic and the company became totally non-liquid.*

*It was a time for some cardinal decisions but the previous management was not making any decisions. It was waiting for the state to bail them out. But the times had changed. The state was in no mood to give credit to anybody.*

*The state had also financed winter supplies to Russia's northern territories but it was no longer able to do that. So despite its high production the company was in a terrible state.*

Andy: *Were people not being paid?*

Zelenin via Grigori: *They were two and a half months in arrears, and since it is an isolated northern territory people need money at certain times to see them through the winter.*

(Think about not being able to pay your heating bill when

the temperature is -50°C outside. Think about your heating company not being able to pay its bills to the gas company. Then think about the gas company being part of Norilsk Nickel, which has no money left to pay any bills…

And then think that a flight out of Norilsk to anywhere costs two months' pay, which you haven't received… because your company has no money. Locked in a cycle of financial breakdown, you can't even leave).

Andy: *Did the workers really understand what was happening to them? Did they understand why they weren't being paid?*

Zelenin via Grigori: *No. The workforce could not understand why they were not being paid. They were used from Soviet times that somebody, the state, somebody, whoever, would help out. No one ever wondered where their wages came from, where the money came from.*

*In Soviet times half of the company's output was handed over to the state precious metals depository and then the state just paid back cash, not at market prices but according to their own idea of what Norilsk Nickel needed at the time.*

*So the workforce lived under the impression that it was the state that was paying their wages.*

Grigori: *I'm trying to imagine Norilsk Nickel as it was at the time. Not in a good state, huge debts, suddenly it was bought by a group of young people. You had to face the workforce. Could you describe what happened?*

Zelenin makes a comedy 'Has someone farted?' face and follows with one of his wry smiles.

Zelenin via Grigori: *It was not my first experience of managing a large production facility. I had managed ZIL the car-maker in Moscow. The workshops are smaller and less impressive but still it's a large industrial production unit.*

*Norilsk Nickel in 1996 had huge debts. Its debts exceeded*

*its annual turnover and the debts included wage arrears, debts to the regional budget and the federal budget and to suppliers.*

*The whole company was nothing but problems and the situation had been created by the previous management. So the new team of us young people had to face and solve these problems on every possible front.*

*The workforce did not take to the idea of these new owners. People in Norilsk are very proud and have a good idea of what they are. And the union there is the best organised union in the whole of Russia.*

*So we had to somehow come to terms with them in the process of pretty difficult negotiations.*

Grigori: *What happened when you people arrived? I heard there was an irate crowd and an effigy was burnt.*

Zelenin via Grigori: *It was much more quiet, much more decent than the stories people tell.*

*But every meeting was very tense both with management and the workforce. There was a special lack of understanding of the new ownership rules because that was very new to Russia then. The employees found it very difficult to understand that new management methods had to be introduced and new ways of budgeting.*

*The introduction of all these new ways met with stiff resistance. We had to take control of everything that was going on, always having to prove that what we were doing was right and correct.*

Grigori: *So you turned the company?*

Zelenin via Grigori: *Yes, the company corrected its situation. It didn't happen at once. It took about a year and a half. Within three to four months of acquiring Norilsk Nickel, an agreement with the unions was reached. Within a year's time, all the problems with the regional and federal budgets had been resolved. In a year and a half all the problems with the suppliers were sorted out.*

*And as Norilsk Nickel exports about ninety per cent of its output, the problem of exports had to be addressed. So we set up a company in London called Norimet as our sales agent to consolidate all the exports so all the sales were coming through a single channel now. That meant that money could be used to fulfil the budget that had been approved beforehand.*

*All the projects begun by the previous management not considered viable were closed down.*

(Interros used its ownership of the government's stake in Norilsk Nickel to oust those of the Red Directors that weren't prepared to bend with the new breeze of capitalism sweeping through the country.

A couple of die-hards, the most senior to be deposed, fought back half-heartedly through the courts but their efforts were small pinpricks on the leviathan of the Interros Group.

It probably didn't feel that way at the time, but the citizens of Norilsk may have got off lightly. The same battle between Red Directors and new investors waging across the country's equally giant aluminium industry was characterised by a bloody and ruthless campaign of intimidation and assassination).

Andy: *How do you persuade 200,000 people that everything they assumed in their lives has completely changed?*

Zelenin via Grigori: *That was not our task. Our task was to manage the company correctly and impose very strict financial rules.*

*The actual production side of the company was quite well set up and organised on a quite high technological level. The only problem was that the company engaged in activities that were not directly related to production. For example, it was responsible for the city of Norilsk and for transport in the region.*

*But it was not our task to educate people in market relationships. That was the task of the entire nation, the whole country.*

*Our employees were learning about new ways of doing things faster and faster. They had to think for the first time. The economy had changed and economic relationships had changed. The state was never going to help them.*

*Output and sales would now define how much money came into the company.*

Andy: *So when you have a former Soviet style city economy, where the company Norilsk Nickel is paying for all the social services, who pays for that now?*

Zelenin via Grigori: *The whole social sphere was handed over to the regional government budget about a year ago but there are still certain things that Norilsk Nickel pays for.*

*It's not just Norilsk. Reform of the communal sector is being decided now in Russia and it has still not been finalised.*

*We had a six-to-seven year programme, and step by step all activities not directly relevant to production were separated from the companies. But at the same time, each employee had a family, of course, which we could not suddenly break up.*

*So we had to think of a long-term strategy as well. That will mean forming work teams in central Russia and sending them to Norilsk to work there for six months. We're trying to test this system right now with repair work.*

*Life in Norilsk is very, very hard and the state we want to achieve is that people work in Norilsk but they actually live in central Russia. In the 1970s Canadian companies solved this problem in this way – they liquidated towns attached to mines.*

(Grigori and I catch each other's eye at this comment. Had we heard that properly?)

Grigori: *So eventually there will no Norilsk?*

Zelenin via Grigori: *Maybe it will take up to thirty years but that is the aim of the company at the moment.*

(Grigori and I are somewhat dumbfounded by this unexpected turn to the interview.

Sergey uses our momentary pause to ask a question. It's about whether Norilsk Nickel reflects the situation in the whole of Russia. Whether the people who can turn around a company like Norilsk Nickel are working in other parts of the Russian economy and government? Given the identity of Sergey's employer, I assume this is the question that Zelenin would like to be asked. He's nodding his head before the question is finished).

Zelenin via Grigori: *It's true we would like to change the situation. The people who have been through the school of working in Norilsk are capable of changing things in the rest of Russia.*

*The city of Norilsk and the company and everything that is happening there is very similar to what is happening in the rest of Russia in the social sphere, in management and in labour relations. It's there in the very consciousness of the people and their attitude to privatisation, the state's relationship to shareholders, to small- and medium-sized businesses, to political processes and to elections.*

*Norilsk is a region locked into itself. It is very isolated and that isolation results in the sense that it is a separate state with its own economic, political and social processes. It is both a small part of Russia but an entity in itself. For the managers who performed well in Norilsk, naturally they have the potential to help similar processes in other parts of Russia and other sectors of the economy.*

*What Russia depends on now is the speed with which small- and medium-sized business will expand. Large companies, large production units will continue working and producing. Nothing will happen to them. It's the small business sector that has all the potential.*

*So now decisions demonstrating strong political will are necessary, special decisions by the government in order to stabilise the whole of the Russian economy. Every possibility is there, we are waiting for the decisions...*

The last words are accompanied by a wink and one of Zelenin's quick-as-a-flash broad smiles. Without having to tell us the interview is formally over, it is clear that he has ended it on the note he intended and stands up to bid us farewell. After

27

brief handshakes we are escorted back out by the PA who has been taking notes throughout the interview.

Grigori and I think it has gone rather well and go to celebrate in a small outside bar, just down the road from the Ministry. However, we are slightly taken aback by one or two of Zelenin's comments. 'Are you sure he used the word liquidated?' I ask Grigori. 'Absolutely sure, I checked with him, you heard me.'

I wonder whether the 200,000 people living in Norilsk are aware of Moscow's plans for their future. I'm not sure how I feel about my 'journey of a lifetime' trip transmuting into a broadcast announcement of my destination's planned 'liquidation'.

I'm also immensely puzzled why a multi-millionaire businessman from the Interros Group is currently working as Deputy Chairman of the State Committee for Physical Culture and Sport. Grigori tells me that physical culture and sport are big things at the moment. The physical health of the nation is a core theme in Vladimir Putin's re-election campaign.

So? I ask Grigori. That still doesn't answer the question of why the Man in the Ministry is in the ministry in the first place. Sitting at a metal table outside a bar with our beers, I persuade Grigori to explain more about Zelenin's current posting for a wider audience.

---

**Transcript.**
**The Man in The Ministry**

Grigori: *I had a chat with some lads outside in the passage...*

(This is obviously a cover story to protect the innocent and all that.)

*... and it transpires that the Interros Group, which is the most powerful industrial and business group in Russia, has a long-term strategy, which is to select bright young people working in the group and place them in every possible local, federal government, and parliamentary*

*administration position, and as far as they can, help them progress in those structures.*

*The aim is that in the next five to ten years the group will have its own agents planted in every government agency, in parliament, everywhere.*

Andy with some incredulity: *Interros is placing its men to take over government?*

Grigori: *Yes. Well, probably. But when you ask people in Interros, they will tell you what they are trying to do is... you see, the situation in Russia is not as stable as they would wish. For instance, there might be a danger of re-nationalisation. So their idea of what they are doing with this strategy is that they are protecting their assets. They are ensuring they will have enough concealed power structure within the ruling elite of Russia to prevent unexpected dramatic changes in policy.*

What matters is what these people really believe. Are they sincere in their beliefs?

Like the man we just interviewed, they believe that their people, people who worked in Norilsk Nickel and managed to turn it round, these people have the potential to change everything for the better in the rest of Russia.

Maybe someone at the top has thoughts of power but a lot of people involved in this strategy believe they are doing a favour to the rest of Russia.

Andy: *Zelenin is Deputy Chairman of the Sports Committee. Is he running things?*

Grigori: *There is a man above him, the actual minister, a former ice hockey player. From what I hear he is not really up to the job, more a figurehead. He's terrified Zelenin has been planted there to push him out and replace him, so whenever Zelenin comes out with a new idea, the guy either kills it right away or pretends it's his own. But without Zelenin's brains he messes it up.*

Andy: *Is that how Russia works at the moment?*

Grigori: *Yes of course.*

Zelenin obviously felt the interview went okay as well. Our permits arrive via Sergey the next day. They allow a maximum stay of one week, starting 25 May.

## Red Director

My relief about getting our hands on the treasured documentation is tinged by nagging frustration that we have to spend a couple more days in Moscow before we can get to Norilsk itself.

Our attentions refocus on trying to get an interview with the other key character we're after for the programme. If Dmitry Zelenin represents the new era of Russian capitalism, Johnson Khagazheev represents the old face of Soviet belligerence.

He joined Norilsk Nickel in 1961 as a smelter worker and rose steadily through the ranks to be head of the company's totemic Nadezhda smelter in the 1980s. He left the company for another huge Soviet metals combine in 1986 and was brought back as general director by the Interros Group, probably as a symbol of continuity with a past paternalist authority.

If nothing else, he's a man who doesn't mince his words, and from what I've read his words are echoes of a *pre-glasnost* age. At the time of the city being closed in 2001, he was quoted as saying[iv] : 'Norilsk is only for Norilsk people... this is the will of the people... people shouldn't be allowed to just come and go freely.' Well, quite! You can't just have people making up their own minds where they want to live and work. Outrageous thought!

Now, Grigori tells me, Khagazheev is working on 'special long-term projects', which if it means anything close to what it means in Western companies, suggests his time left in Norilsk Nickel may be limited.

But Khagazheev is proving maddeningly elusive. A very Russian game of cat-and-mouse has been going on between Grigori and Sergey on one side and 'Former Comrade Khagazheev' on the other pretty much since we stepped off the plane at Moscow airport.

Since it seems a very post-modern thing that if you can't get an interview with someone, you might as well record yourself trying to get an interview, we do so. The interview, like just about everything else in Sergey's flat, takes place in the small kitchen. By this stage we're getting to grips with the conversation-into-the-mike thing but on this occasion the recording is interrupted several times by the fridge sparking unpredictably into life with a general rattling and slightly ominous clanking. Grigori tells me it's the sound of all Russian fridges. Even he starts cursing it, though, after its third uninvited contribution to our conversation.

Grigori leads in with the game-play to date.

---

*Transcript.*
*Moscow.*
*'Comrade Khagazheev'*

> Grigori: *It is 22 May. We are still in Moscow. And we've been waiting for two days now for a meeting with the legendary Johnson Khagazheev.*

Khagazheev was in charge of the construction and start-up of the Nadezdha smelter in Norilsk and he got it done. It's one of the wonders of the world and he had it built against all odds in horrendous conditions of permafrost, hurricane force winds, polar night.

He's been described to me as an explosive mixture of top-notch professionalism and sudden temperament. He comes originally from the Caucasus.

In my mind, he is a leader who can motivate a 100,000 strong workforce to self-sacrifice, a kind of industrial Alexander the Great, a man who can get things done on a major scale.

Until recently Khagazheev was the general manager of the Arctic Division of Norilsk Nickel and now he's in charge of planning the company's long-term strategy. He's moved to Moscow now.

And here a little problem seems to have developed.

(The astute reader will notice those three menacing words appearing again – 'a little problem'.)

Grigori: *Originally, when Khagazheev was first asked whether he'd like to see us, he said he'd be very happy to see people who are making a programme for the BBC. But as far as we understand, he is now having second thoughts, and the way we see it is, he is an old-style Soviet manager and he apparently thinks that as we come from England, from the BBC, so we must be spies.*

*But also it appears that he felt that he could get something out of this and what happened was that he requested an official letter from the BBC asking for an interview. And he said that the letter should specifically say that he is the 'legendary' Johnson Khagazheev and that he is such a genius in administration and played such an important role in Norilsk Nickel, that that's why we're asking to see him.*

*So…*

(Here, Grigori pauses for dramatic effect)

*… I'm afraid that a letter to that effect has been fabricated now. And strangely enough it all goes through the Sports Ministry because my friend Sergey, who is helping us to organise this whole thing, works at the moment for the Sports Ministry.*

*So a BBC letterhead was downloaded from the Internet and the text of the letter was added in Russian, stating that Mr Khagazheev is a legendary figure and that's why we want to meet him.*

*And now for two days the Sports Ministry has been trying to fax this letter to Khagazheev's office but apparently his fax machine is very old and not receiving but we're still hopeful and we probably will see him today after all.*

(Grigori is narrating the tale of the infamous subterfuge with increasing gusto but I'm a little uncertain as to the wisdom of putting it down on the record. I'm not quite sure how the BBC will react to its letter-heading being downloaded off the Internet and used to create what is after all a forged letter. I decide I don't want to know whose signature appears at the bottom of the letter, given the evident ingenuity of the Sports Ministry's media team on the Internet.

I suspect Grigori himself is the originator of the play on Comrade Khagazheev. It has a lot of the hallmarks I've come to know from working with him. Sending the letter from the Sports Ministry fax machine is a particularly nice touch since it lends Zelenin's unwitting imprimatur to our request for an interview.)

Andy: *So does Khagazheev genuinely believe that his fame has spread all around the world and that people walking down the high street in the UK go, 'Oh... Khagazheev... that's the guy who built the Nadezhda smelter?'*

Grigori: *No. He's not as stupid as that. He's creating The Legend.*

Andy: *But what interests me, and I only found this out in the last couple of days, is that in Russian Nadezhda means 'hope'. But of course it was also the name of Stalin's wife, and I guess, you could not have used the name Nadezhda without that reference being explicit in everyone's mind.*

Grigori: *Well, that's quite likely, and also the idea to build Nadezhda, like all the first projects, came in the 1930s, which makes it even more likely that Nadezhda was named after Stalin's wife, who by the way Stalin shot dead shortly afterwards.*

Andy: *Anyway, it is some sort of Soviet era achievement to build a huge plant in the middle of nowhere. I can't imagine a western company at that time doing that sort of thing because it just wouldn't have made economic sense.*

Grigori: *It didn't make economic sense but it made great political sense and that precisely is what turned Russia into a superpower.*

*And to achieve this kind of thing you needed leaders of moral stature no less than Alexander the Great. That's why this man is so interesting. Obviously, he can stoop to this little trick in his self-interest, and at the same time*

*he is the man who, as the Russians say, made Nadezhda,*
*which is hope, spring up in the tundra.*
Andy: *Are you confident that he will talk to us in the end?*
Grigori: *No I'm not… but we'll see what happens.*

I personally think Grigori has been over-egging the pudding somewhat with all his talk of Alexander the Great. After several days of his continuous company, however, I have learnt that he gets over-enthused when talking about the potentiality of the Russian people to do great things. What would otherwise be overbearing nationalism is almost completely offset by his simultaneous scorn that his countrymen have only done so under the threat of extreme coercion.

But Grigori has also been thoroughly enjoying his Moscow break, even if seems to have challenged his preconceptions just as much as it has done mine. The years since he was last here have obviously brought with them a lot of change. I sense he's been wrong-footed right from the start when he had pre-empted our arrival at the airport with gleeful accounts of the layers of bureaucracy we would have to clear and the hours of queuing we'd have to endure. When we'd emerged into the arrivals hall a mere twenty minutes after disembarking, Grigori had stood a moment looking around him in disbelief and, I think, disappointment that I should somehow have got off so lightly.

Our excursions around Moscow have been punctuated with Grigori shaking his head and saying, almost to himself, 'Everyone so calm… everyone so relaxed… so peaceful.' Words that evidently didn't apply to Moscow life in the early 1990s, I can only assume.

Moscow has completely transformed my internal film footage of Russia. I've been wholly unprepared for the sheer sense of capitalist oomph bursting out from behind its Soviet-era façade.

Everyone seems to be on the make here. Step to the edge of the pavement and three cars will screech across lanes of traffic in your direction. Every Muscovite in a car seems to be willing to get a little black-market taxi work.

The city is a heaving metropolis as diverse as any big city

that was once the centre of an empire. But this empire was an eastern one and the faces that crowd the pavements are an exotic blend of Turkman, Uzbek, Armenian and, of course, the universally-dreaded Chechen.

But Grigori was right in his prediction about our wait for our permits. Without quite noticing how or when it happened exactly, I have almost completely acclimatised myself to life in Moscow.

I know this because Sergey has started giving me surreptitious looks of disapproval when I shuffle outside for a smoke in my tracksuit bottoms and slippers. He's far too polite to say so but I know he thinks I'm bringing the block's reputation down a bit. Everyone else has started nodding to me and a few have stopped for a shared cigarette – albeit one without much conversation – so I feel I've settled in nicely.

I guess I *will* see Norilsk like a Russian.

Wise man that Grigori is, though, his trick with Khagazheev hasn't worked. The battle of the broken fax machine has waged for two more days since our taped conversation on the subject and THE LEGEND is proving no less forthcoming about talking to the BBC.

'We'll get him when we come back. You'll see,' breezes Grigori as we board our Demodedovo flight to Norilsk.

i   The Globe and Mail (Canada) 24 July 2001

ii   After the demise of the Soviet Union in 1991 and the emergence of Russia led by Boris Yeltsin, it was decided to apply 'shock therapy' to Russia's crumbling economy. The therapy was a huge dose of financial measures such as cutting all subsidies, liberalising prices and privatising the state-run industry. It was meant to shock the system into jumping across the divide between Soviet centrally-planned economy to liberal market economy. Detractors of the policy joke that Russia got the shock but not the therapy.

iii   See Appendix I

iv   The Globe and Mail (Canada) 24 July 2001

# ARRIVAL
## 'Back in the USSR'

To fly from Moscow to Norilsk takes four hours. Same time as the flight from London to Moscow. We cross four time zones on the way... which doesn't seem right.

After the jet swings north and east of Moscow, the thick carpet of clouds occasionally splits to reveal a seemingly never-ending landscape of dark forest.

This is Russia's land-sprawl, its stretch eastwards from the cramped space of Western Europe. Moscow lies in the West of the country and St Petersburg perches on an outstretched arm on the Baltic Sea. The histories of both are intertwined with the rest of the continent. Over centuries their evolution has been shaped by events in Berlin, Paris and London. Metaphorically, at least, they look westwards, as if fearful of what lies behind them.

And what lies in the East, kept at bay by the Ural Mountains, is Siberia, Russia's 'other'. The forests' brooding presence extends 4,000 miles to the Pacific Ocean. Dividing the landmass between the West Siberian Plain and the Central Siberian Plateau, the Yenisey River springs in the South from the Sayan Mountains near the Mongolian border and flows into the Arctic Ocean in the North.

Look at a map of Siberia, and Moscow is a distant presence at the edge of the page. The cities with their exotic names – Omsk, Novosibirsk, Krasnoyarsk, Irkutsk – are strung along its most southern fringe, linked by the Trans-Siberian Railway, still the only man-made definition of this vast space.

Just about all of them are heavily industrialised, a legacy

of the time Russia wanted its factories protected from military land attack and any close scrutiny from its enemies ... us, for example.

North of these clusters of human habitation the map of Siberia becomes a void, a slab of green and yellow veined with the blue of little-known rivers like the Ob, the Lena and the Kolyma. The city and town names thin out until they become a few tiny-lettered dots seemingly cut off from anything else.

The word Siberia has been described[i] as a mystical mix of the Tatar *sibir* – 'sleeping land' – and the Mongolian *siber* – 'pure'. Both capture the sense of wilderness and obscurity that characterise what covers one twelfth of the earth's land surface.

An affront to the modern paradigm of 'a shrinking world', much of it remains as deeply hostile to human life as it ever was.

Even the Russian credited with conquering Siberia for the Tsars in the sixteenth century – Yermak, a Cossack leader or rapacious freebooter, depending on which version you read – didn't make it back again.

Driven by an insatiable thirst for more land, Russia subsequently wrestled it away from the Tartars and then for many years struggled to find any use for it other than to supply the fur that wrapped a thousand women's shoulders in the capitals of Europe.

It's often been called Russia's very own Wild East and some of the comparisons with America's Wild West ring true. Early Russian immigrants included religious dissenters, peasants fleeing serfdom and frequent famine in the western provinces, fur trappers, traders and vagabonds. Like the Wild West, Siberia had a reputation for lawlessness and defiance of the Tsarist authority that dissipated with every mile travelled eastwards.

But there's one key difference. Unlike the Wild West, a lot of people who migrated to Siberia had no choice in the matter. Almost as soon as it was eaten by its western neighbour, Siberia became the dumping-ground for what Russia regarded as its human flotsam.

When the first gold and silver mines were opened in

the eighteenth century, the Tsars rapidly discovered the convenience of using the labour of expendable 'criminals' to work them. 'Criminal' activity at various times included offences such as begging with false distress, fortune telling and taking snuff[ii]. When there weren't enough criminals, people were just deported and told not to come back. It's estimated a million convicts were exiled to Siberia in the nineteenth century, often followed by their wives and family.

Josef Stalin, who enjoyed a bit of forced leisure time in Siberia himself, simply industrialised the process. The Soviet Union's military machine needed the raw materials that lay beneath the Siberian plains and forests. Stalin's roving paranoid delusions about almost every section of Soviet society at one time or another ensured a never-ending stream of deportees and exiles.

The further north on the map a town is located, the more certain you can be that it was forcibly populated during the gulag years.

This makes Norilsk's history as a prison camp something of a given. Sitting on the ore-rich Taimyr Peninsula it lies in the very far North, about halfway across Siberia from west to east. It is easy to find on a map. With the exception of its port sister Dudinka, it is a lone place-name in a territory the size of Germany and Poland combined, the last outpost in this sleeping giant of a land.

Norilsk is so remote that there are only three ways to get there and two of them are out of the question for most of the year. There are no roads running longitudinally in Siberia so the 'land' route is to travel by boat northwards up the Yenisey River from Krasnoyarsk. It's a trip of more than 1,000 miles but the river is frozen for much of the year, meaning it's a summertime luxury.

The 'sea' route, via the Arctic Ocean, is even more daunting, requiring as it does a nuclear icebreaker. Only Norilsk's precious harvest – the metals it mines and refines – gets such favoured treatment.

Which pretty much leaves only the 'air' route and that's not too reliable for much of the time.

I originally wanted to journey to Norilsk in winter to experience what I told Grigori would be 'the full horror' of mind-numbingly low temperatures and the twenty-four-hour darkness of the polar night.

Unimpressed by what he made clear he felt to be senseless bravado, he explained how unpredictable winter travel is in the Arctic Circle. During the long eight-month winter the airport closes frequently at short notice depending on just how low the temperature has dropped and just what gale force the Arctic storms have reached.

Although I detected something other than just practicality in his answer, I found it hard to argue with him.

One of the few people I'd known who had travelled to Norilsk had found himself stranded for days on end in the middle of winter. He was a tough Jewish-American (in that order) trader following the scent of easy money to be made in Norilsk in the early 1990s when this Soviet city had found itself catapulted into the very heartland of capitalism – the industrial metals markets.

It was a time when, as Zelenin had put it so diplomatically, 'they had a large number of sales agents – there was no consistent and consolidated sales policy'.

Phil, as we'll call him, was in town to score some nickel. Norilsk Nickel's lack of 'consistent' sales policy was in reality a general free-for-all. The company's nickel and copper were seeping through to the Western markets in a thousand different ways, some of them legitimate, most of them highly circuitous with payments deposited in bank accounts in a range of exotic locations.

Phil didn't score. As Phil told it, the then head of the company's Arctic Division had welcomed him into his boardroom with the words, 'If you've come for some nickel, you can fuck off – I've no more nickel to sell.' Instead, they passed the next half hour or so talking about the local hunting before Phil thanked him for his time and went back to the airport…

… which was closed, due to severe weather conditions. Phil was told to try the next day. He did and it was still closed. Phil paid a handsome bribe to someone at the airport to call him at his hotel when it reopened and heard nothing for another two days. By this time, totally unprepared for the Arctic winter conditions outside, Phil was pretty much living in his hotel room surviving on a diet of strong spirits and cigarettes.

The phone call finally came through… the airport had just reopened and a flight from Moscow was expected in a couple of hours. It would return there after refuelling. Phil duly raced off to the airport, only to find the military blocking the road to the airport. They told him it was closed due to severe weather conditions. They wouldn't take his bribes – it was too dangerous, they told him. Phil went back to the hotel. He finally made it out another couple of days later. He told me it was the worst experience of his life.

So I conceded the point to Grigori about not coming here in winter. Our £4,000 budget was generous for one person travelling, so-so for two people but downright tight for the three of us. The thought of finding ourselves stranded in Norilsk in winter with no money didn't really bear thinking about too long. At least Phil had travelled with his customary huge wad of cash. We had no such wad.

But its absolute remoteness in the tundra desert is part of the power Norilsk exerts over me. I am drawn by its very inaccessibility. Its geographic inaccessibility. Its bureaucratic inaccessibility. Its mental inaccessibility… that is, for me at least.

My fascination with the place has grown over the space of sixteen years, each reference in a metal market report adding another drop of darkness to my growing pool of ignorance about what life is really like in a closed city such as Norilsk.

By comparison with the average man in the street, I guess I'm hugely knowledgeable about the place, thanks to my career as a commodity markets reporter. But I know Norilsk only through the prism of the metals it churns out. I know how much it produces every year… well, as much as anyone is allowed to know – bits of the information are still classified as a state secret. I know how it exports its metals. I have a fairly good idea of who buys the metals. I can list a hundred dry facts about the place, but always through the blinkered view of the financial markets in the West. In their maniacal focus on just the information that will affect the price of metal markets, the traders behind their screens in London or New York are as sensitive to the lives of the people living in Norilsk as was the Soviet Ministry of Defence.

However, I now need to know more than the facts and figures. I need to meet these people who live in an environment so hostile it was only populated at the point of a gun wielded by a guard on the other side of the barbed-wire wire.

What sort of Stakhanovite[iii] worker goes to work when it's -50°C, disappears a mile underground to rip metals out of the earth and returns to the surface to find it's been pitch dark all day and it's still -50°C outside?

And what on earth do these Soviet shock-workers make of what has happened since Gorbachev let the hurricane of free market forces through the door?

Once they symbolised the-Soviet-against-all-odds mentality that hurled men sharing rifles against the Nazi invaders in Stalingrad. Now they symbolise the hidden human component of capitalism at its most raw. Today these mystery Russians are going down the mines in -50°C to slake our thirst for the mod cons that we imagine to be so essential to our cosseted happiness.

The metals from Norilsk are inextricably woven into the fabric of our modern existence. Since the new Russian arms industry is a shadow of its monolithic former self, the metals from this Arctic frontier town are sold almost exclusively to us. Each of us is linked by a literal metal chain to these people.

Nickel is unavoidably the metal most associated with Norilsk because the company that runs the city has the name in its title and because it's the largest producer of the stuff in the world.

And nickel is the key ingredient of stainless steel, that ubiquitous modern metal that lines our kitchen sinks, heats our food and turns the water on and off in our bathrooms. Nickel makes stainless steel anti-corrosive and heat-resistant. We need nickel for our cars and trains, we use it in the turbines that drive our power stations and we even use it to manufacture compact discs.

But nickel is just part of the Chemical Table smorgasbrod that's hacked out of the ground beneath the permafrost in Russia's northernmost extremity.

Norilsk's share of the world platinum and palladium production is even more mind-bogglingly total than that of nickel. The two precious metals are most commonly associated with jewellery but they are both essential components of the catalytic converter, that environmentally-friendly component of every modern car. Norilsk is the world's number two supplier of platinum after South Africa and indisputably number one for palladium.

Then there's the cobalt, the copper, the selenium, the gold and the silver[iv]. The last two we use for show, the first three we rarely see in their pure form, but they are there around us, transmitting our electricity or running some component of modern machinery few of us care to comprehend.

Unless you've cut yourself off from the grid and adopted a mediaeval lifestyle of cooking in earthen bowls over log fires and using oxen for transport, you are using Norilsk metals every day.

In this era of soft-focus first-world capitalism, those who can afford it, spend their money on fair-trade coffee and chocolate on the promise that a good part of their hard-earned pay will find its way to the farming collectives in Africa or South America. I've even bought cosmetic products as presents for female friends and been assured by the young assistant in the shop that my money would help the women who harvest the shea nuts in Burkina Faso. 'Really?' 'Really', she'd smiled back.

Funny, then, isn't it that no one asks where their metals come from and who mines them? But that's the personal bit of my 'Journey of a Lifetime'. To meet the mystery people in the closed city in the Siberian wilderness.

## Welcome to Norilsk
The last couple of hours of the flight I can discern very little out of the window through an expressionist whirl of whites and greys. Between the clouds and the snow-clad earth beneath,

only the occasional glimpse of a steel-grey piece of water or the black rock of a mountain offer any identifiable landmarks.

Grigori and Sergey tell me they've persuaded the flight attendant to announce the flight's arrival at Norilsk airport in English. For the BBC, they've assured her.

I don't get the impression she's been asked to do this before but she makes a heroic effort, which with a bit of editing in the studio will come out just fine, I reckon.

I'm hoping to catch some breathtaking birds-eye view of Norilsk as we swoop in to land, but whatever's below is cloaked by dense cloud cover. We descend rapidly through it and it's only at the last moment, at what appears to be near touching distance of the runway, that the clouds part to reveal a line of low-lying snow-covered hills.

The landing is greeted with applause from the passengers. It's a Russian thing, Grigori tells me. It's a nice thing... but one, I suspect, that owes a lot to simple relief at arriving safely on a domestic Russian airliner.

The airport comprises a single runway and a modest, squat terminal building. The only other aircraft are a couple of helicopters at one end of the runway.

Once we come to a halt, there is no frenzied rush to get bags out of overhead lockers or charge down the aisle to gain a few precious yards in the queue to disembark. As Norilsk is a closed city, everyone has to stay in their seats until cleared by the authorities to get out of the airplane.

A group of burly policemen in padded camouflage uniform file through the front cabin door to check papers. They slowly work their way down the aisles, their progress followed by passengers gathering their belongings together and heading for the exit.

I watch their approach nervously, half savouring a flashback to a generic 1960s spy film and half fearful that something is going to be wrong. Incorrect papers and we get to stay on the plane and fly back to Moscow.

One of the cops glances briefly at Sergey's passport and special permit and nods him through. But he closely studies mine and Grigori's for what I feel is far too long. He barks out a few words of Russian, gestures over his shoulder and puts our passports and permits in his pocket. 'We have to get them at the police station inside the terminal building,' says Grigori.

Grigori has a wariness of the Russian police that is undoubtedly justified by years of experience. 'The thing is to never give them any excuse to find anything wrong,' he has told me on several occasions.

As we walk the short distance to the terminal through a biting wind, I can tell he is anxious about the pending visit to the police station. His anxiety rubs off on me. Our mood isn't lightened when we finally locate it, tucked away in a corner at the very back of the terminal. Unlike the rest of the building, which has an early 1970s 'modern' feel about it, this part is poorly lit and badly ventilated. Set in one wall is a giant padded door. Next to it is a small buzzer box.

We wait for the return of the cop with our papers. He eventually walks purposefully around the corner and presses the buzzer, talking to Grigori over his shoulder. The heavy door swings open accompanied by a muffled clanking. He beckons Grigori inside and they disappear down a murky corridor as the door grinds shut behind them.

I'm left nervously wondering whether we're in for the shortest 'Journey of a Lifetime' trip yet seen by the RGS and the BBC.

I smoke two cigarettes in quick succession and it's only when I'm coming to the end of the second that the clanking sound starts again and the door swings open to reveal Grigori chuckling to himself.

---

*Transcript.*
*Police Station.*
*Norilsk Airport.*

The following is a natural recording, which I'll define as meaning we had forgotten to turn the recording equipment off when we had been waiting for the policeman to show up. Grigori also managed inadvertently to record his conversation with the police inside the station. I suspect that this could possibly have amounted to what Grigori in the transcript calls 'naughty' behaviour.

> Grigori: *They are so scary and then when you talk to them, they are very nice, very sweet people.*
> Andy: *It all looks very hard-core.*
> Grigori (laughing): *I said, just to make conversation, is it going to get any warmer? And they said, 'Well… what the fuck do we need summer for?'*

(I'll admit that this is not necessarily my definition of very nice, very sweet people, but maybe it's another of those Russian things.)

> Andy: *So, have we got what we need?*
> Grigori: *We need originals on the way back. We get the originals from the people who invited us. We come in here and then they stamp them.*
> *You see, they're okay unless you do something naughty.*

Our special permits had been faxed through from Norilsk after our interview with Zelenin. The local police obviously don't want to waste any ink stamping documents that aren't the originals. These guys get to do a lot of stamping, I imagine.

It's been a traumatic few moments but the stomach-knotting anxiety that has rarely left me for the last few months pours out of my body. I really want to do one of those athletic head-over-heels goal celebrations, but being far too unfit, I content myself with a grin to match Grigori's.

So, we're in Norilsk!

Or not actually, because when we catch up with Sergey in the middle of the main hall, he is disconsolate. The official Norilsk Nickel minibus that was supposed to pick us up is not there. For reasons I don't fully grasp this is a VERY BIG thing. Sergey has found another one waiting in the car park for a bigwig from the Moscow Public Relations Department. She's due to arrive on the next flight in an hour's time. Sergey and

Grigori agree that it's important we should be on it rather than take a taxi from the airport.

We briefly camp in the small airport café and drink alternate rounds of over-sweet coffee and beer. The airport is sparsely populated, like those in old black-and-white films.

Grigori adds to the sense of time warp when he returns from the toilets and tells me to start the MiniDisc recorder. He has something important he wants to say.

### Norilsk Airport.
### Café/Bar.

> Grigori: *We're still at the bar but I really need my beer now because I've just had a trying and emotional experience. I went into the public toilet at the terminal here and you have to pay five roubles to enter, which is about one sixth of a dollar, about fifteen cents.*
> *And when you pay your five roubles, there is a girl at the entrance and she issues you a length of toilet paper. But it turned out there was no way I could use the toilet paper because there are no toilet seats on the toilets so I had to come back without going.*
> *Anyway, I'll have some more beer.*

We all laugh but it's an early warning sign of Norilsk's lingering Soviet presence. Back in Moscow, the supermarket was selling Andrex. Here you get to buy a few sheets of near transparent paper… just like in the good old days.

I'm about to light up a cigarette when Sergey points out it's a non-smoking building. He directs me to the front steps of the airport. When I get there, I realise why the terminal building looks so deserted. Everyone's out here! Passengers just arrived, passengers waiting to depart, waiting relatives, airport staff, taxi drivers – all of them braving the -10°C to indulge in the Russian passion for smoking. Most of them are wrapped in furs or padded jackets but a few testify to the legendary toughness of the locals by standing around in T-shirts, tracksuit bottoms and trainers.

I'm wearing an insulated jacket padded with some new, state-of-the-art, man-made fibre and a woollen hat. Although I've brought long johns with me, I'm not wearing them right now. I'm aware of a gradual chill enveloping my legs and crotch as the wind swirls around the entrance to the building.

While I'm monitoring its progress relative to the expected time required to finish the cigarette, a taxi swerves to a halt in front of the building and expels a thirty-something woman with peroxided hair. A leather mini-skirt and boob tube leave her midriff exposed to the freezing Arctic wind. I watch in disbelief as she skitters unsteadily on high-heeled shoes across the ice between the car and the terminal building.

Mind you, I guess that by comparison with temperatures as low as -50°C and -60°C in the winter, -10°C is a balmy spring morning for most of the inhabitants here.

Bang on schedule the next flight from Moscow arrives and Sergey springs into action to greet the Moscow official and seek permission to tag along. She's a woman in her early thirties with glasses and a narrow-lipped, tight-set mouth. She's wrapped head to foot in a very expensive-looking fur coat. Sergey jostles amid a phalanx of local public relations people that briefly encompasses her progress through the hall like a human shield.

We join the end of the retinue that trails behind her as she sweeps out of the building and across the car park to the minibus. Grigori and I hunker down right at the back in what we hope is a suitably inconspicuous way. Sergey is chatting to some of the local guys in Russian about the reasons for our trip. The Ice Maiden from Moscow listens distractedly, occasionally making a comment or asking a question.

The airport is some twenty miles from the city and is connected to it by a single road which still has pockets of black ice on many of the corners even though it's late May. The minibus travels at a controlled 25–30 m.p.h. but I feel the wheels skidding gently on some of the bends. There's little other traffic... a couple of cars and the occasional bus negotiating the potholes that have opened up with the spring thaw.

At first the landscape is bleak but not unattractive. Something like Dartmoor on a cold, cold winter day. Signs of civilisation are limited to a single-track railway line and a string of stubby posts holding up what looks very much like an old telegraph wire running alongside the road. All around us the snow-dappled scenery is a patchwork of whites, greys and browns – no trees, just clumps of dark earth emerging from beneath the winter mantle.

The first signs we are approaching Norilsk are the pipes that spring up mysteriously from the ground and start to line the road. First one, then two, then four of them, each easily big enough for a man to crawl down.

Buildings start to appear beside the road. Most of them look deserted. The glass on the windows has long gone, bits of the brickwork have been sucked into the icy ground and metal joists have rusted to the point of disintegration.

The first human habitation we reach is a satellite town of Norilsk, a desolate-looking clutch of Brezhnev-era apartment blocks. Back in Moscow, they had a very run-down feel to them. Here, they look as if they're on the point of final surrender to the hostile elements of the far Russian North.

Next to them is the metal skeleton of a huge aircraft-hangar-sized structure. As the road swings closer, I can see the girders are frayed and tattered as if partially eaten by some steel-eating moth. One of the locals explains to us that it was going to be a furniture factory but that all work had stopped in 1990 – year zero around here.

I'm briefly taken aback by the unfairness of living 200 miles inside the Arctic Circle in a satellite town of Norilsk. It's bad enough living in the main city, from everything I've heard, but the people here don't even get that privilege.

As we pass through the town with no name – I never get round to finding out what it's called – the landscape is slowly but undoubtedly darkening.

More disused or half-built buildings – it's impossible to say which – obscure the barren emptiness. The pipes running beside the road are now legion, writhing and twisting over each other and occasionally coming together to arc overhead across the road.

Something strange has happened to the snow. It's lost its virgin whiteness and degenerated into a series of ugly dark greys. For the first time I see signs that there once was a forest here – but it's all dead now. Just thin emaciated tree-trunks remain like lines of matchsticks stretching across the hills.

The quality of the light has appreciably worsened. It's as if someone has hit a dimmer switch on the whole region. The sky is dark and the sun more a distant presence than a discernible source of light.

The minibus becomes more animated as we round another corner and a huge metallurgical complex comes into view. The size of ten football pitches, its gargantuan chimney stacks are belching plumes of smoke into the air. The Nadezhda smelter! Or maybe that should be The Legendary Nadezhda Smelter! It seems to have that status with the locals, anyway. Even the Ice Maiden from Moscow looks fairly impressed.

A few minutes further on and we pass over the crest of a hill and get the full panoramic view of Norilsk and its satellite towns.

It's a landscape out of a science fiction film. Mile after mile of industrial plant, some of it rusting and discarded, but most of it operating as is evident from the trails of smoke rising from countless chimney stacks. Ore-dressing plants, smelters, refineries, power stations and goodness knows what. I try and do a quick count of the bigger complexes but give up when I realise there are far more here than Norilsk Nickel officially lists. Between them run pipes, elevated slurry chutes, power lines and railway tracks. Lakes of ominously dark liquid lie all around.

The whole dirty vista seems to be set in a broad basin defined by a string of mountains but it's difficult to see through the twilight gloom created by the fumes that pour from scores of chimneys to merge quickly into the dark cloud above.

The city itself is overshadowed, quite literally, by this testament to sixty years of mining and metal refining. It is a concentration of Soviet-style tower blocks, surrounded on three sides by a tundra landscape that has lost any hint of whiteness and has dissolved into a sea of blacks and greys. The remaining side of the city is hemmed in by a string of low hills.

As the road winds its way down the hillside, it runs through a police checkpoint about half a mile short of the city confines. It looks like a border crossing point, a concrete structure with barriers across the five lanes for cars. Several policemen, heavily wrapped against the cold and with rifles slung over their shoulders, are stopping vehicles and getting the occupants out.

Back with the James Bond film sets! Given the physical and bureaucratic difficulties of actually getting to this far-flung outpost of human civilisation, this checkpoint seems faintly surreal. Still, I can't help but notice that the minibus driver removes a wad of banknotes from behind the sunscreen and stuffs it hastily into his trouser pocket just before slowing down ahead of the barriers.

One of the cops waves us through, looking at the company logo on the side of the minibus as he does so, and I realise why Sergey was so keen for us to get the 'official' transport. I suspect that had we taken our own transport, there would have been more problems with the facsimiled special permits and quite possibly some sort of on-the-spot fine.

Norilsk is a very dour place, a symmetrical grid of square and rectangular concrete buildings for the most part. Some have been painted in pastel colours – an attempt to lend some colour to an otherwise monochrome world. But the paint is peeling off in many places and the colours tinged brown by an ubiquitous layer of soot. Rather than cheering the eye the effect is to give the city a run-down, seedy sort of look.

There are few people on the streets, an occasional pedestrian hunched over to lessen the edge of the gusting wind. The traffic is light, just a small number of cars gingerly negotiating the icy streets.

I'm about to comment on one particularly grim-looking monument to Soviet architecture – a beige-coloured modernist monstrosity – when Sergey turns to me with a big grin and announces: 'Our hotel!'

Hotel Norilsk – there is no other in this city – is accessed by three heavily padded double doors. I have the impression of passing through a number of airlocks as if I'm moving between spaceships rather than entering the foyer of a hotel.

The inside of the building does nothing to dispel a growing sense that I've travelled back in time to a pre-1989 Russia. The reception area is a kitsch pot-pourri of fake wooden walls, a couple of black leather sofas from a long-lost age and a plastic grotto fountain in one corner.

The service is another echo of a previous Soviet inefficiency. A single, middle-aged, surly-mouthed woman is making snail-like progress handling what is obviously something of a rush hour by local standards – two flights from Moscow in two hours. As well as the Ice Maiden from Moscow and ourselves, there is a motley group of Scandinavian and Canadian businessmen trying to check in – they're all from industrial equipment suppliers as far as I can ascertain.

Everyone has to fill in forms in triplicate. In Russian. Sergey does the honours for us but it still takes us about forty minutes to be processed and get keys for our rooms. Credit cards are assuredly not welcome. And it's cash up front for three nights in advance.

We decide on a quick spot of lunch in the hotel restaurant which is small and looks and feels like a greasy-spoon café in London.

All of us are in exuberant spirits. I'm filled with a sense of massive achievement at just being here and can't stop grinning inanely. Bizarrely, I can't get the tune of *Oh, I do like to be beside the seaside* out of my head. But it's not just me. Grigori is in fine holiday mood as well, laughing and joking with the waitress as she takes our order. He's all for switching on the recording equipment so we can get down our first thoughts about the place.

***Transcript.***
***Andy and Grigori after arrival at Hotel Norilsk.***

Grigori: *We are sitting in a little bar at the... hey, we always seem to be in a bar.*

Andy: *It's a restaurant.*

Grigori: *Okay, it's a restaurant actually at the hotel. It's a small restaurant and we're about to have our first lunch in Norilsk and Andy is being introduced to some dishes he's never heard of. What's your first course?*

Andy: *Siberian soup with fish... apparently.*

Grigori: *And second course is?*

Andy: *'Appetising pork with mashed potatoes.'*

Grigori: *Well there you are! We'll see how appetising it is.*

Andy: *That may have lost something in the translation though.*

Grigori: *No, it's called exactly the same in Russian so don't worry, we're in the dark as to what it consists of.*
*And we're really having a good time in Norilsk so far.*

Andy: *Yes, but we haven't left the hotel.*

Grigori: *Yeah, and we've been gingerly looking out of the window, and it's a strange sight I must say.*
*So, Andy, what do you make of it so far? We saw the smelters and it's a sight I personally will never forget, the snow and the chimney stacks spewing smoke and those huge buildings looking like a giant threw some pubes into the middle of the tundra and it's really so unlike anything I saw before.*

(I decline to follow the theme created by Grigori's slightly strange use of words to describe the industrial sprawl surrounding the city.)

Andy: *I think what takes me back is the sheer scale of it. I hadn't been prepared for it to be quite as large as it is, and also, what's strange here is half of it's closed and half of it's still open. When they finish with something here they just leave the building standing and build the new one right next to it.*

Grigori: *I was thinking as we drove past, I had never seen so much rusting metal in my life. It just kind of spreads away from you and goes over the horizon. These incredible shapes that the pipelines make, the way they sprawl on the ground as far as the eye can see.*

*All that rusting metal piled up. Probably it will just stay there until it decomposes in a few thousand years.*

Andy: *The irony is it's a huge metallurgical plant. They could recycle it, melt it down again.*

Grigori: *Okay, I'll leave it to you to suggest it to the general manager and see what happens. See how far he's going to throw you across the room.*

Andy to Sergey, as a plate of bread arrives: *We're sharing it yeah?*

Sergey: *Sure, okay.*

Grigori: *Okay, let's turn it off now and have our meal.*

(...)

Grigori: *We've just finished our lunch and...*

Sergey (in English): *... very quickly...*

Grigori: *... and I must say it was very tasty and Andy had his Siberian fish soup. Of course we asked the waitress where the fish came from and she said it came from the Yenisey River. Andy just panicked and asked, 'Did you catch it upstream from Norilsk or downstream from Norilsk?'*

Andy: *I was enjoying it until then.*

Grigori: *I can already see that this place is doing something to Andy. He is undergoing some strange change after he's seen all that black snow and the chimney stacks spewing all that pollution, because he was actually eating an apple rather surreptitiously while I was drinking my beer.*

*And I had to rather forcefully remind him where we are and that we are duty bound to have at least one shot of vodka before we start on our soup. So we've had that now and I think the lunch was pretty delicious, don't you, Andy?*

Andy: *Yes, and just for the record the 'appetising pork', which is truly appetising, is actually a pork escalope with melted cheese and tomatoes on the top. And I only had the apple because Sergey offered me the apple. I didn't order the apple. I'm not going to be caught in some power struggle between you two on this journey.*

Grigori: *Ah ha! He's already apologising!*

Andy: *You represent everything that's evil obviously and Sergey everything that's healthy. This is between you two.*

(Sound of Sergey pushing back his chair.)

*You've already frightened him off, see.*

Grigori: *He's already apologising for not remembering to ask for the vodka. But he will learn. I give him three days in Norilsk and he will not be eating apples.*

Andy: *I'll be on a bottle of vodka a day by that stage.*

Grigori: *Yes, he'll be drinking a bottle of vodka a day and he'll also be saying it makes him much healthier than he was before.*

Fortified by Siberian fish soup, 'appetising pork' and more vodka shots than I really wanted at lunch-time, we decide to try and get some catch-up sleep from the overnight flight, the crossing of four time zones and, in my case at least, the warp effect of being transported back in time by around thirty years.

As I close the door behind me, I realise that it's the first time I've had my own room or space since arriving in Moscow. Although we've gone for the hotel's budget accommodation, I'm briefly overwhelmed by the sense of solitary luxury. I take a quick inventory of the facilities.

## Suspended Animation

---

*Transcript.*
*Andy's Audio Journal.*
*Hotel Room.*

Andy: *The room itself? I'm quite pleased with it. I thought I just broke the toilet there but apparently I haven't. Or rather I did but I've just managed to fix it again. Bathroom's got running water. It came out a nasty brown to start off with but after a bit of running came out clear, so that's quite good. The windows have got massive double-glazing so it's quite a warm room. There's a TV set. I'm not sure I'm going to play around with that. Grigori put his hand on it and got a pretty severe electric shock earlier on. But that may just be him... he's got a weird vibe about these things.*
*I think we're all going to have a quick rest now and regroup for a stroll and spot of dinner later on.*
*I think also that there are some really impressive mountains here. Unfortunately you can't see them because of all the cloud and smoke that's belching out of the factories, but on a clear day I think we're actually in for some quite spectacular scenery. Jury out on that one... we'll have to wait for the air to clear... if it does.*

I look out the window. We're on the sixth floor of a twelve-storey structure. Behind it is a car park with no cars in it. Two dark-windowed, brown slabs of concrete stand at an equal height on the left and on the right, channelling the view across the road to an equally dismal block of buildings on the other side. Most of the snow appears to have melted. Dark puddles crater the car park. What remains of the ice skirts the bottom of the buildings but can offer only a grey border to this void of colour.

The light outside seems caught in suspended animation at that point of a winter day when the quick slide into full night hovers close. It hasn't changed since we first drove into town. I wonder whether it will.

I'm too full of impressions to try any meaningful siesta, and spend my time trying to master the recording equipment sufficiently to get some of them down on MiniDisc. When I play myself back, I'm alienated by the sound of my own voice. The BBC had stressed we have to sound our 'natural' selves and told us not to worry about putting on a posh accent or interjecting the odd four-letter word into the material. It would all be edited out later, they said. I'm unclear how they're going to edit out my bland, nasal, generic London accent.

I'm still tinkering around with the recording when Grigori phones me from his room, suggesting an exploratory reconnaissance mission around the city centre.

Sergey has been busy trying to set up interviews and find out places to go while I've been struggling with a bit of equipment designed for teenagers. Grigori seems the only one of us who has actually managed to sleep.

As we come out of the lift on the ground floor, acrid smoke is swirling through the corridor leading down to the restaurant. The stench of burning plastic follows us into the foyer. 'Is it just me or has there been a fire here?' I ask Sergey and Grigori. 'Well, it certainly looks so,' replies Grigori.

Sergey asks the receptionist and receives a steely stare and a few reluctant words. No, there's no fire, everything's fine, Grigori translates. We look at each other somewhat sceptically before heading out through the airlocks. If the staff is that unconcerned about it, I don't see why we should let it bother us, I reason, as the temperature drops with each set of padded doors we pass through.

Snow has started to fall. The light is still poised somewhere between day and night, apparently unable to make up its mind which one to embrace.

It's just gone seven in the evening. The streets are still sparsely populated... just the odd pedestrian or a couple of solitary figures at a bus-stop, all of them bulked up with thick clothing and most with some sort of woollen or fur hat pulled down around their ears.

Everywhere lie huge pools of blackened slush from melted snow and ice. In the middle of some of the broader roads is a narrow strip of land where, instead of the grass or flowers you'd find in any other city, stick-like skeletons of shrubbery mock any attempt to breathe life into this dark place.

The pavements are wide, which is good. I'm fearful of stalactites of ice falling from the eaves of the buildings twelve stories up ever since I read on the Internet that several of the locals meet their unexpected end every spring with just such a bolt from the grey .

But walking too close to the kerb brings with it the horror of being sprayed by passing cars with the brackish water that in places half-submerges the tarmac. The vehicles are occasional, and most are courteous to pedestrians, but it's almost impossible to avoid sending an arc of evil-looking liquid over the pavement. The cars themselves look as if they've just been in some cross-country rally, caked in sludge, windscreen wipers working furiously to keep the dark spray at bay.

Norilsk is an easy city to navigate, laid out in a symmetrical grid. It's not big. All we have to do is walk down any road for long enough... normally about a mile... and we run out of utilitarian blocks and find ourselves standing at the edge of the tundra and its criss-crossing pipes and power pylons. Or looking up at snow-clad hills towering above us. Except, as Sergey explains, they're not hills, they're snow-clad slag heaps.

This country is playing games with me again. Moscow had shattered just about every preconception I'd had about Russia with its cosmopolitan blend of nationalities, its new-found glitz of neon lights and advertising boards, its evident wealth and va-va-voom.

But in only an hour or so of tramping around the bleak, puddle-infested streets of the city centre, Norilsk is forcing me to 'un-learn' what I'd thought Moscow had taught me. The first little clues as to its sense of difference to the capital – Grigori's toilet paper woes, the strange kitsch of the hotel foyer and the grumpy indifference of the hotel receptionist – are mirrored in the bigger canvas of the city streets.

It looks exactly how I've always imagined a Soviet frontier town in the Arctic Circle to look. There are absolutely no concessions to the frivolous or superfluous in its architecture. It is almost magnificent in its uncompromising utilitarianism.

It projects a total rejection of the last fourteen years of history. The centrepiece of the city is a long, wide boulevard running straight as a plumb line to the fortress of the Norilsk Nickel headquarters at the end. It is lined with the most imposing buildings in town. The colours are less weather-beaten and the stonework is still solid. It has fewer potholes than any other of the roads we've seen so far.

It's called Leninsky Prospekt. Not for Norilsk the 1990s revisionism of changing Leningrad back to St Petersburg and Stalingrad to Volgograd. No, here Lenin still does just fine as a street name.

Instead of Moscow's dripping advertising, Leninsky Prospect boasts giant murals depicting caricature workers joining hands aloft with bannered lettering driving home the message of socialist solidarity. You don't need to read Cyrillic to understand this far-flung part of Russia still has a lot of nostalgia for the time before year zero.

We tramp up Leninsky away from the Norilsk building. We pass the city's department store. It is closed. The theatre is set back from the road behind a square. It is also closed. We look for a list of forthcoming attractions. We can't find one.

It's snowing hard now and we realise Norilsk is not going to offer us any chinks of colourful light in its steel-grey armour. Sergey leads us to a restaurant he's been recommended at the other end of the street.

### Honorary Citizen

We enter another Soviet-designed brick cube through a couple of padded doors and I do a double-take at finding myself in a modern-looking cinema foyer. It's got all the familiar trappings of a multiplex cinema – the cardboard drinks holders, the popcorn dispensers and uniformed ushers.

The restaurant and bar are off to one side. The interior is plush and modern – all gleaming chrome fittings with neon outlining the long, well-stocked bar. The whole place has been done in a nautical theme with stylised oars and prows of boats decorating the walls. It takes my eyes a while to adjust to the biggest infusion of bright colour since I've been here.

With the exception of two or three well-dressed couples, we are the only diners. The food is excellent. I have smoked fish for starters and reindeer with mushrooms for the main course. The vodka is served in champagne buckets filled with ice. The service is extremely professional. Annoyingly, though, our meal is accompanied throughout by a sort of mangled Eurovision pop pap that blares out of the bar's many speakers. While Grigori and I are still somewhat disorientated by the sudden transition from Moscow to the wind-swept, ugly streets of this Siberian city, Sergey is in unrestrainedly chipper mood to be back here again. He rattles through a report card of his afternoon, listing the calls he's made, running off who's said no to being interviewed, who's agreed and who's still thinking about it. At the moment the company itself is in the latter category, non-committal as to whether we can interview any of the top people here or visit any of its facilities. We've obviously got our collective heart set on the Nadezhda smelter but all they've told Sergey is they'll let him know in the morning.

Conversation for us is a strange three-legged discourse since I speak no Russian and Sergey claims to speak no English, although I harbour growing doubts on the latter score. I've spent enough time with him now to suspect strongly he understands perfectly well most of my conversations with Grigori. He's started making the odd sarcastic comment in English which I've begun to find somewhat disconcerting.

But he also shows no intention of engaging any further in English with me, and by now all three of us have got used to Grigori interpreting back and forwards in Russian and English. This sometimes means I can see him react to what Sergey says before he translates it for me. I've already got into the habit of playing little guessing games as to what is coming next in our conversations.

Over the main course Sergey says something to Grigori that makes him sit back in only half-hamming surprise. A quick flurry of conversation follows before Grigori turns to my raised eyebrows and says Sergey's just told him he's an honorary citizen of Norilsk.

He's what? How on earth do you get to be an honorary citizen here? Sergey won't say. I tell Grigori to ask him again, setting off another round of verbal sparring that tails off into a series of monosyllabic *'niets'* from Sergey.

'He says it's too embarrassing and he doesn't want to talk about it,' Grigori finally translates.

To break the silence that briefly envelops us after this revelation, which I can see from his slightly furrowed forehead that Grigori is also digesting, I decide to change the subject to Siberia. Sergey, after all, is a Siberian. He has left a wife back in Irkutsk on Lake Baikal to work in Moscow, a not uncommon example of the migratory patterns of many Russians in this vast country from what I've already seen and heard.

Not wanting to put him directly on the spot, I ask how he thinks people living in Norilsk view the guys such as Zelenin running their lives back in Moscow. The belligerence of the answer causes Grigori to jerk back his head as if reeling from a sudden blow before he translates for me. 'They're all pigs... self-centred... money-grasping... they rob the rest of the country.'

The flash of anger that accompanies this statement is so rare in our experience of Sergey that we drop the conversation and another brief silence envelops us until Sergey returns to his formal self and starts laying out our proposed schedule over the next day or two.

It's about ten o'clock in the evening when we leave the restaurant and walk back to the hotel. It's still daylight or at least still the gloomy half-light that accompanied us on our earlier walk. The snow has lessened in intensity but it has brought with it one unexpected blessing. It has re-cloaked Norilsk's dark hues in a refreshing cover of white.

Off to one side of Leninsky Prospect is a huge square surrounded on three sides by apartment blocks. A group of five or six teenagers is playing an improvised game of football between goals made from piles of jackets. It's a sight you could see just about anywhere in the world but here they're playing amid swirls of snow and in temperatures that are dropping with every step we take.

The incongruity of this all-too-familiar sporting scene transported to this Soviet outpost in Siberia pretty much sums up my disorientation.

Back at the hotel, the fire seems to have been put out and there is now no smoke in the main reception area.

But Norilsk has been keeping just one more little Soviet nugget for me to savour before the day is out. When we get out of the lift at our floor, we see a large matronly-looking woman sitting at a desk reading a magazine. She hadn't been there earlier on. Her hair is peroxide blonde, which seems to be almost compulsory for women of a certain age in this place. We nod at her but receive nothing in return but a slightly disapproving frown.

These 'floor-matrons' had been a feature of hotels throughout Russia in Soviet times. Each floor used to have one, their duties never specifically defined. They were there just to check up on what was going on, and to report back on the comings and goings of those under suspicion of being up to no good, a description that covered anyone in the Soviet Union who could afford to stay at a hotel.

What will she be reporting on us, I wonder? I fear we'll probably be blamed for starting the fire that never happened.

---------

***Transcript.***
***Andy's Audio Journal.***
***Hotel Room.***

> Andy: *Hello again. I just thought I'd give you a little update, later in the day, the first day here in Norilsk which, thanks to someone from the UK reminding me by ringing on my mobile, is 26 May, Monday.*
> *It's eleven o'clock and we've just had a two-hour snowstorm. So! Norilsk in spring then!*
> *And of course it's daylight still. Well, it's sort of daylight.*

*It hasn't really bothered me yet, although I have visions of Al Pacino in that film Insomnia and I worry that I'll be doolally by the third day and I'll just have piled all the furniture in my room against the window to keep the light out.*

*Actually it was Grigori who fell into the 24-hour daylight trap first. For reasons best known to himself he didn't come with a hat. I have no idea what he thought he was doing. Even I realised it might be quite a useful item of clothing for this trip. Anyway, he had to be restrained by Sergey from trying to kick in the door of a department store at eight o'clock. We had to point out to him that it was about two hours after it had closed.*

*I suspect our disorientation will increase over the next three or four days...*

*PS I just wanted to give a little update on the hotel, or specifically my room. Running water in the bathroom, yes. But hot water... no. Which is slightly disappointing. I've already started psyching myself up for my cold shower first thing in the morning... which seems to be very Russian style and will no doubt make me harder and healthier.*

As I lie in bed and luxuriate in being on my own in my own room without the sleeping presence of Grigori a couple of feet away, I try and piece back together my now fractured mental image of Russia.

A week in Moscow had vaporised my preconceptions about modern Russia, but Norilsk in half a day has plunged me back into a world of Cold War spy thrillers full of heavily-clad police at check-points, empty streets blanketed in polluted snow and hotel floor-matrons.

A strong sense of satisfaction that I've made it to this strange city – the 'Journey of A Lifetime' that seemed about to elude us right up to the moment we made it past the airport police – is countered by a sense of being completely lost. Lost in space. Lost in time.

[i]'In Siberia'. Colin Thubron. Penguin Travel

[ii]ibid

[iii]On 31 August 1935, Aleksei Stakhanov, a thirty-year-old miner working at the Central Irmino Mine in the Donets Basin, hewed 102 tons of coal during his six-hour shift. This amount represented fourteen times his quota, and within a few days the feat was hailed by Pravda as a world record. Anxious to celebrate and reward individuals' achievements in production that could serve as a shining example to other workers, the Communist Party launched the Stakhanovite movement. The title of Stakhanovite was conferred on workers and peasants who set production records or otherwise demonstrated mastery of their assigned tasks. At the All-Union Conference of Stakhanovites in November 1935, the man himself thanked Comrade Stalin for 'the happy life of our country, the happiness and glory of our magnificent fatherland'. Stalin reportedly responded with the words: 'Life has become better and happier too.' Widely disseminated, and even set to song, the phrase served as the motto of the movement.

[iv]See Appendix II

# INSIDE NORILSK
## Through the Looking Glass

When I wake up, it is light. I jump out of bed in a panic, convinced I'm late for whatever it is I'm supposed to be doing. I look at my watch. It is four thirty in the morning.

When I next wake up, it is still light, but more by luck than by design it's about the right time to get up.

I go to the window and look out. It might as well be four thirty in the morning. There is no sign of human existence.

I remember with an anticipatory shiver that there seems to be no hot water in the bathroom. With leaden feet I walk slowly round the bed and look nervously at the bath and shower. In hope more than expectation, I decide to leave both taps running for a minute or so. It's a close call as to which is the least cold, but satisfied I can detect a miniscule difference I turn one off and activate the shower switch.

The next few moments are best glossed over. Expletives rip out of me between clenched teeth. I can no more control them than I could a violent spasm of nausea. I refuse to give up though, telling myself I am now in a country where people break the ice for an afternoon swim. Fuuuuucccccck! If they can do it, so can I.

The thought seems to do the trick... but then I realise it's not my psychological resilience that's come to save me. Well, I'll be... after what must be a full five minutes of being run, the temperature of the water has edged up from cold to lukewarm. It doesn't necessarily progress much further up the centigrade scale but it's now bearable.

Silly me! Should have realised that the hot water here would arrive with traditional Soviet efficiency!

I emerge into the corridor at the same time as Grigori. 'Does your shower work?' he asks me. I explain that you have to let it run a long time if you want hot water. He tells me he's had it running for the last twenty minutes and it hasn't moved beyond the original icy cold setting.

'Use my shower, Grigori,' says Sergey who has by now joined us in the corridor. He is positively glowing from some sort of super-charged washing experience he's just enjoyed. 'My shower is very hot… very good,' he tells a slightly put-out Grigori. Huh! Must be something to do with being an honorary citizen of the place, I suppose.

Breakfast, like all meals and all drinks in the place, is served in the small restaurant on the ground floor. Linoleum flooring and six or seven plastic-topped tables. There's a bit of a last-man-stands dash for the available seating among the guests, and those who arrive late have to hang around and wait until places become free.

The food offering, though, is reassuringly familiar, a mixture of the usual pan-global fry-up and patisserie.

People are sitting in national groupings, Russians on one table, Norwegians on another, Canadians on another. There's not much conversation but that's partly because the staff are playing hard-core Russian dance music over the speaker system. Maybe it's to encourage a fast rotation of the available seating space. Maybe it's some sort of anti-jamming device. Who knows?

I'm thankful that Grigori doesn't suggest a vodka over our fried eggs and coffee.

### Soviet Soul

The company's agreed to our request for a visit to the Nadezhda smelter and we're to hook up with one of their representatives over lunch. This is a critical breakthrough for us and puts us all in extra fine spirits.

In the interim, we're off to meet a presenter on the local TV station who's told Sergey she has a whole filofax of local 'characters' for us to interview.

As with the cinema restaurant of last night, the TV station

is heavily disguised as an anonymous grey block of concrete. There are no outer clues to the business going on inside. Only when we push our way through another of those double airlocks do we find ourselves in a bustling modern media environment, pot plants included.

Simona is there to meet us. She's a statuesquely tall woman in her early thirties. Her feminine curves, immaculate complexion and clear blue-grey eyes give her the air of a model.

She leads us into her office and then distractedly moves piles of papers and videotapes off chairs to allow us all to sit down. She talks quickly and enthusiastically, occasionally breaking into bursts of full-bodied laughter. All the time she rummages through index cards and diaries, jotting down names and numbers and giving them to Sergey to contact. He does so on his mobile while Grigori and I chat with her.

She tells us she'd come to Norilsk as a little girl. Her father had been in the air force and been transferred here.

At the time it was probably a plum posting. Norilsk Combine, as it was then known, occupied a very special place in the heart of the Soviet Union, a prized strategic resource run by the Ministry of Defence. The pay was way above the Russian average, there were 'hardship' bonuses for living so far north and guaranteed holidays in the sun in the exclusive resorts of the Black Sea. If you were serving in the armed forces and had the relevant skills, you often got a bit of time knocked off your length of service if you transferred over to the Combine.

And you got to be a pioneer for the Soviet Union, constantly assured that you were working at the fore of the decisive battle against the corrupt capitalism of the West.

Simona tells us she studied psychology on 'the mainland', the description everyone here uses to refer to the rest of Russia… and the rest of the world for that matter.

She'd come back to Norilsk but found no work as a psychologist 'because of the Russian mentality'. She had tried to tell the TV station they needed an in-house psychologist but they had said they couldn't afford one and offered her an assistant's job. That was seven years ago. Since then she'd worked her way up to presenting her own show. It's about animals and plants – 'a family show'.

Just about everyone in Norilsk owns pets apparently. Dogs, cats, fishes, birds. The TV station did a special to welcome in the Chinese New Year of the Snake, and hordes of locals emerged with an assortment of exotic snakes and lizards. Someone tried bringing crocodiles in, but they didn't survive the winter.

Simona reels through a selection of recent editions of the programme. There's a guy trying to get into *The Guinness Book of Records* with the biggest slug in the world. Apparently, the current record is held by a man in the UK. She nods smilingly at me while she says this, as if some of the achievement had somehow rubbed off on me as fellow-countryman.

There's a family that has ducks, geese and chickens and are in dispute with the local airline for not agreeing to fly in their goat.

From what she says, it seems there's a full-blown battle raging between the people of Norilsk and the domestic airline which serves the city. It insists on putting pets above a certain size in the hold and charging a full-price ticket for others. During our interview Simona receives several phone calls from irate viewers, offering her more egregious examples of the airline's callousness.

Then there's the surreal story of the family that found a ladybird on a freshly flown-in apple.

---

***Transcript.***
***Interview with Simona, TV presenter.***

Simona via Grigori: *They called her Valera, which is a popular Russian name, and they created a whole environment for the ladybird. They looked after it for quite a long while but eventually it died because of the harsh conditions. It survived for four months and there was great sadness in the whole town when it died...*

(It sounds like something of an over-reaction to the death of what was, all said and done, just an insect. I look slightly bemusedly at Grigori but he keeps a straight face. Simona smiles at me without a trace of irony. It's hard not to be bewitched by this Siberian beauty. I smile back. And it's only as she goes on to explain more about life here in Norilsk that I understand a little better the symbolic power the ladybird must have held over the city. Its struggle to survive its new environment mirrored that of all life in the Arctic.)

Simona via Grigori: *We all understand the time has come to leave Norilsk. It is very bad for our health. I may look young but we all know that inside our bodies we're quite ill.*
Andy: *Is that a new thing?*
Simona via Grigori: *It's always been like that. For eight months a year it is polar night. Your body's under constant stress because it lacks vitamins and sunlight. We get pills to take to compensate but it's not the same thing.*
*In wintertime this state of the body expresses itself in people being sleepy all the time. When it's dark all the time, it's very difficult to wake up and even when we're awake, we still fall asleep a lot.*
*Things relax in spring but all the disorders in the body that have been suppressed during the winter come to the fore and people fall ill even more.*
*What you see now out of the window...*

(Outside the previous night's fresh snowfall has already degenerated into another layer of black slush. The sun is as ambivalent as to whether it's coming or going as ever. The sky has lost none of its twilight sootiness.)

*... is our spring, and when the ice breaks on the Yenisey river, the tundra begins to blossom a little bit. But it only takes three or four weeks for all the plants to blossom, to bear fruit and to die.*
*Autumn is more like proper autumn. It begins in August, but by the end of September snow comes, and by October it is real winter here.*

(In a world that bursts into life for just a few days every year, animals and plants take on an extraordinary significance for the people of Norilsk. When Simona's show started, they had just covered people's pets but they'd received lots of complaints from plant-lovers so they'd branched out into horticulture.)

Andy: *So as a psychologist, what link do you make between the harsh conditions here and people's love of pets and plants?*

Simona via Grigori: *When it comes to plants, they remove a lot of stress. It's a bright green spot in your life because if you look outside, it's grey all the time. And people crave to do something with the earth. They plant tomatoes or cucumbers on their windowsill. I cannot even describe the feeling when you plant something, no matter what it is, in these kinds of conditions and then see it grow. You don't notice the passage of time so much and a lot of stress is relieved.*

(She gestures around her office and laughs again.)

*Here I don't have much in the way of plants because life in the TV company is so mad. But at home I have a lot of plants. They take the place of children for me. They're friends.*

*The custom here is you can drop in on anybody without any prior warning and they will be glad to see you, so it's quite easy to have friends, but a plant is a better friend because it's always there. It's faithful to you. You plant it and you watch it grow. It's a very profound connection. Sometimes the only thing that saves me is my little flowers on my windowsill and the times I can enjoy these flowers, like in the summer. There is quite a bit of colour then, but we always know that we only have two or three weeks, maximum, to enjoy it because it will all be dead again soon.*

(If the living conditions up here are tough for adults, they pose special problems for children growing up in Norilsk. As soon as the long Arctic winter gives way to the grey Arctic spring, the city's children are sent en masse to stay on the mainland 'so they can get some sunlight and eat some fruit'.)

> Simona via Grigori: *Our children are quite unique. The children who have grown up here, when they are taken to the mainland for the first time and they get off the plane and they see the grass, they throw themselves down on the grass and they kiss it and they cry because they've never seen anything like it.*
> *They don't even know what a cherry looks like, so there's a social programme to take children to the mainland for their summer holidays. A lot of children have to be shown various fruit and have it explained to them. 'This is what a pear looks like... and this is what a cherry looks like.'*

(Simona laughs at our looks of disbelief and nods her head vigorously to underscore the truth of what she is saying. She says that the adults accompanying the children's flights to the mainland now know to form a human chain from the airplane to the terminal to prevent over-excited Norilsk children from running amok across runways to hurl themselves at the alien greenery.

I rewind and then fast-forward in my head our strolls around the city. I realise so far I have not yet seen any natural greenery. Nor have I seen or heard any birds.)

> Andy: *Do you think that if people had the choice, most of them would stay here?*
> Simona via Grigori: *It's a very difficult question. We have this notion of the romance of the North. It draws people in and people stay quite a lot for emotional reasons. Relationships between people are very special here. I have spent a lot of time in places like Vladivostok and Moscow but I never got used to the way people dealt with each other there. I'm used to the closely-knit community spirit and the sort of relationship that is very specific to this place.*

*A lot of pensioners and people who finish their careers and their life here relocate to the mainland and a lot of them just cannot wait to come back here because they cannot get used to the different conditions of life elsewhere.*

Andy: *Do you intend to stay here?*

Simona via Grigori: *I've always run back when I've spent any time on the mainland. I just couldn't wait to get back.*

*It is very romantic to stand somewhere out there in the dark and see the lights of Norilsk at a distance, the whole city blazing with light.*

Andy: *Is there other stuff that people do to keep their spirits strong?*

(She laughs again.)

Simona via Grigori: *They go to gyms a lot, they dance a lot, there are these ballet dancing classes where whole families go and dance. Some people sing. Young people sing the latest hits. People more advanced in years sing after the traditional drinks. I'm not trying to say they're all drunk all the time but that's just the usual thing. Grown-ups sing folksongs a lot when they sit around the table.*

(Sergey has by now got us a couple more likely interviewees and returns to our conversation. He asks her what the company, Norilsk Nickel, means to her life. Good question, Sergey!)

Simona via Grigori: *Once it was the Norilsk Combine and we were all part of it in one way or another. Then, after they started restructuring the company, there were quite a few very unpleasant moments because when people start dividing the money, trying to share the money, there is always a problem.*

Sergey: *What has changed since the Soviet times?*

(I'm aware that Sergey is deliberately accelerating the interview. I sense that it's very important that whatever our agenda this morning, we must not be late for our lunchtime meeting with the company. I trust in his appreciation of the protocol here. It's also obvious that he and Simona have hit it off famously. Probably a Siberian thing.)

Simona via Grigori: *I think all over Russia, things like patriotism and strength of will have become less strong. And people think about the future in a different way, because in the Soviet past we used to think that we are all part of the state and we will overcome any difficulty and in the end we'll have a secure pension. People just felt more secure about everything.*
*That security is gone now and people think about money much more than they used to, but Norilsk more than any other Russian city still preserves that kind of soulfulness and that unity of goals and aims between people.*
*We're very proud of being Norilsk citizens.*
Sergey: *If Norilsk Nickel was only built because of the patriotism and motivation of the Soviet people, what's going to happen now?*
Simona via Grigori: *I want to believe that this motivation and these emotions will survive because, you know, we Russian people are very difficult to get going, but when it comes to the push we can do anything. We can work twenty-four hours and we will not complain. My hope is that we will not lose that.*

(The phone goes. This time the airline is trying to charge someone a full ticket price to take his pet python on the plane. Simona tells him the programme is investigating the whole issue and they're trying to persuade the airlines to be more conciliatory. She notes down his name and details and tells him his story may be included in one of their upcoming shows. It's obviously the standard response to the many irate pet-lovers of Norilsk.

We get to ask Simona one more question before we let her get on with the schedule for that night's show. What does she think of what Zelenin said about the long-term 'liquidation' of the city?

She gives the question a moment's thought before replying with passion.)

Simona: *No, that is not going to happen.*

As we make our way back out to the grey city streets and I run over in my mind the way the interview has gone, I experience a strong sense of double-take on some of what Simona has just said. In the presence of such a vivacious, exuberant, and, let's be frank about it, beautiful woman, it's hard not to get swept up into her aura which cushions you from the impact of her views.

But now I think back to what she said, two words collide into one alliterative ball of confusion. Soviet soulfulness? Not two words you'd normally associate with each other. And not words I'd have expected from a young, highly articulate media professional. From an older generation, maybe, but surely Simona of all people represented a new, forward-looking and forward-stepping Russia. I'm slightly shocked by her evident nostalgia for a totalitarian past.

But if she's in any way representative of the other people here, she's just shed a lot of light on the city's all-too-evident resistance to the symbols of a new world order. It's why the main street is still named after Lenin and why the murals proclaiming socialist solidarity are the most freshly painted walls here.

This, after all, is the city built in the wilderness by Stalin, the synthesis of many Russians' ambivalence about their past. Even Grigori, whose ambivalence at times extends to whether he is really a Russian or not, has admitted to me he grew up admiring the Georgian dictator.

Stalin may have been one of the greatest mass murderers the world has seen but in the eyes of many Russians he's also the man who galvanised this sleeping giant to break the back of the German army in the Great Patriotic War. He's the man who turned the country into a superpower to match the United States of America, even if the contest ultimately proved unsustainable for the Soviet Union.

Stalin, more than any other Russian leader, seems to be credited with creating a sense of Russian self-belief and national purpose, which many Russians feel has been dissipated since.

He also really knew a thing or two about vodka apparently.

### 'Have You Looked Out The Window Yet?'

I ponder again what Simona meant when she talked about the 'soulfulness' of the old days as we stand outside the apartment block of our next interviewee, one of Simona's recommendations.

We're on the very edge of town and, extraordinary though it is to say, this bit looks very run down even by the fairly lowly standards of the rest of the place.

The tower blocks here have a particularly dilapidated feel. Imagine something you've seen on TV about a sink estate, hold in your mind a picture of one of those tower blocks, smash it up a bit, pour soot all over it, smash it up again and you'll come close to how these look.

They gaze out mournfully over a bleak vista of dirty snow and rusting junk. Power lines criss-cross the horizon. Next to the buildings is a huge pool of black liquid, a couple of hundred yards long, gently steaming in the sub-zero temperature.

We enter one of the tower blocks. There are no lights and we stumble up the concrete stairwell. The paint on the walls has mostly peeled away and the whole place has a damp, rotting smell to it.

There are no numbers on the doors and Sergey has to check his notes before we venture to ring one of the bells. But we're confident we'll recognise our intended interviewee when we see her – she's a female bodybuilding champion.

A diminutive young woman answers the door. Just under five feet tall, she's very pretty with sparkling blue eyes. Beneath her tracksuit bottoms bulge thighs that most rugby players could only dream of.

We take our shoes off and are ushered into her kitchen which comprises a small plastic table, a couple of chairs, a portable gas stove and a kitchen sink with a hose-pipe running off it. It reminds me of a flat I once lived in when I was a penniless student. Not the sort of place you'd want to spend winter in Norilsk in, though.

I'm looking around me with a mixture of pity and mild disgust, while Grigori, Sergey and the surprisingly attractive bodybuilder, whom I shall call Mrs Norilsk, chat away in super-fast Russian.

Things take on a different shape, though, when Grigori turns to me and translates. 'She says she's sorry about the state of the kitchen. They're redoing the flat and this is the last room that they've got to work on.'

With a girlish bounce and a sweep of the hand, she invites us to see the rest of the apartment. We are accompanied by her toddler son and two small, yappy dogs. As we enter the main room, I blink as if I've just emerged from night into strong daylight.

It's like one of those apartments that you see in Hollywood films... all minimalist designer furniture and pine floors... the sort I always think no-one ever really lives in... until now, anyway. A state-of-the-art flat-screen TV and speakers sit along one of the walls. Lighting comes from a series of elegantly designed lamps and lights, all fashioned from gleaming chrome. Shipped from Moscow, she tells us.

The three of us follow her into the bathroom, which is also immaculate and boasts a huge round sunken bath approached by a set of three tiled steps.

And so the tour continues. Through the master bedroom, the kid's bedroom, the latter done up in jaunty blues with sailboats on the wallpaper.

Then there's the orchid room. Tray after tray of orchids, stacked from floor to ceiling. We've already seen them lining all the window shelves around the apartment, small explosions of colour wherever you look. But this is the mother-lode room, with hundreds and hundreds of orchids.

Well, actually, two thousand, it turns out. This is her other obsession apart from bodybuilding. It is also her connection with Simona and her show about plants and pets, of course.

I've been attempting a running commentary of our progress

through the apartment. It's not proving very easy. One of the dogs keeps attacking my ankles. I'm absolutely hopeless when it comes to a coherent, intelligible description of home furnishings. And Grigori, Sergey and our hostess keep bursting into animated fusillades of Russian. Only in the orchid room do I suggest to Grigori an attempt at a slightly more structured take on our thoughts.

---

*Transcript.*
*Grigori and Andy.*
*Orchid Room in Mrs Norilsk's Apartment.*

Andy: *So I think we're all a bit surprised and slightly awestruck by what a nice flat it is inside. Certainly there's nothing on the outside to give us any indication of what to expect once we got into the apartment.*

Grigori: *I just asked her whether it is a trying emotional experience every time to open her front door and go on to that horrible staircase. She said yes, it is horrible, especially as her neighbour is an alcoholic and he gets drunk and shouts all the time.*

*It's a world in itself, locked into itself, with some pretty terrible stuff going on right outside. All you have to do is open the front door and you step out into a totally different and very unpleasant world.*

Andy: *Have you looked out the window yet by the way?*

Grigori: *No, I'm not looking out the window because again, it's such a contrast... I'm looking now and, ugh... it's twisted rusting metals, huge lakes of some horrible steaming liquid and a very bleak landscape beyond it. Then I look at these fantastic flowers and very cheerful light fittings and this woman who is so fit and full of life and I cannot reconcile the outside with the inside. It must be some kind of personality split going on.*

We troop back into the kitchen, the false signifier for the rest of the apartment. I get one chair, Grigori gets another, and

Sergey gets to sit on an upturned crate. Mrs Norilsk stands by the sink to make us a cup of tea. She's frequently distracted by her young son and by her enthusiasm to speak to these strange foreigners from the mainland.

She's been growing orchids for three years, she tells us. It 'puts some kind of beautiful barrier between life out there and my home'. She's been bodybuilding for ten years, since she was sixteen years old. Her then boyfriend, now husband, introduced her to it. He runs a local gym. She is now female bodybuilding champion of Norilsk. 'Mrs Norilsk!' Her husband is local male champion. 'Mr Norilsk!' They are both going to compete in an international competition in Spain later this year.

---

***Transcript.***
***Interview with Mrs Norilsk.***
***The kitchen in her apartment.***

Mrs Norilsk via Grigori: *I was born in Norilsk. My parents, when they were young and members of the Komsomol[1] youth organisation, they came 'to build Norilsk'. That was in 1971.*

(As well as using the armed services as a filter for the most potentially useful workers, the Soviet leadership launched frequent campaigns, urging the country's brightest young communists to move to Siberia and help make socialism blossom in the tundra. The propaganda used just such phrases as 'to build Norilsk'.)

Mrs Norilsk via Grigori: *I've got a medical education already and I'm now studying at the Krasnoyarsk Pedagogical Institute, physical education department, Norilsk branch. I'm in my first year. I just took a biomechanics exam and got the highest mark.*

(Sergey, who is obviously quite taken with Mrs Norilsk, tells her flirtatiously he can understand why she got such high marks. I can't work out from her answer whether she's registered the implied compliment.)

Mrs Norilsk via Grigori: *I found it quite easy to do well in the exam because there are very few athletes of my calibre in the city. And of course I get a bit of preferential treatment. Since I won the Mrs Norilsk bodybuilding contest, I am the pride of this town.*

(And will the pride of the town be staying here or moving to sunnier climes?)

Mrs Norilsk via Grigori: *Yes, I want to move away. I grew up here, it's my home city, but…*

(And here she gestures out the window.)

*… it's a bit of a shit-hole.*
Andy: *The things that we have no experience of in the UK are the long winters here and the twenty-four darkness. How on earth do you get through that every year?*
Mrs Norilsk via Grigori: *It is very hard. There is very little that is pleasant in the winter. When I was small, the environment was much better, so much better that reindeer used to walk through the town. We used to go out. There was a forest right next to this building with mushrooms and we used to go mushroom picking, but the pollution from the smelters burnt the forest and the mushrooms are long gone.*
Andy: *When did that happen?*
Mrs Norilsk via Grigori: *It happened gradually. I can remember when I was small seeing the reindeer wandering down the streets. But now they've gone a long way off from here because there is nothing for them to eat and they cannot cross the big gas pipelines.*

(Reindeer! I wince at the word. Our trip to Norilsk is meant to be the antithesis of a programme about Siberian reindeer. Why are we all so obsessed by reindeer? I've watched several shows on TV in the few months preceding our visit, tuning in to anything and everything I could find in the schedules about Russia.

The last one I'd seen had taken a particularly dry comedian to a small village of Siberian indigenous people who attempted to train him in the art of driving a sleigh with reindeer.

I have to say I found the programme very funny. But I'm also immensely frustrated by our media's repeated reduction of this huge country to a tiny family-viewing-friendly pinpoint. One of my driving motivations for making a radio show on Norilsk is to try and capture something of the many millions of people living in Siberia who don't actually herd reindeer.

Grigori had agreed whole-heartedly when we'd discussed our ideas before contacting the RGS and the BBC. 'Who the fuck cares about the reindeer?' he'd exclaimed theatrically before launching into an impressively impassioned rant against the dreaded beast. Somewhat ruefully, I suspect that just about everyone listening to Radio 4 at eleven o'clock in the morning probably cares about the reindeer. But we'd agreed at the time that the closest we were likely to get to reindeer in the industrial mining town of Norilsk was via the dinner plate. Not so apparently…

Enough of the reindeer! I switch the subject back to Mrs Norilsk's plans to leave Norilsk).

Andy: *And where are you planning to go?*

Mrs Norilsk via Grigori: *We're planning to move to Moscow as a first step. Then it's in the gods' laps. I've already got an invitation to go and work in St Petersburg but I'm not that keen. I don't like the climate. It's too humid there. I couldn't live in the city.*

Andy, more to Grigori than Mrs Norilsk: *Don't you reckon any climate's going to be a bit warm and humid if this is the one you're used to?*

Mrs Norilsk via Grigori: *I really love central Russia. The climate there is just perfect for me. Last summer we went to south Russia for a holiday and that wasn't as hot as I expected either.*

One thing is puzzling me, though, about Mrs Norilsk. She and her husband have obviously already spent quite a lot of time thinking about their plans to leave. Why, then, are they spending so much time and money making their apartment into a Hollywood penthouse? The property market is so new an idea here in Russia that the current British obsession with buying a house to work on it to sell it for more money to buy a bigger house and so on simply does not exist. And even if it did, this particular flat is always going to fall foul of the property mantra, Location, Location, Location.

As Mrs Norilsk attends to her son for a moment, Grigori tells me he's equally surprised at the luxury they've lavished on their apartment. He was brought up in an age when such creature comforts were a distant promise, something that would be achieved when the rest of the world had seen the error of its ways and come round to Socialist enlightenment. Luxurious home furnishings were not high on the agenda of the Soviet's ramshackle economic system. Not when they could have more missile launchers and tanks to show off at the May Day parades!

The result, Grigori tells me, was that no one really gave much of a damn about their surroundings. Even if you did, you just got to choose along with the rest of Russia from the same limited choice of furniture and wallpapers churned out by a couple of huge industrial combines.

And people didn't give much thought to the future anyway. Why bother, when the future was always postponed?

Grigori turns to Mrs Norilsk and starts off on a long, meandering speech in Russian. The question is no doubt lurking in there somewhere but he seems to have gone off on one of his poetic verbal excursions. When he's eventually finished, it takes Mrs Norilsk about a quarter of the time to answer.

Mrs Norilsk via Grigori: *My husband and I don't want to spend our best years in a pigsty. Yes, we are planning to leave. But it might not happen this autumn. It might happen in a few years' time and in the meantime I don't want to sit on my suitcases dreaming of leaving one day and doing nothing about my surroundings.*

Our tea has been made and drunk by this time and Mrs Norilsk has to go to the air terminal. Her latest purchases for the apartment have just arrived from Moscow.

Leaving her flat and going back into the stairwell I get some sort of insight into what Adam must have felt like when God told him to get out of the Garden.

As we re-emerge into the wasteland outside the tower block, I look back and try and catch any visual clues to the sleekly designed interior we've just seen. There are none. I look around the dismal horror-scape that stretches away from the block and try and imagine a forest with mushrooms where the barren, rusted-junk-strewn tundra and steaming pools of black sludge lie. I try and imagine reindeer wandering between the sooty tower blocks. I can't.

### The Reindeer and the Wolf

We trudge back into the centre of town to meet our next interviewee, a woman who runs the local embroidery club. 'Quite a character' is how Simona had described her. So far, our highly limited straw poll of the merits of leaving or staying in Norilsk has produced a one-all draw. Looks like the next Norilsk citizen, the last one we've got time to see before lunch, is going to have the casting vote of the morning.

REINDEER WOMAN, as I will call her for reasons that will shortly become clear, lives close to the central Leninsky Prospekt. It's a relatively swanky part of town, at least in comparison to the part we've just visited. Here the apartment blocks are only four or five storeys high. They date back to the 1960s. The architecture is less austere than the anonymous slabs of concrete that were obviously all the rage in the 1970s and 1980s. Some of them even have ornate designs worked into the stonework, although they've been eroded almost to the point of invisibility by the Arctic conditions.

The apartment is in a block that looks as if it's just had a very fresh lick of yellow paint. But, once again, the stairwell is a dank, gloomy place. The walls are bare concrete that are cold to the touch. However, I'm starting to get to grips with the inside-outside conundrum of Norilsk and I'm less surprised when we're shown into a homely, richly-decorated apartment by a sprightly woman in her fifties.

The living room-cum-kitchen is a large and bright space. Huge pot plants spread their fern-like green leaves from all four corners. A cream-coloured three-piece suite surrounds a glass-topped coffee table.

The walls are adorned with a selection of striking paintings – bright-coloured flowers set against white backgrounds, Christmas-card snow scenes of churches, St Petersburg in the nineteenth century and abstract modernist kaleidoscopes of shape and colour. It's only when I go to look more carefully at one of them that I realise they're not paintings at all. They're intricately woven embroidery patterns, encased behind glass.

An elegant Persian cat sits purring on one of the cream chairs. Reindeer Woman makes us freshly ground coffee and serves us slices of camembert cheese and chocolate biscuits, all the while chirruping away animatedly. She seems to be positively buzzing with excess energy.

Grigori, whose simultaneous translation skills have impressed me mightily on this trip so far, struggles to keep up with her. She speaks in rapid machine-gun bursts and leaves him little space to try and translate into the microphone.

We're here to talk to her about the local embroidery club but that gets forgotten when she tells us what she does. She is a botanist working for an agricultural research institute. In fact, she's head of the botany department.

She and her husband, who works 'high up' in 'the company' – there is only one company here – came to the city straight after graduating from university in St Petersburg. That was twenty-six years ago. They were drawn by the higher salaries being offered by the Soviet state at the time for working in places like Norilsk, part of a concerted effort to populate the Far North of the country. She doesn't use the word but the profile is spot on for Komsomol membership.

Hold on, though! My mind does a little somersault. The thought of an agricultural research institute in this pollution-devastated city is so surreal I have to hide a smirk when I ask through Grigori what exactly her work involves.

She laughs. 'Reindeer, of course.'

I briefly catch Grigori's eye. I can foresee no escape from the reindeer story. Completely fortuitously it seems we're now going to get the chance to interview the local expert on the subject. Looks like the Radio 4 listeners won't be disappointed after all.

Reindeer it will be then.

-----

**Transcript.**
**Interview with Reindeer Woman.**
**In Her Living Room.**
**Punctuated by Coffee and Camembert Interruptions.**

Andy (somewhat resignedly): *That's interesting, because we've just talked to someone who said they could remember as a small girl that there were reindeer here in the town.*
Reindeer Woman via Grigori: *Yes, I can also remember the time. In the early 1980s there were reindeer wandering through the town.*
Andy: *And there was a forest here as well?*
Reindeer Woman via Grigori: *Yes. There was a forest here when they were building the town. The first housing was built right next to the nickel smelter and then the town started spreading and the forest disappeared.*
*The death of the forests was as much due to 'the axe' as anything else. It's natural that areas of countryside are destroyed when a city develops like that.*

(Decades of heavy pollution didn't help either, I think to myself.

She explains that there is nothing for the reindeer near the city now and their migratory patterns have shifted to accommodate it and its surrounding spider's web of gas and water pipes.

I picture a half-starving reindeer trekking across the far northern tundra and ask how many there are now).

Reindeer Woman via Grigori: *About twenty years ago there were around 370,000 reindeer. Now it's close to 1,200,000. The population has exploded.*

(It's not the answer I'm expecting. I can see a similar reaction on Grigori's face even before he turns to me and the microphone to translate.)

Andy: *Over a million reindeer! Where?*
Reindeer Woman via Grigori: *All within the Taimyr Peninsula. It's the largest population of wild reindeer in the world here. It's one of the things my institute is studying.*
Andy: *Why do you think it's grown so much over that period of time?*
Reindeer Woman via Grigori: *Well, it's difficult to say. There is a natural cycle in a wild animal population like that, it increases and decreases naturally.*
*But also there was a Soviet industry to breed reindeer for meat. Not the tame reindeer, which the indigenous people here herded as domestic animals. It was a full-scale industry and it collapsed with the fall of the Soviet Union. The industry had been a way of culling the wild herds, and since it's stopped, the reindeer population has just carried on growing.*
Andy: *I suppose there's no natural predator for reindeer here.*
Reindeer Woman via Grigori: *Wolves. The wolf population is exploding as well...*

(Here she laughs at us and her eyes twinkle.)

*... so you be careful when you walk down the street tonight.*
Andy: *No, seriously now, do the wolves ever come near*

*places of population?*
Reindeer Woman via Grigori: *No, the wolves generally follow the reindeer. They migrate together across the tundra.*
Andy: *How far do they migrate?*
Reindeer Woman via Grigori: *Thousands of kilometres. The reindeer and the wolf. They walk together hand in hand across the tundra.*

The reindeer story is turning out to be a little more interesting and surprising than I had imagined.

I realise that I had jumped to conclusions about what Mrs Norilsk had told us about the reindeer vanishing from the streets of Norilsk. Leaving aside Grigori's and my attempt to avoid the whole subject, I guess I'd assumed that they were simply another victim of the pollutants being pumped daily into the Arctic ecosystem, another sad story of ecological blight.

But it seems they, and the wolf population, have been unintended beneficiaries of the Soviet economy's collapse.

It's hard to exaggerate the scale of the changes that took place in Russia after the collapse of the Berlin Wall. It's no coincidence that a lot of people around here call 1989 'year zero' to try and capture the sense of economic upheaval that gripped the country through much of the 1990s. The Moscow government spent much of the decade teetering on the brink of bankruptcy, state enterprises were collapsing like dominoes and those that remained were largely paralysed in a glue-pot of collective unpaid debt.

Places like Norilsk were particularly affected because they had previously relied on heavy subsidies from the central system. When those ran out, the impact sent destructive waves rippling through Russia's most far-flung regions.

In this case, as Reindeer Woman explains in some detail, what went first was the domestic air cargo company that had flown the reindeer meat to the mainland. That in turn led to the bankruptcy and closure of the local reindeer meat industry which had served to keep the reindeer population in check.

At the same time, the state system of paying bounties for wolf hides also collapsed. A male wolf hide in the old days would bring a hunter the equivalent of a month's average salary in Norilsk's mines. Without that incentive, only the wealthiest of citizens could afford the fuel for the helicopter needed to track the wolves across the tundra.

Reindeer Woman via Grigori: *It requires a special skill and art to kill a wolf. Very few people can do it. It takes a lot of work to track it down and kill it. It's not like in central Russia where there's a small forest and they drive a wolf into a small corner with red flags and kill it. Here you have to cover really long distances, so it's got to be worth your while.*

This complex chain reaction of events and consequences may have turned out to be good news for the local reindeer and wolves, but there is an ugly flipside. Along with the disappearance of the various subsidies to the local indigenous people went the one to herd domesticated reindeer.

There are only two domestic herds left in the area and they're struggling, according to our expert on the subject. The state-funded herding was managed on collectivist principles drawn up by Party technocrats not reindeer herders. Many of the indigenous people became dependent on the handouts and turned their back on their elders' more traditional nomadic lifestyle.

They now find themselves in cultural and economic limbo, having been forcibly integrated into a system that no longer exists. They live in settlements with no banks, no infrastructure and no supplies, reduced to a subsistence level of survival, and plagued by alcoholism.

There are three main indigenous peoples in the Norilsk area – the Dolgans, the Nganasan and the Entsy. The last publicly available survey of their population compiled in 1989 put the population of the Dolgans at over 6,000, and at just 300 in the case of the Entsy[ii].

Reindeer Woman tells us she has worked a lot with the indigenous people because she uses them as guides on her expeditions to the tundra.

'I know a lot of them personally. I count them as good friends. They're lovely people. But their life is very tough and it's our fault for what we've done to these people.'

Sounds depressing, I say, but she doesn't agree. 'Without optimism there is no life.'

She says that the new governor of the Taimyr Region – a certain Alexander Khloponin who was not entirely coincidentally former general director of Norilsk Nickel during the period of crisis management in the late 1990s – has started a campaign to try and halt the decline of the indigenous population.

> Reindeer Woman via Grigori: *Now the state has begun to support domesticated reindeer breeding. It has started paying a certain amount of money for every reindeer head because the authorities have realised that the basis of the indigenous people's economy is reindeer breeding. Not hunting. Hunting is very insecure and too unstable a livelihood. Today you may kill a reindeer but tomorrow you may not. But when you have a herd, you have some security.*
> *The main thing is, these people don't need another easy infusion of cash. What they need is the creation of conditions where they can build up their own economy and look after themselves.*

(Her institute is also studying the economics of reintroducing a wild reindeer industry along the lines of that which existed before year zero.)

> *In principle, it makes sense. There is great demand for reindeer meat because it is believed to have very good qualities for your health. And we're also developing technologies to utilise everything the reindeer has to offer, the horns, the hooves, everything. The indigenous people are showing us how. They use everything the reindeer has to offer for clothes, footwear, food, even for medicines. The tradition is already there and our institute is trying*

*to work out how to do it at an industrial level. So why not?*
*There is a chance for the industry to be rebuilt.*

(A similar programme is underway to study how to regenerate a local eco-system that has been ravaged by decades of industrial pollution on a scale we in the West can barely imagine.)

Andy (slightly sceptically): *Could the forest ever return?*

Reindeer Woman via Grigori: *That may be a bit too difficult because what you must remember is that northern eco-systems are very slow to return to their original state. Even the slightest disturbance in the eco-system balance causes very lasting effects in systems like that around Norilsk. The seeds of plants and trees have been damaged to such an extent that they grow much slower now.*

*It's what my institution is doing right now, studying the seeds and seeing what conditions they are in now and how to change them, how to improve them. We've also developed a technique of creating a new topsoil and planting grain in it. It grows quite well.*

*But there are no sources of organic fertilisers here because there is no cattle breeding, although we've discovered that sewage processing sites produce material which can be utilised as fertiliser.*

Andy: *Reindeer shit also springs to mind.*

(She dissolves in uncontrollable fits of laughter and struggles for several seconds to regain her composure enough to reply. Grigori and Sergey are also laughing in sympathetic merriment, which I think is a bit disloyal, since I know for a fact they know exactly as much as I do about reindeer shit. I don't see why my comment has produced such collective mirth. These days there seem to be enough of the damned beasts around! Eventually, she manages to answer me, still giggling between the words.)

Reindeer Woman via Grigori: *It would be very difficult. You would have to wander around a territory of over a*

*few thousand square miles looking for reindeer shit with
your pooper-scooper!*

(Yeah, okay. I hadn't thought of that.)

*Getting forests back is probably too ambitious for now. But
in this city, even getting shrubs and grass to grow again
would be a major achievement.*

(Having now had a crash course in everything I could ever
have wanted to know about the local reindeer population, I
decide it's time for our interviewee to cast her vote on the
attractiveness or otherwise of living in Norilsk. Her laughter
tinkles around us again.)

Reindeer Woman via Grigori: *I've lived here for twenty-six
years, what do you think?*
*We've a grown-up son but we decided our son, who is
twenty-four now, should start his life on the mainland. He
has bad eyesight so he's been exempted from army service.
He's working in St Petersburg, which is one of my favourite
places. My husband and I have a dream one day, when
we're finished here, to go and live in St Petersburg. It's the
city of our dreams.*
*But as long as my husband and I can work, as long as
we're strong and capable, we will stay here. I love the
tundra too much.*
*When the summer season begins, everyone here cries, 'Let's
go to the tundra!' We take sashliks with us, kebabs, and we
go for walks in the forest and then we cook our meal in the
open and have a good time.*
*There are mountains here near Talnakh with a beautiful
waterfall. That's one of our favourite spots. We go there
often.*
*To understand the beauty of Norilsk, you should come here
in summer because there's so much more to do. In spring
it's a very unpleasant city because everything melts and it's
quite muddy and grey, but in the summer it's a fantastic*

*place. Particularly near Talnakh. The winds hardly ever*
*blow that way so the area is not polluted at all.*
*Sometimes, like the summer of 2001, we were on an*
*expedition out in the tundra and there was a lake there*
*and the water was very warm and we bathed all the time.*

(The memory of my shower experience is still too fresh for
me not to shiver at the very thought of skinny-dipping in an
Arctic lake.)

Andy: *Really?*
Reindeer Woman via Grigori: *The water warms up to a*
*depth of about one metre. So the main thing is not to dive*
*in but just to stay on the surface of the water.*
*I just love the tundra. It's my workplace but it's also my*
*home.*

Looks like 2:1 for 'staying' then!
Sergey is nervously starting to look at his watch. We're already
running late for our meeting with the company representative
and we've not even asked about the embroidery which is the
reason we'd come to interview her in the first place. Out of
politeness more than interest, we do a quick skim along the
dozens of framed embroideries that decorate the walls of her
apartment.

In the process she shows us her home gym, comprising
an exercise bike, a rowing machine and various weights. I'm
impressed by her evident energy levels and the fact she thinks
nothing of going for a dip in a lake in the Arctic Circle.

We turn our recording equipment off and start to back out of
the flat whilst making our excuses. She never stops talking and
I'm not convinced she stops even after the door has closed on
us and we're exiled back to the dark stairwell.

As we make double-quick time to the restaurant rendezvous,
I look more curiously at the functional, weather-beaten facades
of the Soviet-era apartment blocks that line our route.

I'm not sure if I'd thought too much about what an average
Norilsk apartment would look like on the inside. Flaking

wallpaper, peeling paint and shoddy carpets, I guess. But what I hadn't expected was anything like the two I've just visited. I've obviously seriously underestimated the power of consumer capitalism over those to whom it was so long denied.

Also, something that our last interviewee said keeps looping through my thoughts as we hunch up against the icy wind that is cutting like a knife through my padded jacket. We'd asked her what she did in winter. She'd sighed with vicarious contentment. 'The winter is very long and our world is here at home. Here we feel just fine.'

Spring may not be a great season to visit by the sound of it, but winter must surely be worse.

I was living in Berlin when it had its coldest winter for fifty years. The temperature dropped to -25°C for a few days. I was sharing a flat with a Brazilian and we used to cut a pack of playing cards to see who had to face the walk down to the supermarket to get provisions. The combination of wind and cold literally burnt any exposed bit of skin.

The average temperature here in Norilsk is a few degrees colder than that for around three months of the year. Fairly significantly, I feel, the figure does not include any wind-chill factor from the winter gales that sweep across the tundra.

I suspect there are a lot of quiet nights in if you live in Norilsk, particularly with the twenty-four-hour darkness in the middle of winter. Your home must assume immense importance under such conditions. No wonder people take such care of their immediate surroundings. Norilsk is not the place to let yourself go, particularly in winter.

We turn the corner into the street with the restaurant. On doing so, we find ourselves facing a big power station, two arms of smoke powering upwards into the sky from the massive chimneystacks. I try again and imagine forests and reindeer wandering through the town. I still can't.

Bloody reindeer!

[i] The Komsomol was in essence the youth wing of the Communist Party, the central skeleton of power in the former Soviet Union. Like its big brother, it sprang directly from the 1917 revolution and was formally subordinated to the Bolshevik party in 1919. The minimum age requirement was fourteen and the maximum twenty-eight. It was primarily used as an organ of 'education' of Socialist principles for the nation's younger generation. But it also proved a surprisingly efficient mechanism for pooling youthful labour resources at short notice. If a special project, such as Norilsk, needed a new injection of energetic workers, Komsomol was effective in raising the cry for socialism and exhorting hundreds of volunteers to sign up to help. Needless to say, Komsomol members received a range of privileges and preferences in promotion. At its peak, membership is estimated to have been around forty million in the 1970s and early 1980s. The Party's tentacles spread all the way down through Russian society. The Komsomol was complemented by two other organisations – the Pioneers for children aged between nine and fourteen and the Little Octobrists for the very young.

[ii] 1999 Paper on 'Economic Development and the Environment: Sakhalin Offshore Oil and Gas Fields', Hokkaido University, Japan.

# FIRE AND ICE
## 'Welcome to Hell'

The restaurant is down a flight of stairs in front of another Soviet realist expression of concrete. Three people – two men and a woman – are waiting for us just outside the entrance. There's a burst of Russian conversation – apologies for being late on our side tumbling over and into an introduction by the younger of the two men who is the representative of the company's public relations department. He simultaneously bustles all of us down and into the restaurant.

Yet again, my mind registers a slide between two realities as I look around. As with the restaurant last night, this one has also been themed but this time as some sort of underground grotto, which seems appropriate given the fact we're in the middle of a huge mining area. It's all fake stone walls and hidden orange lighting, which gives the impression of a distant fire – a bit like hell, although I'm sure that was not intended.

The only incongruity in the subterranean décor is a giant TV screen showing what appears to be some sort of cable TV fashion programme. It takes me a while to work out the appeal of this latest example of the Russian multi-media restaurant experience, but then I register most of our fellow diners are single men, all watching scantily-clothed models parading up and down a catwalk between mouthfuls of lunch. As I'm growing accustomed to by now, the sound is turned down and has been replaced by high-decibel Russian pap-pop music.

Lunch is ordered for me, and since most of the conversation at our table is in Russian, I'm left to my own thoughts about our lunch companions.

The guy next to me has been introduced as a photographer for a local newspaper. He's a bear of a man – young, mid twenties but several stone heavier and several inches taller than I am, and I'm no slender waif. He's bearded and I just instinctively know from the hair bursting up from under his collar that his whole torso is unimaginably hirsute.

The woman is in her late forties. She has carefully coiffured red hair, which makes her almost unique after what I've seen of the Russian fondness for peroxide. She represents a local magazine, I'm told. She seems quite personable but whether it's latent Russian sexism or just her own shyness, like me she is largely left out of the conversation.

To me the most interesting of our companions is the young man from the company's public relations department. I'm starting to discern some classic Russian stereotypes in terms of faces and this guy has one of them.

A round face, rosy cheeks, lips just the right side of fleshy, strong nose, pale green flashing eyes sunk into the skull, bullet-shaped forehead and close-cropped haircut. His skin is faultless, which strikes me as incongruous in this most polluted of cities.

I spend quite a lot of time wondering what I would cast him as in a film and I eventually decide he'd be in a World War II film – or rather a film about the Great Patriotic War since we're in Russia – and he'd be the young Russian army lieutenant.

The conversation between him, the bear-like photographer, Grigori and Sergey is animated. The woman makes occasional comments and smiles a lot. I say nothing but try and give the impression I'm following whatever is being said with interest.

An almost complete silence falls around the table when the food starts arriving. This is another thing I'm starting to notice about the Russians in groups. Food is not there to be enjoyed; it's there to be attacked. I've been criticised many times in the past for bolting my food, but I'm the slowest eater at this particular table.

The service is timed accordingly. As soon as the first course has been deposited in front of us, the waitress has gone off to the kitchen to fetch the main course. It doesn't matter if you haven't finished your starters. The plate just gets shoved next to you anyway.

Conversation dries up as everyone gets on with the business of tucking in at a furious pace. Three courses from start to finish take no longer than ten minutes to be consumed. I surreptitiously time us on my watch.

Only when the coffee is served does everyone start to relax again and the conversation resumes with reinvigorated joviality. I can tell Grigori is just itching to order a round of vodkas but the company is hosting and the offer is not made.

When we exit the restaurant a company minibus is awaiting us. It's only as I take my seat next to Grigori in the back that he gives me a quick catch-up on the planned afternoon events.

Now, I had been under the impression that we were going to be given a guided tour of the highly symbolic Nadezhda smelter, which, as we all now know, was built almost single-handedly by the legendary Citizen Khagazheev, the bastard who gave us the 'sorry, my fax machine isn't working' run-around back in Moscow.

It seems, sadly, that his legacy in the Arctic tundra is going to be as elusive as the man himself, since Grigori tells me we are not going there at all but rather to another of the many metallurgical complexes dotted around the fair city of Norilsk.

I ask Grigori why we can't go to Nadezhda. He turns all Russian on me and avoids the question altogether, just assuring me that, 'Don't worry, we're still going to one of the plants'. 'Which one?' I ask. The copper smelter, he tells me. What's its name, I want to know. 'Just the copper smelter. Everything will be fine, you'll see!'

Sometimes Grigori's breezy insouciance infuriates me, but I get no chance to start an argument with him since he's sucked back into the post-prandial jollity that is washing over the rest of the party. A sort of school outing excitement has seized all the Russians in the vehicle. Everyone's trying to talk at once and there's a lot of laughter and backslapping going on.

I feel excluded by my total inability to follow the conversation. The BBC had been insistent that I shouldn't make any attempt to learn even rudimentary phrasebook Russian before the trip. They said my dependence on Grigori as translator and guide would add to the sense of drama in the programme. There's no sense of drama if your guide doesn't talk to you, I muse to myself, as I hunker down and gaze sulkily out of the minibus window.

## Matrix

The journey from the restaurant to the copper smelter takes all of five minutes. The young public relations guy, or Lieutenant Ivanov as I have now decided to call him, explains that when the first permanent structures in the city of Norilsk were built in the 1950s and 60s, the metallurgical plants were built as close as possible to the housing for the workers.

Apparently, the city administration thought it was the most practical measure. After all, no-one wanted a long commute in mid-January in this Siberian city. No-one knew much about the effects of emissions from Soviet-designed metals plants on the health either, apparently.

The smelter is divided from the city proper by another of the huge lakes of steaming liquid that are scattered around the place. It's around three hundred yards long and a couple of hundred yards wide. I assume that it's something to do with the metals facility itself, but when I eventually manage to ask Grigori between all the joking, he says that it's just the city's sewage plant.

The smelter is an enormous building. It must be all of half a mile long and several hundred yards wide. Its massive chimneystacks tower above us. Giant plumes rise up into the sky to form part of the hazy cloud that smothers the whole city.

We pull up in front of an administrative building. It's the usual concrete structure, about eight storeys high, but relatively modern looking. Lt Ivanov gets out to liaise with whomever it is he needs to liaise with.

I look out of the window at the monstrosity and wonder whether it's the same smelter I saw featured in a photo journal of the city on the Internet. The only picture of 'The Copper Smelter' was of a wall inside the plant on which someone had scrawled in English: 'Welcome to Hell!'

Or maybe that visitor had been lucky enough to get inside

the Nadezhda smelter.

Huh! I feel that the ghostly presence of Citizen Khagazheev is dogging our footsteps. Has he called Norilsk and told them not to let us anywhere near HIS smelter, I wonder?

Lt Ivanov returns and we drive through a barrier, operated by a large-framed female guard, to a side entrance near the front of the smelter. There we get out and stand in a small human huddle dwarfed by this metal-making monster. There's more liaison work to be done by our young friend before we're allowed to step inside. I look around.

Sergey is in a state of almost feverish excitement. He's been in exuberant form ever since we arrived in Norilsk but I haven't seen him as animated as he is now. He leans over towards me, grinning, and says, 'Matrix!' That's the film he went to see back in Moscow. It was the time Grigori and I had got lost on returning to the apartment. And I know immediately what he means. The place looks like a set from a Hollywood film, a terrible futuristic man-made dystopia.

I've been to metals plants before – it came with the job to some extent – and they tend to be rather bland, anonymous structures. Huge, it's true. But most developed countries now have such strict rules on emissions from metal smelters that they are literally self-contained, capturing and purifying any noxious fumes. To the untrained eye many of them simply look like big aircraft hangars.

This, however, is quite a different matter altogether. There are massive pipes running higgledy-piggledy across the ground, up the walls, over our heads. The casing appears to be falling apart just about everywhere. Steam leaks from a thousand cracks and holes, some of which have been haphazardly stuffed with lagging. The background hissing sound is so loud that it's impossible to use our recording equipment.

Seen up close, even the walls of the giant building are rusting away in parts and it looks as if the whole mammoth edifice is a living thing, breathing out steam and smoke through the pores of its shell. Had they had industrial-scale copper smelters in the time of Dante, this is what they would have looked like.

Our young lieutenant returns with obligatory hard helmets

and we push through heavy plastic doors to the interior of this fuming leviathan.

We find ourselves in a long workshop, populated by groups of workers, those at the far end reduced to the size of matchstick men such is the scale of the place. It is the part of the plant where the finished copper is being loaded and prepared for shipment. It's 99.97 per cent pure, electrolytically refined copper cathode. It's just starting its own journey of a lifetime, destined to travel many thousands of miles to manufacturers in distant countries. They'll metamorphose it into wire or cable, tubes or bars. Semi transformed, it will then travel on to be further manipulated into an end-product that will make our cars start, our homes light up and our mobile phones work. Copper is a metal with myriad uses but most of them derive from the fact that it is such an efficient conductor of electricity – the life force of our modern technological era.

A big display on the main wall shows how much copper has been produced this day, the numbers ticking over at regular intervals.

There are slogans emblazoned on the other walls. Grigori translates for me. 'Your family awaits you! Healthy and Smiling!' And my personal favourite: 'I love you life!'

So much do the workers love life that all of them are equipped with oxygen packs to compensate for the polluted atmosphere inside the smelter. These packs comprise a heavy-looking black satchel belted around the waist and a straggling nozzle with mouthpiece. All the workers are taking deep drags of the life-enhancing gas as they walk around. Amid the clanking of machinery and a more sonorous constant rumble emanating from somewhere deeper inside the plant, the image adds to the feeling we have indeed just entered some antechamber to hell.

### Workers Unite!
Without too much ceremony we're shown into a side-room, which is obviously where the workers take their breaks. A heavy smell of stale tobacco smoke permeates the air. Three tough-looking members of the workforce eye the visitors

warily through three plumes of cigarette smoke rising from three ashtrays on the table in front of them. We all stand there slightly ill at ease, no one quite sure what to do next.

Seems as good an opportunity as any for an interview, I say to Grigori.

He goes over to the trio and starts a lengthy explanation of who we are and what we're about before asking for their permission to interview them 'for the BBC'. Their collective expression of world-weary scepticism doesn't change throughout his speech.

When he stops talking, there's an uncomfortably long silence before the largest member of this morose triptych nods with a 'why the fuck not?' shrug of the shoulders. He's obviously the alpha male among the boiler-suited brethren and most of the answers to our questions come from him – his sidekicks occasionally murmuring their assent or just nodding.

------------

***Transcript.***
***Copper Smelter.***
***Interview with Smelter Workers (actually Contractors, see below).***

Andy: *How long have you been working here?*
Alpha Male via Grigori: *I've been working at this plant for twenty-one years.*
Andy: *Is that all your working life?*
Alpha Male via Grigori: *I used to work on the mainland before that. I'm a construction worker.*
Andy: *Family?*
Alpha Male via Grigori: *Wife and two children. They're here in Norilsk.*
Andy: *How has life changed for you in the last ten years?*
Alpha Male via Grigori: *It's exactly the same as it was before. The same conditions, except now we have to work more and get paid less.*

(There's a general low grumble of agreement from the other two.)

Andy: *How long are the shifts and how many hours per week?*

Alpha Male via Grigori: *Seven hours per day. Five days a week. It's continuous production here.*

Andy: *And how often do you get a break like this?*

Alpha Male via Grigori: *It's right at the end of the shift now. But we decide ourselves when we have time to have a break. It's up to us.*

(There's a quick interchange between the big guy, Grigori and Lt Ivanov.)

Grigori: *Ah! Okay! You see these guys are actually contractors. They're not employees of the smelter. They are just contracted to do jobs for the smelter.*

Andy: *And which is the first thing you go for on the break... the oxygen or the cigarettes then?*

(For the first time, the big guy breaks into a laugh, a trigger for his two sidekicks to chuckle in accompaniment.)

Alpha Male via Grigori: *When we work, we take the oxygen. But when we have a break like this, of course, a cigarette is the first thing.*

Andy: *And would you mind if I asked how much you get paid per hour?*

Alpha Male via Grigori: *Eighteen thousand roubles per month, it's about the average.*

(Grigori does a quick bit of mental calculation and says it's about £500.)

Andy: *Overtime?*

Alpha Male via Grigori: *Not bloody likely! That's the policy of the middle level of management. We don't get much chance to do extra work and earn extra money.*

(There's another collective round of monosyllabic grumbling.)

Grigori to Andy: *As far as they're concerned, nothing has changed since the company was bought by this young team from the Interros Group.*
Andy: *Did they expect it to?*
Alpha Male via Grigori: *Yeah... we had high hopes.*

(The interview comes to something of a standstill for a few moments. Grigori has increasingly been fleshing out the silences between what have become mostly short two- or three-word answers. I'm acutely aware that we may be treading on very touchy ground with this line of questioning, particularly in the presence of a representative of the public relations department. But finally one of the sidekicks can't restrain himself any longer.)

Grigori to Andy: *This guy just said that every year things are getting worse and worse.*
Andy: *As contractors, do you have a union to represent you?*
Grigori to Andy (after a flurry of comments from all three): *They have that small union, the one whose leader went on hunger strike very recently.*

Valery Melnikov, head of one of the trade unions at Norilsk, had led twenty-five other union officers on a hunger strike in February, just three months before our arrival. Negotiations on a new labour agreement for workers at the mines and smelters had foundered at the stage of 'the conciliation committee', which in Melnikov's case appears to have been something of a misnomer.

Melnikov was asking for pay rises for his members, more paid holiday, profit-sharing and detailed information about the company's financial status. He may have been pushing his luck on the last two demands, given the opaque nature of Norilsk Nickel's ownership structure, but the story of his hunger strike got picked up by the Russian media and from there by the international media.

The global metal markets twitched when they heard the 's'

word – a strike! For traders sitting in front of their price screens in London, New York and Tokyo, the 's' word set alarm bells ringing. Norilsk Nickel dominates the world's production of many of the most volatile metals markets. Any problems at the source of this metallic chain will always cause prices to start swinging wildly at the other end.

What those traders didn't know is that while there is a long tradition of hunger strikes in Siberia, dating as far back as the original gulags in Tsarist times, total down-tools, 'we're all out, lads', strikes are very rare indeed.

The last time there was a full-blown strike here had been in 1953 – the year of Josef Stalin's death. What were then gulag prisoners had miscalculated the time it would take between the death of the gulag's godfather and a change in administrative policy. The strike hadn't gone too well. Several prisoners had been killed, although a mass slaughter by the encircling army units had been avoided by a subterfuge. The prisoners, who had barricaded themselves into their camp, had been lured out on a promise of amnesty. Then the ringleaders had been separated out and sent to even harsher punishment[i] camps.

A total strike was the worst of all crimes within the gulag because it affected work quotas and production – the benchmarks against which every camp commander and every guard was judged. It had by no means been uncommon for camp guards to find themselves on the other side of the wire for failing to fulfil quotas. Reaction to total strikes had therefore tended to be extreme.

Hunger strikes, though, with their strong symbolic resonance, were a constant ubiquitous feature of the camps, having started as a form of protest among the very earliest political prisoners. They remain common even now in Siberian political life. Norilsk miners staged several underground hunger strikes in the mid-1990s, normally to protest at the fact they hadn't been paid for several months.

Melnikov's own protest lasted two weeks[ii], during which time the number of hunger strikers rose to fifty-seven. The company kept up a media barrage against him. The leader of the largest trade union at Norilsk – with 43,000 members

– publicly called on him to give it up.

I'm moderately impressed by the fact he kept it up so long, but it seems that by the tougher standards of the locals it wasn't up to much.

Andy: *How did they feel about that?*

Alpha Male via Grigori: *We're disappointed in Melnikov and the other union leaders. He didn't achieve anything, He just came out with a lot of fine-sounding words.*

Andy: *But even in the West we heard about it because of the hunger strike, so that was a good action, no?*

Alpha Male via Grigori: *It all ended up in a general meeting of all the employees. And then the big boss came down and simply chose the people who were to represent us at the meetings with management.*

*And whatever happened at that meeting didn't represent our interests or our needs as workers.*

*That's why we're disappointed. Maybe you people heard about us in the West but we haven't seen anything change for the better because of it all.*

Andy: *And do you have any hope for any changes?*

Andy to Grigori: *They seem quite bitter and pissed off from what I can tell.*

(Grigori translates the question and there's a collective shaking of heads.)

Grigori (for the sake of the recording only): *No, they're all shaking their heads. They are quite bitter.*

Andy: *So you think it's going to be the same for ever here really?*

Alpha Male via Grigori: *Yeah! Promises, promises and nothing but promises. As far as anything actually happening, all we hear from management is 'if you don't like it, resign!'*

Andy: *Would any of you consider standing for union leader yourselves? If you're unhappy with the one you've got?*

Alpha Male via Grigori: *What's the point? The bosses should take positive steps to improve our conditions. Whatever we do makes no difference anyway.*
*Each of us has a family and children. So we all keep silent. We're all scared. That's why we don't take any action. We are only working here because of our children, to get them out of here.*

(Now it's become quite clear over the course of the last few minutes that these particular guys have quite a long way to go before they fully grasp Russia's new 'market relationships', as Dmitry Zelenin would say.

The local female journalist has been dutifully taking notes all through our interview, while after a couple of snaps, the local photographer has been listening with a somewhat detached air. Sergey is looking serious.

Lt Ivanov has been growing palpably more and more disconcerted at the course this particular interview has been taking and has just exited the room during the last exchange.

Not sure what to make of this development, I decide to try and turn the conversation towards lighter topics.)

Andy: *What do you do then to relax when you're not working here?*

(At this stage the unofficial spokesman breaks into laughter again. It's a signal for his two partners to start guffawing in theatrical unison. Grigori starts laughing and before we know it, everyone's laughing. Finally the big guy controls himself and manages to answer the question.)

Alpha Male via Grigori: *We engage in sports!*

(There's a lot more general laughter.)

Andy: *Would that be the drinking variety?*
Alpha Male via Grigori: *Spot on! That's the one.*

At this point Lt Ivanov comes back into the room. He looks flustered. He explains to Grigori there's someone we should interview outside in the main room we had first entered.

We thank the disgruntled threesome and receive slight nods in return as they each go for another cigarette from the three packs laid out in front of them.

Outside Grigori translates for the company representative. Why had we been talking with these people? They are just contractors after all... why hadn't we asked to meet a proper smelter worker... like this one?

A 'proper' smelter worker has indeed miraculously materialised. He is in his mid-forties, his hair still free from grey and his face dominated by a big bushy moustache. He looks a lot less dishevelled and grubby than the three comrades back in the rest room. He has an easy-going manner and appears comfortable in his own articulacy. I imagine he would be an entertaining storyteller after a few shots of vodka.

---

***Transcript.***
***Copper Smelter.***
***Interview with Model Worker.***

Grigori to Andy: *Now this is a proper smelter worker. Not like the people we've just spoken to. They're just contractors.*
Andy, with a heavy trace of sarcasm: *Alright! How long has our proper smelter worker worked here?*
Model Worker via Grigori: *Twenty-seven years.*
Andy: *Was it your first job?*
Model Worker via Grigori: *Yes. I did my army service first and then I came here. And I've been working here at the smelter for the last twenty-seven years.*

(The female journalist pipes up at this stage. She had been almost totally silent during our interview with the contractors. She asks him about his alcohol consumption, which I take to be something of a hot local, and for that matter, national issue.)

Model Worker via Grigori: *A reasonable intake of alcohol saves your sanity in this place. A hundred grams of vodka a day is good for your health anyway.*

(In response to another question from the female journalist.)

*Yeah, unfortunately, I smoke as well.*
Andy: *What brought you to Norilsk?*
Model Worker via Grigori: *When I was in the army, I was given a choice. I could be demobilised early but only if I agreed to go a particular place from a list given me by the armed forces. I chose Norilsk.*

(He laughs.)

*So, the only reason I came here was to get out of the army a couple of months early.*
Andy: *What's your position here?*
Model Worker via Grigori: *I'm a general supervisor at the smelter.*
Andy: *How many men do you have reporting to you?*
Model Worker via Grigori: *One hundred and eighty.*
Andy: *And how many people are working in the plant in total?*
Model Worker via Grigori: *This shop has 900 people. My section is 180 of that workforce.*
Andy: *And what are your work hours?*
Model Worker via Grigori: *Officially I'm paid for seven point two hours a day.*

(It seems a very Soviet answer. I'm still trying to work out what this is in any non-decimal system of time as he carries on speaking. It's only afterwards I calculate it's seven hours and twelve minutes.)

*But that doesn't happen very often. It's more like eight or*

*nine hours a day. Five days a week.*
Andy: *And how much holiday do you get?*
Model Worker via Grigori: *Every thirteen months I get ninety days off.*

(There we go again! What's wrong with the twelve-month calendar that the rest of the world uses?)

*I can break it into two sections of forty-five days.*
Andy: *Where do you go on holiday?*
Model Worker via Grigori: *Either abroad or to central Russia. Well, I say 'abroad', but I mean Ukraine.*

(This produces a general round of laughter among the Russians which seems the intended aim of the remark.

The resorts down on the Crimean 'Riviera' by the Black Sea have long been regarded as the luxury Russian beach holiday destination. The fact they now exist within the confines of an independent country called Ukraine is something of a running joke among Russians. You'd get the same reaction if you told a Brit he'd need a passport to go to Cornwall or an American that the ski resorts of Vermont had just been moved into Canada.)

Andy: *Have you seen big changes over the twenty-seven years?*
Model Worker via Grigori: *Yes, the technology we use has changed a lot over the time. Some of it has changed very radically.*
*When they take out the smelted metal in that section over there…*

(He waves to the middle section of the room in which we're standing.)

*… it's still exactly as it was twenty-seven years ago and sometimes it takes four workers to move the container with the metal out. But there's another section over there…*

(He points in the direction of a second set of heavy plastic doors leading to another room.)

*... in there we now have some of the world's most modern technology.*
Andy: *How did things change here specifically after 1989?*

(At this point the attention of our model smelter worker is drawn to a statuesque woman, wearing a full-length fur coat and high heels, who is gliding across the factory floor. Everyone follows the object of his gaze. There is a flurry of laughter and comment among the Russians.)

Grigori: *A brilliantly dressed woman in a fur coat has just walked past us. Everybody's pointing to her and saying, that's one of our top metallurgy experts.*

(The joke presumably sounds better in Russian. Our Model Worker's back with us now.)

Model Worker via Grigori: *As far as the organisation of labour is concerned, there have been significant changes since then.*
*The new owners are counting their money all the time. So the big thing here was to get rid of some of the excess workforce. There were lots of people just providing back-up and ancillary roles. So they were all got rid of and productivity shot up as a result.*

(The Model Worker is asked by Lt Ivanov about the recent threats of strike and Valery Melnikov's hunger strike. Just to 'put the record straight', as it were, you understand.)

Model Worker via Grigori: *I cannot speak for everybody but I can tell you my own personal view.*
*It's a natural desire in people to get paid more but we have to understand that nothing comes out of the air. My team*

*is paid an average $1,000 a month and I have virtually
no problems or unrest in the team. Basically, they don't
have anything to complain about.*

*These other guys, the people you've just spoken to, they're
different. Because they don't have stable jobs, they are
quite insecure. They are external contractors, so whenever
there is a job for them, they are invited in and they do the
job and then they go back home and they are practically
unemployed. So their life is very insecure. Basically they
work, maybe, two or three months in the year. It's not much
so they don't get paid much and they are discontented as
a result.*

(It's a fair bet that the sub-contractors would have been fully
paid-up employees of the Combine until the Interros Group
started spreading the capitalist news at Norilsk Nickel. The
total workforce had declined from 115,000 in 1998 to 89,000
at the end of 2001. That's a cut of 26,000 workers, or just over
one in every five in the space of three years. Productivity up!
Insecurity up as well, I would imagine! Particularly if you're
now classified as a contractor, not a full employee!)

Andy: *Have you got a family in Norilsk?*

Model Worker via Grigori: *Wife and two children. My wife
doesn't work any more. She's on pension. She was working
very hard and not being paid much so I insisted that she
stop work.*

Andy: *Is this your home? Do you see yourself staying here
always now?*

Model Worker via Grigori: *A lot of my friends talk all the
time about leaving Norilsk and going to the mainland.
They're dreaming that maybe one day they'll have a happy
contented life somewhere.*

*Personally, I believe that's all bollocks. You live today
and you have to make your life as good as possible today
instead of indulging in dreams of maybe living a perfect
life somewhere else.*

Andy: *And do you want your children to follow you into*

111

*the copper smelter?*

Model Worker via Grigori: *My daughter said she doesn't want to live here because it's too cold. So I've bought her a one-room apartment in the city of Vladimir in central Russia. She's studying in the university there.*
*As for my son, well...*
*You see, my daughter is a responsible woman. She knows how to look after her money and how to spend it. So I had no problem with buying her a flat.*
*But my son! He's altogether different from his sister. I fear he'll be with me as long as I am here in Norilsk. If he doesn't go to university, he'll have to go into the army and that could ruin the rest of his life. So, I'm keeping him at home and I've told him he can choose any university in Russia and I'll pay his way. Then he can do whatever he wants with his life.*
*But I'm insisting he stay at school. He's in year ten so he has one more year to spend in school. If he does that, I've told him he can go and study at any university.*

(Model Worker's family woes tail off amid a rolling of the eyes and a multilingual 'Kids! You know what they're like!' resigned half-smile.)

Andy: *How do you cope with the conditions here, the polar night? Is this a Russian thing?*
Model Worker via Grigori: *No. Why should it only be Russians? There are all nationalities here. We've got Ukrainians. We've got Tartars. We've got guys from the Caucasus.*

(I feel put in my place. That old map of the Soviet Union learnt as a schoolboy had insinuated itself so far into my formative views that I am still struggling to weed out its multiple tentacles. The one-dimensional splurge of red spreading from Western Europe across Asia to the Pacific masked a hugely divergent number of peoples, each with its own history and its own culture. I've already had enough clues in Moscow, the multicultural centre that continues to suck in fortune-seekers from all the corners of the once vast empire.

Sergey comes to my rescue. He leans into the mike and says something in Russian, smiling mischievously at me.)

Grigori: *Sergey puts in a little remark. Just like some of his other remarks. 'If you Brits had had a Stalin of your own, you would have built a smelter like this in a place like this!'*

Our allotted time with the Model Worker is up… and I feel that Dmitry Zelenin would have been proud of him. He bids us a cheery goodbye and walks off back through the second set of plastic doors.

It appears we are not going to follow. This is as far into the smelter as we're going to get because Lt Ivanov starts walking us to the exit. I'm more than a little frustrated. It's like being shown into someone's fifty-bedroom mansion only to never leave the hallway.

I detect again the unseen hand of Citizen Khagazheev. I'm not sure whether there had ever been any intention to let us see inside the smelter proper. Our unplanned discovery of the divisions within this once Socialist workforce had almost certainly not aided our cause, I suspect.

I disappointedly follow the others out and surrender my hard hat, looking wistfully again at the massive building stretching in front of me. What other mysteries does it hold? Not ones that we will discover, I fear.

I flirt with the boyish urge to make a break for it, running back into the first room and through the second set of doors. I wonder how far I'd make it before being run down and rugby tackled to the ground. The adult in me pictures us being driven straight back to the airport bound for Moscow, winners of the shortest 'Journey of a Lifetime' ever likely to be recorded for the BBC.

The grown-up joins the others on the minibus for the short trip back into town. The two representatives of the local press are dropped off first before the three of us are returned to the hotel.

Once there, we share a cigarette with young Lt Ivanov on the steps leading up to the hotel. I learn that my casting of him as an army officer is not far off the mark. He tells us he had tried to join the police force in his home city of Kirov but not got in. So he'd come to Norilsk and joined the force here.

You see! *Police* Lieutenant Ivanov then!

But he'd got bored. There's not a whole lot for the police to do here apparently. So he'd taken a job in the public relations department of Norilsk Nickel. He says he likes it. 'It's an interesting change.'

Seems a weird career path to me, but I wonder what a normal one is here?

So Officer, what's the truth about Norilsk 'closing' itself then? Had the city been invaded by criminal gangs from 'abroad'? Had it been swamped with drugs and violence as the authorities claimed at the time?

He nods pensively. Yeah, he says, a lot of 'foreigners' had come to Norilsk, particularly from the south – Armenians, Georgians, Azerbaijanis, even the Chechens.

They had been drawn by the high wages Norilsk Nickel pays – the company pays well for skilled labour by the standards of the rest of the country. There are hardship benefit payments for living in the Arctic as well.

But most of the 'foreigners' hadn't had the right skills for working in mines or in metals plants. Few of them had got jobs with the company. They had started street trading and become associated with selling drugs and a host of other real or imagined crimes.

According to Lt Ivanov, tensions between these new arrivals and the locals had simmered for some time before coming to a boil. As is so often the case, all it had needed was a trigger and the trigger had come from an incident involving a group of 'foreigners' who were living rough in a derelict tower block. They were accused of starting a fire to keep warm and inadvertently burning through a power cable, which deprived a large part of the city of electricity.

No electricity spells a lot of trouble in the middle of the Arctic winter and, not entirely surprisingly, the entire city had been thrown into crisis. Once the cable was fixed, residents, company and local authorities decided they'd had enough and made the request for the city to be closed to all outsiders again.

Police work had got a lot easier since and a lot more boring, hence Lt Ivanov's move to the company.

Our young cop friend says he'll try and join us for dinner if he can. He's got to go back to the head office now. He'll let us know later.

## Looking Through Doors

As the minibus pulls off through the ubiquitous sludge that covers the roads here, I ask Grigori where we're going for dinner tonight. He tells me the Russians earlier recommended the restaurant right next to the hotel – it's got live music apparently!

'Where?' I look across the street and try and discern anything that could feasibly be the entrance to a restaurant.

'Well…' Grigori steps out to the edge of the street and looks up and down.

'Come to think of it, where's the delicatessen?'

Reindeer Woman had told us she'd bought the fresh camembert at the delicatessen right next door to our hotel. 'We all laugh about it,' she'd said. 'In the old days it only used to have six or seven loaves of bread… on a good day!'

All three of us look around bemusedly. There's no sign of a restaurant and even less of a delicatessen. Just the same grey blocks of brick and concrete in various stages of exhaustion in their battle against the elements.

Sergey is designated to go into the hotel reception and ask. They tell him he can't miss either restaurant or shop. They're right next door!

We look around us again. For the very first time I notice that next to the heavily-padded double doors with reflective glass leading into the first of our hotel's airlocks there are two more sets of double doors.

All three sets are almost identical and they're spaced just a couple of feet apart. The other two sets hardly look promising.

Faced with no other choice, though, we try the ones in the middle. They're locked, but the right-hand set leads, via an airlock and a second set of inner doors, into a large shop, about twenty yards long, stuffed full of little luxuries like chilled meats and cheeses, fancily wrapped boxes of chocolates and biscuits and a whole range of juices and soft drinks.

Wow! I've received enough clues today but this is a particularly strong Road to Damascus experience. I have to walk back outside and look again at the three anonymous sets of doors. I realise that on first arrival I'd not questioned which set hid the hotel. I'd just got out of the minibus and followed everyone else through the left-hand doors.

With those firmly fixed in my mind as the hotel doors after that, I'd not given any thought to the other two. To the casual eye there are no outwards signs that they lead anywhere. Their proximity to the 'front entrance' of the hotel had me thinking they were service entrances to the same building.

I push my way through the right hand sets of doors again, through the airlock and the inner set of doors, and am still overwhelmed by the Aladdin's cave of goodies piled high up the walls of the shop.

We spend a good deal of time carefully looking over the merchandise. We might as well be Soviet citizens suddenly fast-forwarded in time such is our amazement at the luxury on display.

I end up buying a small bottle of fizzy drink and a Lion Bar as two little Western treats. They cost me over four pounds. The River Yenisey hasn't thawed yet, which means they've had to be flown in.

Now I feel a bit guilty about eating so much of the camembert earlier on.

We go back to our rooms for a steaming hot shower (in Sergey's case), a warmish one after several minutes (in my case) and what will possibly be the world's attempt at the fastest shower (in Grigori's case).

Later, lying on my bed, staring at the grey sky outside, I ponder Norilsk's inside-outside conundrum. Every time I've entered one of the grim concrete blocks here, I've been assailed by the sensory opposite to what I had been expecting. My brain is literally hurting, it's done so many reality back-flips over the course of the day.

From the outside everything looks terrible. A forlorn showpiece of Soviet town planning, the place is a grid of anonymous concrete. To the uninitiated, there are no clues to what lies inside any of the bleak buildings. There are no signs, not even in Cyrillic. There are no windows to take a peek inside. Just an endless series of ominous doorways barred by heavily padded doors. It's a little too close to the stuff of nightmares for comfort.

I realise that had I been travelling on my own, I would have struggled to find the hotel, given my lack of Russian. Even shown the building, I would have been baffled as to where the entrance was, just as I wouldn't have been able to find the delicatessen or for that matter the restaurant where we had lunched earlier that day.

It ties in with something one of the Norwegians had told me when we were all hanging around in the hotel lobby on first arrival. There were lots of good restaurants and bars here, he had said with a conspiratorial air. The only issue was identifying them. The locals knew where they were but you wouldn't find them by yourself. I'm starting to see what he means. Or at least I'm starting to see that I'm not seeing.

I conclude that the practical answer to this puzzle comes in two parts.

One: These heavy anonymous doors and the airlocks behind them are here for a reason. It's called Winter, with -50°C temperatures, not counting wind-chill factor. Shop glass frontage and normal doors are not going to do the trick in terms of keeping the cold out.

Two: Norilsk is a city of just over 100,000 people but its isolation gives the place the feel of a small village. Everyone knows where everything is here. If you don't know, you just ask someone and they'll know. That, and a certain pre-1989 disdain for commercial advertising, means there are no bright neon signs outside the bars, no displays outside the shops, no concessions whatsoever to the outsider.

Lurking somewhere behind the practical, though, I'm starting to pick up a strong psychic reaction to the desolation outside, not just the man-made horrors in the immediate surrounds of the city but the bigger desert of the tundra beyond.

Reindeer Woman may enjoy summer treks across the tundra, but I already know she is in a minority. Most people here, if they can afford it, migrate to the south, to the 'mainland'.

The 'outside' in Norilsk is a hostile place to be. It is not there to be prettified. It is there to resist. Why waste any time and money on trying to make the 'outside' look nicer? The only requirement is that it puts up a reasonable fight in the never-ending war of attrition with the Arctic winds.

The 'inside' is sanctuary. It allows you to live here, quite literally, during the long winter months, and symbolically it's the one environment people can in any appreciable way alter. The 'inside' is there to be nurtured and tended, like Simona's little plants on her windowsill. It is a safe place. It is a human place.

---

***Transcript.***
***Andy's Audio Journal.***
***Early Evening.***

Andy: *Anyway… where was I… ?*
*… ah, yeah, just leaving the copper smelter.*
*There's quite an amusing postscript to our visit. Apparently the company was so upset that we'd interviewed those three disgruntled contractors that the head of the public relations department has just called Sergey and said that 'obviously', while we can use the material, they would basically ask us… and I think that might be an interesting use of the word 'ask'… to emphasise that these were contractors and not really Norilsk employees. And therefore everything they told us should be put in that perspective.*
*Right!*
*I think we're getting a little bit of an over-reaction here… and an interesting throwback to former times, shall we say?*

*I'm not completely surprised when we meet up later and
Grigori tells me our young friend will not be able to join us.
I imagine there's still a heated post-match analysis going
on in Norilsk headquarters about our interviews with the
very un-united workforce.*

## The Challenger

I sense we may have inadvertently stumbled across the very
issue that the company would have preferred we didn't find.
For the BBC, of all people!

Valery Melnikov is a very sensitive issue with Norilsk Nickel
right now. A union firebrand with what seems like a good eye
for a media 'story', he is waging a one-man war against the
company. He is presenting Norilsk Nickel with a decidedly
unwelcome and uncomfortable challenge to its administrative
credentials.

It runs this town. It's as simple as that! It runs the power
stations that provide the heat and light. It runs the water and
sewage system. It runs the telephone system. It runs the petrol
stations. It is town-planner, architect and building contractor. It
runs the schools. It even runs a near monopoly over the supply
and sale of alcohol[iii].

In short, it decides what happens here. It may have pushed
some of its social obligations on to the local municipal authority,
but since the latter's main source of income comes from taxes
from the company, this amounts to as much a bout of spring-
cleaning of the financial books as it does to a change in power
flows.

Without the company there would be no Norilsk. For that
matter, if Zelenin is anything to go by, with the company there
may be no Norilsk either.

It is not used to anyone questioning its authority. In very
un-Soviet style, it has already slashed the workforce. It has
introduced new working practices. It is twisting the arms of
pensioners to leave the city for the mainland. Until Melnikov
there was no counter-weight to its self-appointed role as
ultimate arbiter of all things concerning Norilsk.

Melnikov's threat of calling a total strike was not that

far-fetched. He even waded through the deliberately labyrinthine process of declaring a labour dispute, the first stage of initiating a walkout. One of the later stages requires the convention of a general assembly of the entire workforce. It was to this that our disgruntled threesome back in the rest and recreation room at the smelter had scathingly referred.

What the model worker said about their insecure contractor status is all true, but their allegations about what had happened at the general assembly are not unique, either. The *Moscow Times* carried the union's allegations that 'management handpicked the candidates to the conference and rigged the voting', sidelining the union's own officials[iv].

Melnikov's hunger strike was at least in part a protest at the course the assembly had taken. Although the newspaper quote is not attributed, it's a fair guess as to who may have supplied it.

By the time of our visit he has just upped the ante again by standing in the elections for city mayor on a platform of 'Let's get Norilsk Nickel!' He won the first round of the elections with a forty-seven per cent share of the vote. The local authorities have responded by trying to declare his candidacy null and void on the basis he infringed campaigning rules.

The issue is unresolved at the time of our visit in May 2003.

I've suggested a couple of times that we should try and interview Melnikov. Sergey's consistent view, and one fully endorsed by Grigori, is that it would jeopardise the goodwill of the company, which is of course the sponsor of our special permits to visit Norilsk. Fearing that what the all-powerful Interros Group gives, it can just as quickly take back, I've reluctantly accepted Sergey's caution as wise.

But the whole subject of Melnikov remains so touchy that it's easy to understand why Lt Ivanov had been upset at the way our first interview at the smelter had gone. That's why Norilsk Nickel is so keen to stress that they were not 'real' employees of the workforce, just a bunch of malcontent contractors. And that's why I'm not surprised that Lt Ivanov will not be joining us for dinner this evening.

Which is a shame, because he is also an interesting, articulate man, and I've been looking forward to hearing more from him.

## Mirrors

But the three of us still set out for the restaurant, which involves leaving the hotel airlocks, turning left, taking two paces, turning left again and trying the middle set of padded doors which are now unlocked. We go in, and after another airlock we enter a long extended entrance foyer, all done up in red velvet and mirrors. A grandiose staircase with gleaming metal balustrade and gold-framed mirrors on the walls leads up to the first floor.

There we enter a huge bar-restaurant with a dance-floor and small stage. The place is sumptuously decorated with glossy finishing and subdued lighting. We choose a table on a slightly elevated section looking down on the dance-floor over which a mirror-ball is slowly rotating. Our chairs are fake Louis XVI with pink cushions embroidered with blue fleur-de-lys.

There is only a handful of other diners, most of them seated in the darker recesses of the place against the wall.

Although I'm getting into the swing of this 'what lies behind the padded door?' malarkey, I'm still taken aback by the TARDIS-like size of this particular establishment and spend a good part of the evening contemplating what seems to be an impossible spatial relationship between our hotel and this place. It's something that becomes increasingly difficult to fathom as the evening wears on and the vodka rounds accelerate. The Russian spirit-of-life is brought to the table in chilled carafes, like white wine at an Italian restaurant back home.

We celebrate what we appraise as a pretty successful day – some interesting people, some good interviews and a great exposé of life among the workers.

The conversation turns to our companions of the afternoon – the lady from the local press and the photographer – the man I've described as a bear. Except he's not a photographer from the local press, Sergey says. He's a spy.

Grigori and I are sceptical but Sergey confidently laughs away our dubious looks. Of course he's a spy, he says. Maybe from the company. Maybe from the Federal Security Services, the successor to the KGB. Maybe both.

After all, Sergey explains, don't you think they're curious as to why these two guys are wandering around their smelters asking questions for the BBC? Particularly when they're not technically employees of the BBC?

Our resulting conversation provokes a lot of vodka-fuelled merriment, during which I point out that the best spy on our doings would surely be Sergey as he would have the ultimate cover for keeping a close eye on us. This produces another long round of joking and laughing.

Our hilarity is interrupted by the start of the live music act in the form of a guy who's derived his costume from a late-career Elvis Presley and a woman whose outfit seems more suited to the role of magician's assistant. He sings to backing tapes, she joins him on every third or fourth number. The rest of the time she just hangs around having the occasional cigarette.

I assume he's singing in Russian until I discern a mutilated version of a Tom Jones number. I strain to catch the words. I turn to Grigori. 'Is he singing Tom Jones in Russian?' Like me he strains his ears. 'No, it's English… I think…'

The guy on stage obviously quite fancies himself as something of a multi-gifted musician as well. It's patently clear he's recorded his own backing tapes. I know this because he's inserted a five-minute guitar solo of his own devising in the middle of Hotel California. He's obviously one of those frustrated musicians who heard what is one of the best-selling records of all time and thought: 'Okay song, but what it really needs is me playing in the middle section.'

We last as long as we can but finally surrender and get the bill and leave.

The peroxide-haired floor-matron is back at her desk when we get off at our floor of the hotel. She barely acknowledges our greetings before going back to her magazine.

Before turning in for the night, I make an entry in my audio journal. It's probably not best BBC recording practice to make a recording lying on your bed when you're drunk. But, hey! they can always edit it. And I need to make an editorial correction about the water status in my room.

---

***Transcript.***
***Andy's Audio Journal.***
***Late.***

Andy (Following a rambling account of my shower tribulations, which I'm convinced at the time is extremely humorous but is of course nothing but the inanity of a man who's drunk far too much vodka): *And the reason I mention all that is that it quite nicely sums up my impressions of Russia and my impressions of Norilsk as well. Your initial reaction is quite negative. You get taken in by appearances here. So when we were in Moscow, for example, my initial reaction to the estate on which Sergey lives was, 'Jeez, it's a place where I wouldn't even drive through quickly let alone walk through quickly', but then, of course, I ended up really enjoying it and seeing another side of it.*
*So too with Norilsk. It does look like hell on earth. It looks like your worst nightmare. But the longer you stay here, you start to blank that out and get on with the business of meeting people, and just getting on with things.*
*So that's why I mention the shower. A nice little summing-up of my whole experience so far. Initial impression – nightmare! Then turns out to be okay after a few minutes. Anyway, that's about it for today…*
*… oh… almost forgot… we have been promised an interview with one of the top people tomorrow. But at this stage, frankly, I'm not holding my breath because these things prove very elusive, I've found so far. It would be good if it happens, but if it does, I suspect we'll get ten minutes at most.*
*But I do know we're going to get the full environmental public relations exercise from Norilsk Nickel tomorrow… which should be quite interesting.*

[i]Anne Appelbaum, Gulag: A History. Anchor.
[ii]Pravda, 21 February 2003
[iii]See Appendix III
[iv]Moscow Times, 6 May 2003

# SECRETS
## Ghosts In The Machine

After a sound night's sleep uninterrupted by light-induced confusion, I wake up at a time which is as close to normal as I'm probably going to manage during my stay in Norilsk.

I may just have discovered the benefits of drinking vodka before retiring for the night. Maybe that's why all the Russians say it's good for their health.

Vodka does have another big benefit though – no hangovers. When drunk neat – and the Russians joke that it's a criminal offence in their country to drink it any other way – the local hooch seems to bring with it none of the devastating after-effects associated with a big night out on just about any other spirit. A certain sensation of numbness and a slight detachment from reality maybe. But no blinding headaches, no churning stomach and no spasms of nausea.

While I wait for Grigori or Sergey to knock on my door, signalling the start of the day's activities, I tinker around with my audio journal, playing back the recordings and deleting the worst of my drunken meanderings of the night before.

Initial mistrust of my own incompetence with the equipment has given way to possibly dangerous over-confidence.

I'm starting to enjoy the exercise. Grigori and I had used some of the waiting time in Moscow to make double conversational recordings about our thoughts and impressions. 'All very relaxed,' as Grigori would say.

Here in Norilsk, though, we haven't done so since our first lunch. Grigori's translation skills are fantastic but it's starting to take it out of him. We've already crammed a lot of interviews into an incredibly short period, and he's in no mood to make more recordings when we're 'off duty', so to speak.

I'm growing used to talking into my mike alone in my bedroom.

---

**Transcript.**
**Andy's Audio Journal.**
**Hotel Room.**
**Morning.**

Andy: *Sergey threw something of a curved ball into the conversation half way through dinner last night by suggesting that one of the local journalists who was with us yesterday... in fact the guy I think I described as a bear of a man... might have been a government... how shall I put this?... well, a government spy on us. No point in beating about the bushes, is there?*

*Which obviously produced a huge amount of joking at that stage of the evening given the amount of vodka we'd had. And then of course it struck me that he quite possibly was.*

*It is easy to forget that the precious metals part of Norilsk Nickel's production in particular is still pretty much a state secret. So it would make a lot of sense that someone is keeping an eye on these two foreign journalists wandering around this town. So joking aside, I can't necessarily say it's not true.*

*I did also point out that the best spy on us would be Sergey himself... something which also caused its fair share of good humour and which I notice he didn't actually deny. Which gives you food for thought...*

*It shows how easy it is, once you start thinking in those terms, to get paranoid about who is or who isn't watching you and listening to you, and you do start looking at virtually everyone you know in a different way.*

*So, a nice little insight into what it must have been like here up to the year 1989, I think.*

*Just as a little postscript to that comment, I believe that we are going to go ten-pin bowling with this gentleman this evening.*

*Grigori, who is much better versed in these things than me, says it's the best way of dealing with the issue. You might as well just get to know them really and not worry about it.*

## Of Geese and Men

Breakfast is a detached affair for us this morning, for which read the aforementioned after-effects of vodka. 'Breakfast' is mostly coffee for the same reason. But I'm genuinely looking forward to the next part of our trip.

The company is holding a big press conference on the environment. Since I've seen precisely zero natural flora and fauna here since I first arrived, it promises to be an interesting test of the public relations department's grasp of the Western principle of spin.

Ironically, the weather is really nice on our walk to the press conference. Bright blue skies and a fresh wind blowing away the smell of sulphur that otherwise lingers around the streets. It even feels quite warm... relatively. The short walk from the hotel into the centre of town raises all our spirits.

The conference is in a lecture hall. We're the last to arrive and there's a general low hubbub coming from the assembled TV cameramen, radio reporters and local press and an almost equal number of Norilsk Nickel's public relations people. I look around and note the absence of Lt Ivanov.

The ICE QUEEN, whose courtesy minibus we'd gate-crashed on the way in from the airport, is standing by the lectern in one corner calmly viewing the scene. Looks promising.

'What's on the agenda?' I ask Grigori as we sit down towards the back of the sloped hall, giving us an elevated view of the twenty or so members of the Norilsk city media. He squints at the programme he's been given and translates slowly and carefully, 'The... lesser... white... fronted... goose'.

'Are you sure?'

'Yes... maybe the word is 'chested'? The lesser white chested goose?'

I neither know nor care about the correct nomenclature for the beast. But whatever it's called, a big poster of one is being tacked up on the wall behind the podium. I look again at the serried ranks of the media sitting in front of us. Is news really that scarce here? Or does any pronouncement from the company that defines this city amount to a three-line whip on the local newspapers, magazines and TV station?

A hush falls over the room as the person who is apparently The Chief Ornithologist of the Region starts his presentation. Not inappropriately, he looks very bird-like. Around forty years old, his brown hair and beard seamlessly encase a beaky nose in an oval furry head. Common Garden Sparrow?

Obviously, I can't understand a word of what he is saying, but Grigori explains that THE SPARROW is conducting research on said goose which was once found all over the Russian Arctic but is now extremely rare and seen only around this area. Not too close to the smelters, I would hope.

The point of the press conference, tomorrow's headlines as it were, is the launch of an expedition by our friend to the Putoran Plateau, a nature reserve about a hundred miles north of Norilsk. He will be studying the habitat and migration patterns of the lesser white fronted goose. The expedition is being funded by the company which is keen to show off its environmental credentials.

The Sparrow talks for about twenty minutes in a quiet, slightly monotonous voice. Grigori, who had started translating for the benefit of both me and the microphone, gives up after a few minutes and he and Sergey follow the proceedings with a slightly disinterested look on their faces.

I feel deflated. Based on years of professional disappointment, I'm worried the company is dead-ending any further interest we may have in the subject of Norilsk and the environment.

Good news though it undoubtedly is for the lesser white fronted goose, this is not what I want know on the subject. There are some more obvious ecological issues around here. The snow is black, the forests have died and the reindeer have devised their own migratory bypass system.

And I want to know about the guys in the smelter with the oxygen packs and how long they're going to have to go on wearing them.

In short, I want to know what the company is going to do to put right what it has so evidently done wrong.

I whisper my dissatisfaction to Grigori, sparking a murmured conversation between him and Sergey. To anyone looking, and the Ice Queen has carefully positioned herself so she alone can monitor the audience, we no doubt identify ourselves as the potential trouble-makers sitting at the back of the class. The upshot of the whispered three-way conversation is that Sergey says he's already been working on the public relations people and we should be able to get an interview with The Ice Queen herself. As the representative of the Moscow head office she apparently outranks anyone else here. The fact she's the deputy head of the Moscow public relations department gives her truly regal status.

As The Sparrow winds up his presentation, fielding an array of questions from the local press people, Sergey slips down the aisle and renews with added urgency his solicitations on our behalf.

The press conference breaks up into a series of small conversations between assembled media and Norilsk representatives. Grigori and I find ourselves standing in front of The Sparrow, who is putting his presentation paper back into a weather-beaten briefcase.

Now feeling guilty about what I fear was our all-too-evident lack of interest in what he has been saying, I suggest to Grigori we do a quick interview with him. Seems only fair.

The Sparrow's name is Alexis. So what brought Alexis to Norilsk?

------------

*Transcript.*
*Interview with Chief Ornithologist, aka THE SPARROW.*
*Norilsk lecture hall.*
*After presentation on the lesser white fronted goose.*

The Sparrow via Grigori: *I came to Norilsk in 1980 to begin working on the Putoran Plateau. At the time this very extensive territory in northern Russia had not been explored by ornithologists at all. Once I started doing it, it became the best thing I ever did. I love that territory. That's where I work and that's where I intend to continue working.*

*The whole meaning of my work there is not only about my emotional personal liking for this territory but also it's the fact that this very interesting region has hardly been explored.*

Andy: *What are the main problems in your work at this time?*

The Sparrow via Grigori: *Getting finance for research is the main problem. Any expedition into the area needs helicopters. It's the only way to get there. And even if you have a helicopter, a second and very major problem is the weather. On the way you can hit fog or a snowstorm and you cannot even get there, let alone start the expedition.*

Andy: *What's your relationship with the company?*

The Sparrow via Grigori: *Norilsk Nickel has adopted a long-term ecology programme. The company supports my research, especially research that will result in practical measures to preserve the environment in this area.*

*I think that it is essential that all nature-preservation agencies co-operate in a constructive way with the company.*

(It strikes me that the company has a slight advantage in this, because, if the agencies don't 'co-operate in a constructive way', they can't physically come to Norilsk, its sister port of Dudinka or any of the surrounding area.

Its geographical and bureaucratic isolation has preserved the company from the prying eyes of hostile environmental lobby groups. It's going to take an extremely hardy eco-warrior to make it across a thousand miles or so of taiga and tundra to protest at what has been going on here.

It's not possible that Alexis doesn't see the paradox of being funded by one of Russia's, possibly the world's, biggest polluters. But, no 'constructive co-operation' and I guess he doesn't get to explore the Putoran Plateau any more.)

The Sparrow via Grigori: *As for the relationship between the company's technology and the environment, I cannot tell anything in great detail. But what I do know is that the environmental programme adopted by the company in the next five to seven years will result in dramatic improvements in the environmental situation in this area. That I know for certain.*

Andy: *What is the long-term effect of Norilsk Nickel on the environment here? What irreversible changes have taken place?*

The Sparrow via Grigori: *The main negative effect is in the degradation of forest, and it's mostly seen in the hundred-kilometre-square area between Norilsk and the Putoran Plateau. The western edge of that Plateau is like a fortress which protects the Plateau itself.*

*Even if certain species have disappeared in the area, it is a complex phenomenon and it cannot be entirely ascribed to the pollution from Norilsk Nickel.*

*In the 1980s the white-tailed eagle population was drastically reduced, and although the pollution was enormous from Norilsk Nickel at the time, it was not the only factor. The other big factor was the poaching in the area.*

Grigori to Andy: *He was saying in the presentation there are a lot of hunters in Norilsk. They are not very well educated. That's one of the things they are trying to do, educate the people so at least they don't damage rare species and don't shoot them to extinction. But that was a factor then. There was no control, and poaching was really having as serious an effect as the pollution.*

Andy: *And has there been an improvement in poaching?*

*The Sparrow via Grigori: There is less of it now because there are fewer birds and people are more knowledgeable, especially about rare species. They try not to destroy them.*

He also confirms what we have already heard, that the reindeer now bypass the city on their migratory wanderings and... yes... there has been a population explosion.

At this stage I'm running out of questions. Ornithology is not one of my strong suits. When I'm reduced to asking him what his favourite bird is, both Grigori and I know we've come to the end of the interview. Not least because Alexis starts listing slowly just about every bird you can name... and a few you cannot... and I get the strong impression that he's spent many an hour in his tent on the Putoran Plateau doing just this... listing every species in order of preference.

It's pretty clear that we've just got some soft spin on the company and the environment, but I can't begrudge the man, since it's the company that's allowing him to chase his dreams out in the unexplored tundra.

The Ice Queen is still not ready for us and we (or specifically Sergey) get chatting to a young woman in her twenties who is here from Radio Norilsk. Apparently she wants to interview us later that day. Apparently we've just said yes. I ponder how this whole trip is starting to take an increasingly bizarre turn as I watch the audience gradually thin out.

## Legacy

Within a few minutes only a handful of people remain. Just us and a few guys from the public relations department. The Ice Queen comes over and signals she's ready for our questions. The radio reporter makes her excuses and leaves.

Without the fur coat that bulked her up when I first saw her, The Ice Queen is a less intimidating presence. Nevertheless, her black-rimmed glasses and short black hair lend her a stern air. At no point in our conversation does she smile or laugh.

In another era she would have been a card-carrying member of the Party. Now she is a card-carrying official of Norilsk Nickel. I can't help trying to rile her out of her cool composure. The furthest I get is lukewarm. Like the shower in my hotel room.

So what's the big cleanup plan, Ilyena?

---

*Transcript.*
*Interview with Ilyena Kalakova, deputy head of public*
*relations department, aka The ICE QUEEN.*
*Norilsk lecture hall.*

The Ice Queen via Grigori: *In March this year the company*
*approved a long-term programme until 2015. And under*
*this programme the company will invest every year between*
*$300 and $400 million dollars on improving technology*
*and production processes, which will have a very positive*
*effect on the environment.*
*We expect within the next five years to reduce the emissions*
*of sulphur dioxide by seventy percent. That's the main*
*polluter here.*
*The ore in this area has considerable sulphur content,*
*and the technology that is being used today in the metal*
*production facilities needs replacing because pollution*
*regulations today are much stricter than they were at the*
*time the technology was created.*

(Today is the first time I've seen clear skies in Norilsk. Up to
now it's been cloaked in grey haze. The smell of sulphur has
been a constant olfactory companion whenever we've gone
outside, although its distinctive chemical sting has overlaid a
heavier, almost metallic, presence. I've got into the habit of
rinsing my nostrils every time I get back to my hotel room and
am still shocked when the water runs out dark grey.

In the year 2000 Norilsk Nickel emitted more than two million
tonnes of sulphur dioxide into the air[i]. That was one-fifth of
all Russia's sulphur dioxide emissions. It was also Russia's
biggest chlorine polluter and emitted around 17,000 tonnes of
'dust', an innocuous little word that I fear covers a host of truly
unpleasant chemicals and metallic compounds.

A fuller appreciation of the scale of those figures comes from
Norilsk Nickel's other Arctic mining division. It's located 1,000
miles west of here on the Kola Peninsula, another outcrop
of land in the Arctic Sea. Originally there were two separate

companies called Severonickel and Pechenganickel, but in the first reshuffling of state assets in the early 1990s they had been thrown together and subordinated to their bigger eastern sister. In typically prosaic Soviet style, they were named Kola Mining Company.

Parts of the Kola division are located just over the border from Finland and Norway and the same harmful emissions have caused major deforestation both there and in northern Sweden. Once Russia parted the Iron Curtain, the Scandinavian countries were quick to club together and offer Norilsk Nickel a lending financial hand to clean up its act in their ecological backyard.

But the Kola division is a baby in terms of harmful emissions. In 2000 it emitted 'just' 200,000 or so tonnes of sulphur dioxide a year. Its 'dust' discharge was half that of the main Norilsk division. Even in the bad old Soviet days of 1980 it had managed 'only' half a million tonnes of sulphur dioxide, a quarter of what Norilsk was pumping out twenty years later.

But Kola is close enough to the rich North-East of Western Europe to have drawn attention to itself. The city of Norilsk is a long, long way from anywhere at all. Out of sight, out of mind.)

The Ice Queen via Grigori: *In the Kola Peninsula there is quite a unique relationship between the production facilities and nature. The border of the nature reserve there is within seven kilometres of the Pechenga nickel smelter. So we have to apply especially strict environmental standards there. By the year 2006 we intend to reduce emissions by ninety percent. There is a joint Russian and Norwegian project to help achieve that.*

*Norilsk Nickel is an international company today as opposed to what it was when this equipment was installed. We see the practice and application of international standards as a basic necessity now. We are adopting the international ISO 14001 specification[ii], and we expect by the year 2005 to have come up to that standard here in the Norilsk area and by 2014 in the Kola Peninsula division.*

Andy: *So given that you're going to cut emissions here, when will your workers stop having to wear oxygen packs when they're at work?*

The Ice Queen via Grigori: *We are planning that within the modernisation programme the improved technology will allow us to improve labour conditions.*

Andy: *When?*

The Ice Queen via Grigori: *By the year 2010.*

Andy: *So, for the next seven years oxygen packs are going to be absolutely compulsory in the copper smelter?*

The Ice Queen via Grigori: *There are specially polluted production units and there the workers need oxygen packs, but gradually, and it will be a gradual process, we will reduce the number of such units and replace them. The facilities in the Kola Peninsula were built in the 1930s and here in Norilsk in the 1940s and 1950s. It's very old equipment and it takes time to replace it.*

Andy: *Is it true the average life expectancy here is below the national average?*

The Ice Queen via Grigori: *I met people in the health department of the local government yesterday and they told me that the birth rate here exceeds the death rate.*

Andy: *It's not really what I asked.*

The Ice Queen via Grigori: *I don't know where these figures come from. But one thing I can say is Norilsk Nickel has a programme to move pensioners to the mainland and that will certainly extend their life expectancy. A lot of people have already moved to the mainland so it's quite difficult to calculate exact life expectancy here. Where did you see these figures?*

Andy: *On a couple of places on the Internet.*

The Ice Queen via Grigori: *The level of health care in Norilsk is on a level with any large Russian city. Norilsk does not have more serious diseases than any other major Russian city. Of course, Norilsk is in a special situation because of the climactic conditions here but it has the same figures here as the average.*

Andy: *What about the clean up of the waste from the past?*

*Because you've had sixty or seventy years of mining here.*

The Ice Queen via Grigori: *Before you start reconstituting the soil you have to stop the current emissions.*

Andy: *Do you have any concern that as Norilsk Nickel becomes more international, you could attract much more aggressive environmental campaigning?*

The Ice Queen via Grigori: *All we can say is that we're trying to improve the situation. We're not saying that we are satisfied with the situation as it is.*

*We have to work with the equipment from old Soviet times, and in those times the very words 'ecology' or 'environment' didn't exist in the Russian language.*

*There was a slogan then that the state is the most effective owner. If that slogan had been a reality and not just a slogan, we would not have to go through all these dramatic changes now.*

*The basic process is the introduction of market relationships and market technology.*

*Russia is on the way to becoming part of the international economy, so we are very conscious of the fact that without us making a major effort to improve the environmental situation, we will never achieve our aims internationally.*

Hmm, that bit about 'the introduction of market relationships'. Now, where have I heard that expression before?

I feel sorry for the guys with the oxygen packs in the smelter. Another seven years of sucking from a rubberised mouthpiece to survive the noxious fumes of hell. Let's just hope that the other reference I made – the bit about life expectancy – isn't true, because I seem to remember a very similar number for how far it is supposed to be below the national average for males in Russia.

Norilsk and the area around it are in environmental crisis and that's not just my opinion but that of UNEP, the United Nations Environmental Programme. It says that concentrations of pollutants in the local rivers exceed the permissible levels by 106 times for copper, 2 times for zinc, 13.8 times for ammonium, 6.6 times for nickel, 11 times for phenols and 150 times for iron.

So I don't know, incidentally, why Grigori made such a big joke of me asking where my fish came from at our first lunch in the hotel. The area in the immediate vicinity of the industrial plants is designated an anthropogenic desert, meaning complete loss of vegetation cover and eroded topsoil due to the activities of mankind. The forests are degraded in certain directions at distances up to 150 miles away.

There is also concern about nuclear contamination in the local seaways from the use of nuclear-powered icebreakers to ship the metal out of Norilsk. Mind you, we can probably all be thankful the experimental nuclear research reactor was shut down in the early 1990s.

The terseness of some of our exchanges in the interview may give some indication of just how strong an instinctive dislike I have developed for The Ice Queen. But setting aside personal animosity, I'm also forced to concede, reluctantly, the core truth of what she has said. I'm itching to point the finger of blame at 'them' for what they've done in the past, but their 'it wasn't us' response is at least partly true in a typically convoluted Russian way.

What's happened here is a legacy of the Soviet times, when Norilsk Nickel was called a combine, when it was subordinated to the Ministry of Defence, and when The Ice Queen probably hadn't yet been born. Even if you wanted to try and take someone to court for this gigantic act of ecological vandalism, you can't. The Soviet Union is no longer a legal entity. Nor are any of its former ministries. There's no one to sue. Year zero!

The USSR may have had 'soulfulness', to use Simona's word at the TV station, but the system did not produce state-of-the-art technology and it couldn't have cared less about the environment.

The area around the city looks as if it's just come off the losing end of a major military battle. Rusting scrap and junk litter the barren earth for miles around, an ongoing reminder of the Soviet Defence Ministry's method of recycling. There was none. Once something came to the end of its useful life, it was just left to disintegrate over time and a new facility was built next to it. Used pipes were simply thrown a few yards out into the tundra to make way for a new set. Slag from the smelters, much of it massively contaminated with heavy minerals, was piled up at the nearest convenient distance, most noticeably on one side of the city itself.

The same policy applied to pollution from the mines, smelters and power plants... one of absolute disregard for anything that did not directly result in more strategic metals being produced and delivered to the military factories scattered across the Siberian 'waste' lands. Raw volume production, not productivity, was then the name of the game.

The new entity that runs this city now, Norilsk Nickel, and the powerful Interros Group behind it, may be sitting on a metaphorical gold mine in terms of how much money they can earn every year but there's a price to be paid as well.

It helps that the short-term costs will pay off in future profits.

New technology will indeed go a long way to solving some of the ecological issues here. The party of Norwegians staying in our hotel are visiting the company to discuss industrial flue systems, and it seems that if you're in the business of environmentally friendly gizmos for industrial plants, there's something of a Siberian sales bonanza underway right now.

New technology, of course, will also make the smelting and refining process more efficient and require fewer workers. That means lower production costs and more money to drop to the bottom line. It also means less money to be spent by the company and local authorities heating people's homes and supplying them with power and water.

The company is even trying to work out how to get rid of the mountainous ice-covered slag heaps dotted around the city. Sergey says it's working on ways it could extract the metal from them. But the material comprises what are known in the business as 'complex' residues, with traces of large numbers of hazardous minerals, making them an unattractive prospect from both a financial and environmental viewpoint. The company has also considered just digging the stuff out of the permafrost and chucking it down one of its worked-out mines, Sergey says. But that might cause a few problems with the water table, which is not going to help Norilsk Nickel achieve its coveted ISO status.

But while the company ponders this all-too-physical reminder of its Soviet legacy, it does seem to have embarked on an attempt at a massive tidy-up. The appliance of 'market relationships' to the company, to use Interros-speak, is designed around a win-win solution to this testament of Soviet environmental recklessness. Investment in new technology equals better profitability and a better environment. It's disarmingly simple but hard to argue with.

I bet it's a few years before the reindeer come back, though.

## Ghosts

Before we can leave the lecture hall, another functionary from the Norilsk public relations department introduces himself to us. He tells us he will be arranging our trip to one of the mines tomorrow and will also try and facilitate an interview with the top man here. Sergey's been trying to get an appointment with The Man since touching down at Norilsk airport. So far it's been 'promises, promises, nothing but promises'.

I get the distinct impression that after our interview with the contractors at the smelter yesterday, we've just been moved up a level of minder. The new guy is a few years older than Lt Ivanov, in his early- to mid-thirties with a thin face and jet-black hair. But he's friendly enough, in a reserved sort of way, and we spend a few minutes with him outside while he and I smoke a cigarette. He promises to call us later with more details.

We walk back to the hotel for lunch under still-bright blue skies.

Lying on my bed that afternoon – Grigori has gone for 'a little lie-down' – I think about The Ice Queen. I can tell that she's just as much a foreigner from the mainland as we are. She has something of the Moscow intellectual about her, a standoffishness that marks her out in this place.

Talking to people here is surprisingly easy. Well, assuming you speak Russian or have a translator, it's easy. As with all isolated islanders, everyone we've met so far has been desperate for news from the mainland and equally enthusiastic about describing their own lives here in Norilsk. They're chatty in a way that city-dwellers are not.

The Ice Queen stands aloof from this sort of rural community spirit.

I'd be flattered to think that her visit has somehow been timed for our benefit, but she's part of a to-ing and fro-ing between Moscow and Norilsk that is apparently building to a crescendo of activity.

Our new public relations minder has already moaned to us that the local department is rushed off its feet right now with the growing number of visits from the Moscow bigwigs. The climax of all this hoo-ha will come in the autumn with the official celebrations of Norilsk's fiftieth anniversary.

Even the city centre has been given a new lick of paint apparently, although this particular bit of news comes as some surprise to me and leaves me wondering what the hell it looked like before being tarted up.

And it's only now, as I try and picture this pending anniversary, that I realise that there's something wrong with the mathematics here. If the official fiftieth birthday party is scheduled for this year, it implies that Norilsk came into existence in 1953. But I know it started out in the late 1930s as a labour camp, part of the mammoth gulag system that spread its tentacles through sleeping Siberia.

Ah! But of course! That would be it! 'Norilsk' didn't exist as a city prior to 1953. Before that particular year zero, it was a prison camp with a minimum of actual buildings. Not a city. A penal colony.

In fact, Norilsk was one of the biggest camps in the whole system. It had started out in 1933 as a geological expeditionary camp under the authority of the Soviet Heavy Industry Ministry. The camp struck nickel in massive quantities. Then, as now, nickel's main use was in stainless steel, something the Soviet military was keen to get its hands on at the time.

In June 1935 Norilsk was transferred to the administration of the NKVD, the Soviet Union's political police. The top-secret document covering the transfer ('About Norilsk Nickel industrial complex construction') noted that existing infrastructure was 'minimal'[iii]. Think tents!

The NKVD was awarded the contract for two reasons. Thanks to Stalin's paranoia about the enemy within, it could supply an almost infinite stream of workers. It had also developed a reputation for taking on and administering projects in Russia's extreme regions, unlike the civilian ministries that shied away from them. Indeed, the Heavy Industries Ministry had specifically requested it be relieved of the Norilsk project.

'Norilsk Correctional Labour Camp' (acronym, Norilsk ITL, but generally referred to as 'Norillag') was one of only six projects at the time directly under the control of the central gulag administration rather than regional divisions of the NKVD. All six were considered critical to the state's strategic interests.

The first thousand prisoners arrived by boat from Krasnoyarsk within weeks of the order authorising the NKVD to set up Norillag. Their job was to start building the infrastructure that would support a mining and metallurgy complex. As was often the case, they arrived in the clothes they had been wearing when arrested and were weak from the hardship of the journey to the Arctic North.

An idea of what life was like for these first Norilsk workers comes in a highly atypical descriptive passage buried in the dry administrative language of a 1936 special report[iv] from the directors of the camp, explaining delays and cost overruns to the central gulag administration.

It should be noted that materials of the annual report and its narrative reflect insufficiently the circumstances of construction work under absolutely abnormal conditions: 'In 1935 an advance group of workers was sent to undeveloped tundra without necessary materials to prepare for expanding construction in 1936. This contingent had to do difficult and time-consuming preparatory work under permafrost conditions, under the most severe snowstorms, which dissipated their energy and mental state. Only a person who had experienced it himself knows what it means to preserve the necessary vitality and working energy after months of constant winds with a force from 18 up to 37 meters per second that blow continuous clouds of snow, so that visibility is about 2 meters. Stray workers were lost due to loss of orientation. They had to work in temperatures reaching 53 degrees below zero. Workers were dispersed in the tundra to prepare new areas for habitation and to prepare the area to receive new labor force, create stocks of materials, and to equip work places. In these conditions, Norilstroi workers conducted the first operations in making tractor and cart roads from Dudinka to Norilsk.

Prisoners died from starvation. They died from overwork. They died when they got lost in the snow blizzards. Construction work in the permafrost was done with hand-held shovels and pick-axes. The movement of earth and rock was accomplished with wheelbarrows. Women prisoners assigned to work on conveyor-belts had to jump up and down on them to keep them going in the freezing temperatures. Convoys of food and raw materials didn't make it in time before both the Arctic sea route and the Yenisey river route froze up during the long winter months.'

The first general director of Norillag was arrested in April 1939 for non-fulfilment of norms and sentenced to death, commuted to a 15-year jail sentence[v]. The 1935 decree ordering the construction of Norillag stipulated production of 10,000 tonnes of nickel by the year 1938. The figure was only achieved in 1945[vi].

Those first thousand 'enemies of the state' were followed by countless others. Because of the harshness of the conditions and the virtual impossibility of escape, Norillag was the favoured NKVD destination for hard-core subversive elements – anti-Soviet partisans from the Baltic countries and the Ukraine, professional criminals deemed beyond rehabilitation, and, during the Great Patriotic War years, those convicted of war crimes against the Soviet peoples.

Because of its strategic importance to the military, Norillag also became one of the largest penal colonies. From just 1,200 prisoners at the end of 1935 it grew to 19,500 at the end of 1940 and to 68,850 in 1952[vii]. Those figures, though, cannot capture the total number of people who worked in Norillag since the turnover was extremely high – both due to the mortality rate and the successive waves of amnesties and new arrests that characterised the Stalin era.

Conditions remained unimaginably grim throughout. A 1948 inspection of Norilsk by a central gulag team found that only seventy-five per cent of prisoners had warm boots and only eighty-six per cent had warm clothes[viii]. In the 1940s there was a children's prison, housing over 1,000 youngsters[ix]. They were put to work in a brick factory. Even the hardened gulag administration was shocked by this and ordered the children to be relocated to another camp in less harsh conditions back on the mainland.

Norillag remained a penal colony until 1956 – three years after Stalin's death. The strike and uprising mentioned in the previous chapter took place in 1953. The prisoners had gambled that the death of the tyrant would lead to general amnesties. They got it wrong by several years.

Norilsk Nickel's official birthday celebrations effectively consign its history before 1953 to nothingness. The many thousands who died here building the city will not even merit a footnote in the history books. They have simply been erased from the past, like those shining lights of the Soviet Union who were scrubbed out of the official photographs once they had fallen from grace and been arrested for anti-Soviet activities.

Instead, the official history of Norilsk will be of the many patriots from the Communist Party and its youth brigade, the Komsomol, who came here in the 1960s and 1970s to make Nadezhda, 'hope', bloom in the tundra.

There is nothing unilateral about the company's approach to its past. Not one person we've met and talked to so far has made any reference to it. There are very few living survivors and most of those are non-Russians. If any still live in the city, we can't find them. For most of the people working here, there is simply no reference point in their day-to-day lives to what went before.

Even Grigori's generation of Russians has a stoic, black-humoured view of the bad old years. Maybe the taboo is still too strong. Nobody asked about political prisoners at the time. No one does now.

A friend of Grigori's in Moscow had regaled us with an after-dinner story about an unfortunate co-worker. At the factory collective's annual dinner dance, he had got a bit too drunk and a bit too exuberant in his floor moves, inadvertently knocking over a plinth of Lenin. Despite hasty apologies at the time, a couple of weeks later he and his family had disappeared. No-one asked why. No-one asked anything. To do so would have been to associate oneself with an anti-Soviet element and risk the same fate.

There is a ghost in this story – the person who had reported the hapless dancer.

Life in Soviet times was pervaded by fear of the anonymous neighbour or co-worker or even friend... the one who was prepared to file a report in the full knowledge that his or her action would send their target off to a highly uncertain future in some distant penal camp.

Grigori's friend Uly had told the story as if it were a joke, laughing uproariously at key moments and inviting us to join him. His wife occasionally scolded him to 'keep it down' in case the neighbours heard. 'Very Soviet woman!' Uly had bellowed at her.

But the point is that you didn't know then and you don't know now who played the elided role of state informer. Best not to say anything. Best to keep your head down. Best to stay out of trouble and hope that the gulag administration hadn't requested a new batch of workers with your specific qualifications. For the system worked in reverse too! Arrests would be made to fulfil specific quotas for trained personnel.

Nobody asked any questions then and nobody seems to want to know about the gulag prisoners now. From what I've read, it appears to be the same all over Russia. After a brief deluge of memoirs and biographies from former, often 'celebrity', dissidents in the early 1990s, Russia appears collectively to have yawned and decided to get on with things.

It's not like holocaust denial. No one's denying anything. It's more a national shrug of the shoulders. 'Yeah, it happened, so?'

And before that happened, life hadn't been that great under the tsars either. In fact, it had been so bad, they'd had to have a bloody revolution to get rid of them.

And if they had been bad, Russia had earlier been run by a guy whose name is always accompanied by the words 'the Terrible', which must say something about how good life had been then for most of his countrymen.

When I once asked Grigori about the reaction to the financial crisis of the early 1990s, involving – but not limited to – a massive cut in everyone's pensions, he told me that what I forgot was that life had always been 'shit' for most Russians and they didn't expect anything more. The point being, there is simply too much awful history here for people to want to remember. Thomas Hobbes' dictum that life is 'poor, nasty, brutish and short' has been too good a description of their existence for too many Russians for too much of the time. It wasn't Stalin who invented the Siberian penal camps, after all. He just brought them up to a scale made possible by the advances of the twentieth century.

But no matter how I try and find an emotionally correct explanation for Russia's insouciance about the gulag system, I am still deeply shocked by the fact that twenty years of history will just be removed from this city's consciousness. It doesn't seem right. It doesn't seem right at all.

The fact that Norilsk Nickel has chosen as its official birthday the year of both Stalin's death and the prisoners' revolt is purely coincidental. The uprising will not be officially celebrated, although Ukrainian survivors of the camp will hold their own ceremony later in the year. All members of the anti-Soviet Ukrainian Rebellion Army and the Ukrainian Organisation of Nationalists, they had been the instigators of the uprising and view it now as a nationalist revolt. Their anniversary bash will be held in Ukraine, not Norilsk.

### Transmitters

I'm just in the middle of recording such thoughts on Norilsk's spectral past when there's a tap on the door, quickly followed by Sergey's bushy moustache and broad grin.

I've completely forgotten that we are due to give an interview on the local radio station. Rather, I am due to give an interview. Grigori will be translating.

The radio station is located at the top of yet another dank and dingy apartment block. It has two employees, the producer and the reporter. Both are in their early twenties. He, the producer, is a slightly bookish looking guy with hair neatly parted. She, the reporter, is an attractive brunette with blue eyes and wide cheekbones. I suspect they are also boyfriend and girlfriend.

He says they've just received some new equipment, but to my uninitiated eye the technology in the room looks like that used by a moderately well-run pirate station back home.

We are offered cups of tea and chocolate biscuits and they tell us about Radio Norilsk. It's mainly music – and an Elvis Presley poster on the wall suggests which era – with the odd bits of reporting and, more rarely, the odd interview with an outsider.

I'm a bit unsure as to whether we're doing the right thing here.

Firstly, it all seems a bit self-referential, like one of those over-intellectualised French novels from the 1950s. So, we're going to be on radio talking about us making a radio programme. Then they're going to send us the tape so we can be on Norilsk radio on BBC Radio 4. Eh?

Secondly, I'm concerned that we're attracting an increasing amount of attention from the company's public relations department, and, if Sergey is to be believed, from other more sinister forces as well. I'm not sure after our interview with the contractors yesterday and a fairly feisty interview with The Ice Queen today that we should necessarily be heard broadcasting over the entire city of Norilsk.

My sense of unease is heightened after being embedded in the claustrophobic interior of the recording studio – a wardrobe-sized room which barely holds the reporter, Grigori and me.

We start with a couple of disarmingly bland questions such as, 'Do people in the UK also have pets?' and 'What's your favourite dog?' I start to relax in the premature assumption that I can't get into any trouble here, at least not with the authorities. I guess a few of Norilsk's passionate pet owners may not like my choice of 'Saluki!', but I can live with that.

'Do you think Norilsk Nickel is wholly responsible for the environmental damage to this area?'

I'm almost winded by the question as my brain registers that I've just been softened up for what is going to be the meat of the interview.

Grigori translates the question and then looks at me unhelpfully, awaiting my answer, so he can translate back. The reporter is also nodding at me in a presumably encouraging way. I look through the glass window of the recording room and see both the producer and Sergey looking expectantly at me.

But what, exactly, are they expecting?

To my mind, the answer's a pretty unequivocal 'Yes!' with a few important caveats.

But I'm not sure whether this is the sort of thing I want to be heard broadcasting to the good citizens of Norilsk. I don't have any feel for whether I'm being set up, and, if so, whether I'm being set up by friends or enemies. I am powerfully struck by the realisation that not speaking or understanding any Russian has robbed me of so many nuances of understanding. I get hit with another sudden sensation of being hopelessly lost.

After a drawn-out hesitation, I manage a meandering 'on the one hand... on the other', duck-and-dive, circuitous response and try not to think of an unseen hand notating my answers next to a monitoring set in one of the city's bland concrete buildings.

The rest of the interview proves to be an uncomfortable mix of the anodyne and the potentially dangerous. 'Where do people in the UK go on holiday?' 'What do people there now think about Russia?'

After half an hour of this torture, we finish up and say extended goodbyes to Radio Norilsk. I hardly register what's said. My mind is whirring back through the interview as I try and re-locate the mantraps and imagine how they might be edited.

When we're back outside trudging down the street, I ask

Grigori and Sergey what they thought. They shrug off my fears. What's there to worry about? After all, we're now due to go ten-pin bowling with the man identified by Sergey as a government agent. Now's the time we might want to choose our words carefully.

THE BEAR is waiting for us outside the ten-pin bowling alley, a relatively new addition to Norilsk's leisure facilities from what I can gather. He's beaming amicably and laughs away our apologies for running late.

He leads us into a brightly lit building with neon bar and restaurant and we sit at one of the benches adjacent to the bowling alleys. He explains that 'a friend' is going to join us, and after a first beer, during which the conversation is a relaxed catch-up, our second evening companion arrives.

By now I'm only too aware of the dangers of judging this country and this city by outward appearances, but 'the friend' does nothing to dispel the doubts I have about the authenticity of the local 'photographer'.

He is a young guy – I would guess middle to late twenties – but one of those types who through their superficially youthful features exude the personality of a sixty-year-old. He has the haircut of a much older man. His thin, fair hair is already receding and he's combed it very carefully over the middle to disguise the fact. Frameless steel glasses slightly magnify his thoughtful brown eyes. A finely chiselled face tapers down to a set of thin, cruel-looking lips.

He's the archetypal secret police interrogator, an amalgam of a hundred different interpretations in a hundred movies. He's the quietly terrifying character who gets to do horrible things to a gagged and bound hero. He always gets the best lines. 'If you do not co-operate with us… well… I'm afraid this is going to be a lot more painful for you than it is for me, my friend.' The twisted irony of that last word is always intended to leave a lingering chill in the viewer.

I keep a wary eye on the new arrival as more beers are ordered and we get down to business, which apparently is going to be an interview with the local magazine, assuming it exists, of course. The Bear takes the main role, interviewing

Grigori and Sergey in Russian and taking down notes. Hmmm! Not just a photographer then, I see!

His friend, The Inquisitor, occasionally interjects a comment or a question. I am largely left out of things. Without Russian I can only detect the odd familiar word in Grigori's detailed personal history. The whole thing lasts several rounds of beers.

I have no choice but to trust Grigori's judgement that the best way of dealing with the authorities here is to give them all the information they want and then let them decide what to do with it. Our invitation courtesy of someone as high up as Dmitry Zelenin gives us a comfort zone with 'the local people', he's explained.

## The Locals

The 'local people' are almost certainly the Federal Security Services, successor to the KGB. Although Norilsk stopped being a closed strategic city in 1989 and the mines and metals plants were 'privatised' in the mid-1990s, the state has never stepped away completely from its former asset.

Much of the Interros Group's tenure of Norilsk has been spent trying to loosen the vice-like grip of the other men in suits, those in the hidden corridors of Russian power. The two ghostly combatants have been locked in a shadowy tussle for real control of the company since the day Interros came on the Norilsk scene.

After years of lobbying, Norilsk Nickel has only this year wrested from the state reluctant and partial permission to tell people how much metal it produces. Until 2002 everyone in the company was prohibited from giving away such sensitive information. Every annual report to shareholders until the one for 2003 gives only percentage year-on-year comparisons such as 'nickel production was 104.1 per cent of that achieved last year'. A miniscule footnote states: 'Absolute figures may not be shown due to restrictions imposed under the Russian Federation's Law on State Secrets.' Which is a major pain for a company trying to gain credibility in the global financial markets. 'We're a big company.' 'How big?' 'Unfortunately, I can't give you that information.' Not the sort of answer to whip up the interest of the smart young men and women working for Wall Street banks.

Now, for the first time in its seventy-year history – and I'm personally going with seventy rather than fifty – it can say how much copper and nickel it produces every year. But not how much platinum or palladium. Information on those metals remains a state secret. It seems someone thinks they're still just too sensitive a subject to be openly discussed. A bit too valuable as well, it should be said. One of the first clashes between company and state was over the government's annoying habit of regarding Norilsk's precious metals as a useful piggy bank to be raided at times of financial trouble.

When Russia fell through the door of the capitalist club and immediately smashed its head on the floor, Norilsk was told it could do what it liked with the base metals – the copper and the nickel. The result was the chaos of the scatter-gun sales patterns in the early 1990s.

The state got to keep the precious metals – the platinum and palladium – to sell as it saw fit. It managed to surpass its protégé in terms of financial anarchy. First it raided its own stockpiles as part of a fire sale to keep itself afloat, forcing down international prices and putting most of the world's producers under immense financial pressure, including of course its own favourite daughter.

Then, one year the annual law authorizing the state export licences somehow failed to get passed in time for the start of the year. No licences, no exports, no sales – at all.

The law was eventually signed and the exports flowed again, but not before a tidal wave of uncertainty had crashed through the global markets.

The same happened the next year. This time it took months to get the law passed. It looked like a fairly blatant attempt by the Russian government to manipulate the global markets for platinum and palladium.

What was actually taking place was a very Russian bout of internecine warfare between ministries and the central bank as to just who should sell the precious metals and who should get the money. The battle raged behind closed doors in Moscow and over the floor of the Duma, the Russian Parliament, which had to approve the export licence war. At its fiercest in 1999, in some sort of bureaucratic blocking move that exceeded the originator's intention, the Duma passed a law prohibiting indefinitely all exports until further notice. No money for the state. Much less money for Norilsk Nickel, which ruefully conceded in its annual report that year that things might have been better had it not been left with over $300 million worth of unsold platinum and rhodium at the end of the year.

It took Interros another three years to be allowed to sell its own production of precious metals to customers outside Russia.

That was just one victory in a long, long battle. The state is still here. It is not yet ready to relinquish control of this last bastion of the Soviet system. After all, it fathered Norilsk, from the very start of Norillag as a penal colony.

And since the state is still here, so too are its eyes and ears in the form of the Federal Security Services. Which is probably why we're being interviewed at a ten-pin bowling alley by The Bear and someone who looks as if he's walked straight out of a spy film.

The lengthy process finally comes to an end, and we have snacks from the Americanised restaurant – all burgers and hotdogs – and more beers, and engage in some ten-pin bowling.

The last time I played was when I was nine and all I remember about it was that it was a hopelessly frustrating sport. My technique has deteriorated since then and I soon give up trying and just hurl the balls in the direction of the pins between getting stuck into the beer. Sergey contrives to be even worse than me, which is some comfort. Our two Russian friends take it immensely seriously, particularly The Inquisitor.

I'm relieved when the sport is over and we go our different ways amid much good-hearted handshaking. Our two companions stroll off down the street through the half-day, half-night gloom which has recently returned to the city. They are chatting to each other. My uneasy impression is of two people who can now relax having just successfully completed a potentially tricky mission.

---

**Transcript.**
**Andy's Audio Journal.**
**Hotel Room.**
**Night.**

Andy: *I found the press conference slightly surreal to be honest. Bear in mind that just yesterday… woah!… hold on!… let's put this into perspective… bear in mind every comment I've made about what this place looks like.*

*… and specifically when it was brought home to us yesterday, at the copper smelter. When you see the guys in the plant wandering around breathing from oxygen packs…*

*… I did find it slightly surreal that the promotion of the company is about a very little known bird which, in fact, is not even found in Norilsk per se, but is found on a neighbouring peninsula…*

*… but whatever!*

[i]'Russian Smelter Emissions' by S.V. Edimov, I.V. Samodova, Dr I.M. Petrov, Dr V.V. Troitsky and Dr M.A. Burstein as appeared in Mining Journal, 23 Nov 2001.

[ii]ISO. The ISO is the International Organisation for Standardisation. It is a non-governmental organisation based in Geneva, Switzerland and is a network of 153 national standards institutions. The abbreviation ISO is not an acronym but derives from the Greek word 'isos' meaning 'equal'. Built around consensus and voluntary recognition ISO has published more than 15,000 International Standards, from nuts and bolts to computer protocols. The ISO 14000 family of standards is specifically concerned with environmental management, stipulating parameters by which to measure a company's impact on the environment.

[iii]Behind the Façade of Stalin's Command Economy. Ed Paul Gregory,

Hoover Press. Chapter 7, 'Building Norilsk' by Simon Ertz.

[iv] ibid

[v] ibid

[vi] ibid

[vii] Anne Appelbaum, Gulag: A History. Anchor

[viii] ibid page 214

[ix] ibid page 303

# INNER SANCTUMS
## 'BBC or British Intelligence?'

---

*Transcript.*
*Andy's Audio Journal.*
*Hotel Restaurant.*
*Afternoon.*
*Killing Time.*
*Waiting on Norilsk Nickel.*

Andy: *I'm just sitting in our breakfast-room-cum-restaurant-cum-bar and I thought I'd share with you the combination of the radio and TV which are playing simultaneously.*
*Also, quite curiously, the people working in the kitchen here... let me rephrase that... the woman working in the kitchen here... is dressed like a dental hygienist, which gives the overall impression that she's just rushed next door from a second job, leaving the patient sitting in the chair. And it being Russia, who's to say she hasn't just rushed from next door where she has in fact left a patient in the chair?*
*So this is what we have every morning. It's a hell of a way to start the day. TV in one ear, which confusingly enough is also music at the moment, and radio in the other ear. They're actually being quite restrained because I'm the only one here. They usually play it louder. It makes morning conversation quite difficult. Maybe that's the point. Who's to say?*
*All the music sounds like stuff from the Eurovision Song Contest, and after a while I find it really does my head*

*in, to be honest. I had quite romantic notions that people*
*would be playing Russian folk music on the radio.*
*Obviously not!*
*Right! That's quite enough of that. I don't think I can stand*
*very much more. I just came down for a coffee.*

## Need to Know

This morning at breakfast we're brusquely interrupted by our
new friend from the public relations department who comes to
find us to tell us we're late for the minibus. It's waiting outside
to take us on our visit to one of the mines.

We're not late. He's early.

There's a bit of an all-hands-on-deck scramble back to our
rooms for recording equipment and other assorted bits and
pieces. When we emerge flustered in front of the hotel, I fear
we give a far from professional BBC impression.

Already ensconced in the minibus are our two companions
from the smelter visit. The Bear is full of hearty hail-fellow-
well-met bonhomie. The female journalist remains her quiet,
withdrawn self of the previous day. I examine her with
renewed curiosity, unsure any more as to whether she is really
a journalist or just another layer of security to watch over us.
For that matter, I'm a bit suspicious of the driver now I come
to think about it. Is he part of all this as well?

I'm not usually the paranoid type but Norilsk seems to be
the embodiment of that old hippy mantra – just because you're
paranoid doesn't mean they're not watching you.

The mine visit is one of the cornerstones of our trip here.
The BBC had been very keen on getting some recordings of a
Russian mine – the 'dirty geography' as the producer called it.

For me, it crystallises all my fascination with this place, all
the unanswered questions that have accumulated over the
years, all the difficulties getting here.

Sergey's pulled off something of a coup with the company.

Unlike Western mining houses that are only too keen to
whisk favoured financial analysts and journalists off to remote
parts of the world to showcase their achievements, this type of
glasnost is pretty new to Norilsk Nickel.

Only a few years earlier you would have been lucky to get them to admit they had any mines at all. When I started as a journalist covering the world's industrial metals markets in 1987, trying to extract market-sensitive information from the Soviet system was just as difficult as you'd expect.

Raznoimport, universally known at the time as Razno, was the Soviet state entity that handled all sales of base metals such as copper and nickel outside the Soviet Union. What was on offer was normally remaindered stock from the Ministry of Defence's own annual requirements.

Razno maintained a small London office staffed by... well, who do you think the Soviet state was going to trust with living abroad and trading the USSR's natural resources?

One of my colleagues waged a three-month campaign of ringing Razno's office every couple of days to try and 'break' a source there. It took him a month to get the guy on the other end of the phone to admit he even worked for Razno. It took him another two weeks to confirm Mr X was indeed the nickel trader. Mr X refused to give his name – 'you can call me the nickel trader'. By the third month, The Nickel Trader was prepared to chitchat about the weather or even the football. But as soon as the conversation seemed in danger of turning to anything of potential commercial interest, Mr X chuckled and hung up with what had become his trademark parting shot: 'That's enough information for you today, my friend.' My colleague gave up around that stage but told me it had been good practice for his basic conversational Russian skills.

Things had not improved much by the mid-1990s, even though other parts of Russia were going through an orgy of openness and Norilsk Nickel was emerging as the primary source of raw metals for our markets in Western Europe, albeit one that regularly redefined the word 'chaos'.

Metals prices rocketed in late 1993 on rumours that one of the power plants supplying Norilsk and its mines had blown up or suffered some equally cataclysmic failure. Such a power loss would have spelt major trouble, not just for the unfortunate citizens of the city, but also for the company's metal-making operations. Without power, miners wouldn't have been able to go down the mines, or even more disconcertingly, wouldn't have been able to come back up. Without power, the giant slurry pipes connecting the matrix of crushing and ore-dressing plants would have frozen solid. Without power, the huge smelters and refineries would have ground to a complete halt.

What, traders wanted to know, had actually happened and what did it mean for this newly emergent source of metals supply, which by now was feeding the stainless steel plants of most of Europe? The fate of the citizens was of secondary interest to the world's big trading centres with their ranks of desk-soldiers glued to every tick of every price. The marketplace, whether for gold or gasoline or grain, is a very hard place indeed.

The market's search for accurate information could have been answered easily if the accident had taken place at just about any metal producer other than Norilsk Nickel. The US-derived culture of market regulation means a big public metals company such as Rio Tinto, or an oil producer such as BP, can actually be fined by the regulatory authorities for NOT telling investors about that sort of disruption to cash flow.

Not, alas, Norilsk Nickel at the time. Still run by its former Soviet management, it was not yet ready for this, to them, highly unusual press and market scrutiny of its home island up above the Arctic Circle.

Norilsk Nickel's head office in Moscow had responded to the financial press requests for information with a combination of the absurd – 'there are no problems at all at our operations' – and the sublime – 'we do not have any operations where you say we have them'.

World prices for nickel and copper, platinum and palladium gyrated wildly for weeks on end in the face of the company's stonewalling and the resulting swirl of rumours, half-truths and outright lies. What the markets hate most is uncertainty – and that's exactly what they got from a company for which glasnost was something that was happening somewhere else in Russia.

It was literally months later that the whole truth emerged. One of the power stations had indeed stopped working. The Ministry of Emergency Situations had airlifted something like 60,000 people – around a quarter of the town's then population – to central Russia so power could be prioritised for uninterrupted production of the all-important metals. And no one outside of Norilsk knew anything about it! If you're into keeping secrets, being located on the northern tip of Siberia obviously has advantages.

Yeah! So I'm up in a big way for this particular instalment of my Journey of a Lifetime. I'm going to travel to the underground heart of the secret city of a previously closed country! How's that for a holiday trespass?

Years of dealing with belligerent, unhelpful and at times downright mendacious Norilsk officials, and I'm here ten years later, to come and have an emotional gloat. 'Couldn't keep me out, could you, you ******ers?'

The fact that at least one of my travelling companions is probably a government agent is a minor blot on my otherwise luminous sense of achievement.

## Descent

Most of the company's mines, unlike the smelters and refineries, are located around the satellite town of Talnakh, about twenty miles from Norilsk itself.

The minibus trip there is a journey of two contrasting halves. The first twenty minutes are spent driving, with the customary jolts and corner-skids, through the man-made apocalypse to which my eyes and nose have now just about fully acclimatised.

But a strange and unexpected thing happens then. The bus crosses a frozen river on which rest a number of boats in varying degrees of weather-beaten disintegration like stranded whale carcasses. Once on the other side, the landscape quickly starts changing, throwing off the blanket of soot and grey that cloaks Norilsk.

Suddenly we are weaving through still-living fir forests. Set back slightly from the road in small clearings sit wooden dachas in all shapes and sizes, anything from a simple shed-like structure to two-storey multi-bedroom houses.

A sprinkling of snow – white snow at that – makes the

whole place feel a bit Christmassy.

I can't take my eyes off the trees. They are the first ones I've seen since I've been here.

The public relations guy – I haven't thought of a nickname for him yet, but I'm working on it – explains that the emissions from the city don't cross the river due to a combination of prevailing wind and local topography. The river separates desert from forest.

I start to visualise what Norilsk itself must have been like before the forests died around it. The idea of a couple of reindeer wandering into town doesn't seem so far-fetched now.

Which mine are we actually going to, I ask via Grigori. The Taimyrski mine, I'm told. It's named after the Taimyr Peninsula on which Norilsk is located.

And how many mines does Norilsk have in total, I ask. Without intending to, I spark a protracted and heated discussion among all the Norilsk people in the minibus. The public relations minder, the Bear, the female journalist and even the bus driver start counting them off on the fingers of their hands and arguing with each other.

There are in fact seven mines[i]. The information is publicly available on Norilsk Nickel's website. But I'm highly amused by the debate I've unwittingly started. It continues, without clear resolution, until we come to the outskirts of Talnakh.

Although designated a satellite town of Norilsk, it has about the same size of population with just under 100,000 people. It is characterised by the same rows of dirty apartment blocks that blight most of Norilsk. The only difference is that Talnakh is situated on one of the hills that surround this area. Amazingly, it manages to appear even grimmer and more smashed-up than the main city.

We bypass the town centre and pull up in front of a modern, two-storey building. We're still running late apparently. The lift to the bottom of the mineshaft is due to depart in around fifteen minutes, and if we miss it, we either have to wait another four hours or forego the whole trip.

We dash through the front doors of the building and into

a changing room, where we strip off to our underwear. A couple of burly miners stand around smoking, offering bits of advice and the occasional helping hand as we struggle into our kit – full heavy-duty overalls, various belts and straps and Wellington boots.

Somewhat worryingly we also each get an individual power pack for the lamps on our helmets and emergency rations 'in case anything goes wrong', as Grigori translates for me.

The half-mile or so down a sloping corridor to the main shaft entrance is done at a gentle jog, ensuring that all of us are out of breath by the time we arrive at the huge steel cage that will take us a mile below the permafrost. A small group of miners, kitted out like us, is already waiting in the lift, chatting animatedly.

We step into the cage, which is about the size of a modest family-home garage, and a door of steel casing is slid shut. Amid a shrill hissing and a heavier grinding of distant machinery, the descent starts. Slowly at first… but then faster and faster. Both ends of the cage are open so we can see the bare rock of the shaft accelerating upwards past us at ever more mind-boggling speed. Our guide – a heavily-built man with a huge beer gut – warns us not to try and put out our hands near the rock – they will be completely smashed. My ears pop three times on our descent into Norilsk's dark heart.

The braking of the lift is so strong that when we finally come to rest one mile underground I subconsciously lift my eyes to look for my stomach, which feels like it left my body about half way down.

The cage door is opened and the other guys in the lift disappear down one of the many tunnels leading off from the cavernous waiting room in front of us.

We follow our guide down another, poorly-lit tunnel. It's about the size of a London tube tunnel, an impression reinforced by the fact there is a single track of rail running down the middle of it. It's only after we've been trudging along for a hundred or so yards that our guide tells us not to stand on the rail – it's got 600 volts of electricity running through it.

As we walk along, struggling with the unaccustomed weight

of our battery packs and provisions, Grigori translates for me the occasional slogans on large posters nailed on the walls. They're a mixture of Soviet exhortation for greater work norms and somewhat absurd health and safety warnings. 'In the event of locomotive coming, get off the tracks' is just one example of the bleeding-obvious nature of the latter.

Our tunnel walk lasts fifteen minutes and then we come across a squat vehicle which will take us down further into the depths of the mine. It looks a little like those toy trains you get to ride around fun-parks in, and the way you get locked into your seats with a metal safety bar adds to the sense of a funfair ride. It's pulled by something that looks like a cross between a Jeep and a Humvee. On a thumbs-up from our guide it growls into life.

Although our drive is very slow – a couple of miles per hour at best – the floors of the rock-hewn tunnels we're now traversing are so rough that we're thrown around inside in truly alarming fashion. Within seconds I'm thankful we're wearing the obligatory hard hats. Without one I would have been knocked stone-cold unconscious at least twice, such is the violence with which my head has come into contact with the metal roof of the vehicle. And that's with the restraining bar!

The drive seems interminable but is probably only twenty minutes or so. The direction is downwards about eighty percent of the time. There is virtually no room for error on the part of the driver – the vehicle clears the sides by a matter of mere inches. Occasionally, a slight miscalculation heaves us all to one side or another like the crew of the early Star Trek TV show when they hit an asteroid belt. The tunnels are now unlit and the only light comes from the small lamps on our helmets. The sound of the diesel engine as it slides up and down its gears is gratingly loud.

We try recording the experience but give up after a couple of minutes of breathless commentary regularly interrupted by curses and oaths as we're flung around in our seats.

## Underground

When we finally arrive at our destination, I get out of the transport and stagger around for a few seconds until I find sufficient confidence to walk again. I feel as if my bones have been dismantled, shaken in a big bag and roughly reassembled. I notice that it's not just me. Even our public relations minder seems to be unused to this sort of experience.

We walk into a chamber carved out of the rock. It's around fifty feet high and fifty feet wide. Seven thin beams of light from our heads criss-cross the blackness, which is darker than any night sky I've ever seen. Where the beams hit the walls of the cavern, the rock glints and glistens with the metals embedded in raw form within them.

The 'ground' here is covered with six or seven inches of black mud, meaning everyone apart from our guide is slipping and sliding. I nearly drop the MiniDisc recording equipment at one stage, bringing a stern telling-off from Grigori who is already pissed off with me because I've managed to delete his dramatic recording of our descent in the lift. He's been sitting in silent fury since I told him. I tell him we'll just do it in reverse going back up. I can't help twisting the knife in his wounded theatrical pride a bit further. 'It'll be alright. You'll see!'

The temperature seems suddenly to have soared, like someone's just flipped the heater switch. It was slightly warmer when we walked down the original rail tunnel but there was a cooling breeze back there. Just standing still here now, I can feel rivulets of sweat streaming down my back and legs. It's impossible to believe that it's permafrost one mile above us. I feel as uncomfortable as if I'd just entered a sauna in full overalls and boots.

We're going to be given a display of the mining technique here, the guide explains via Grigori, pointing as he does so to small sub-chamber off to one side.

On cue, an approaching rumble reverberates around the chamber announcing the arrival of the drilling machine. The noise gets louder and louder until a huge bit of machinery roars out of a pitch-black tunnel I'd not even noticed.

It looks like an over-sized tractor with four outlandish metal arms, each of which has an over-sized pneumatic drill on the end. It positions itself at the end of the sub-chamber and lifts the arms until the drills are touching the ceiling.

The guide starts to speed up his explanation of what's going to happen and Grigori's translation becomes an accelerating burst of gasped phrases. He's still talking when the air is split like a knife by a screaming drilling sound that causes everyone apart from the guide to wince. Think of your worst dentistry nightmare and then multiply it by a factor of several hundred.

The 'mining technique' used here is a deceptively simple routine of drilling holes in the ceiling, placing explosive in them, exploding it, and then sending another diesel-powered monster that's straight out of Thunderbirds to scoop up the resulting rock-fall and whisk it off to a crusher somewhere else in the mine.

'Deceptively simple' because any miscalculation on the part of the explosives expert and there's a mile of solid rock waiting to fall down on you. You had just better hope the guy didn't have a big night out on the vodka last night!

Alas, we don't get to see the fun part which is the controlled explosion. After ten minutes or so of the aural assault, the guy with the drills switches off the machine and swings himself down for an impromptu photo-shoot with The Bear. The resulting silence is deafening, a verbal cliché I've never truly experienced until now.

Holiday snaps taken, as it were, we're led back to the funfair ride for another bone-jarring drive through the maze of pitch-black tunnels until we come to a second slightly smaller cavern carved out of the rock.

A controlled rock fall has already happened here and the guide tells us we're now about to see how the glistening boulders, rocks and debris are removed. It all has a very 'here's one I prepared earlier' feel to it.

There's an infernal roar from the tunnel behind us and we have to jump out of the way to avoid a monster-sized scooping machine that trundles around the corner out of the inky gloom of another side tunnel. Its shovel, which can hold thirteen tons of rocks, is so big it grazes the sides of the tunnel.

Entertainingly, the controlled explosion here has been a bit off target and the rider of this mechanical leviathan struggles to position his monster in such a way that he can get at the rocks that are piled on the floor. For several minutes our ears are assaulted by the beast's thunderous cries as the driver shifts up and down through the gears. He repeatedly reverses and adjusts position in a giant version of negotiating a particularly tight parking space in a car park. The engine is diesel and the belching fumes sting our nostrils and make our eyes water.

The huge scoop is finally placed in idle as the driver gets out to consult our guide as to how best to tackle what seems to me to be the impossible geometry of a finite space with tight angles and something the size of a tank.

Thankful for the resulting reduction in noise, Grigori and I try and record our sensations.

---

**Transcript.**
**Taimyrski Mine.**

Sergey: *Hot*

Andy: Very hot. *Yes, Sergey. Hottest we've been since we've been in Norilsk. We've all got sweat pouring down our backs.*

Grigori: *The guy told me something happened today to their air supply system. We can see bits of it here… this kind of rubberised cloth is actually a conduit for air. And it's empty. Just hanging limp here. So today they say there is no air supply in the mine. But it's just one of those things… no one pays any attention to it…*

*… but it is hot…*

Andy: *It's a very Russian one-of-those-things… oh well… ho hum… it's a very Russian approach to health and safety I think in these places…*

…

Andy: *This is quite modern mining technique. I have actually been down a mine before and seen them do this but, hey, think what it would have been like fifty years ago without any of this modern equipment.*

Grigori: *They would have just been hacking it and taking it back in wheel-barrows.*

Andy: *Absolutely! Maybe with a few pit ponies underground, but I don't think so even then. Unfortunately human labour was just too cheap in those days, wasn't it?*

Grigori: *Yeah, they just arrested another few hundred people and brought them down here and made them work.*

*But they tell us that it's one of the more modern mines here, and certainly to a non-expert mind, it doesn't look that modern.*

Andy: *The mining technique is modern and you said it's got a workforce of about three hundred people?*

Grigori: *Yeah. At any given time there are three hundred people.*

Andy: *That means it's quite heavily automated and you can see that for yourself. They've got all this heavy equipment. Modern drilling equipment and what you call the huge monsters to move the stuff away. If you had a more primitive mine, I think you'd find the number of workers would go up exponentially. That's probably much more hand drill stuff. I don't know whether they've still got that here, but it's no coincidence we've come to the most modern showpiece mine they've got.*

*And this is it! So imagine what the less modern ones are like. Fucking hell!*

(We'd been ignoring the huge scooping machine which by now had restarted its engine, disappeared off into one side corridor only to reappear at speed from another one hidden in the all-enveloping blackness of the mine.)

Grigori: *The monster just came quite near us, scooped up some glistening rock and retreated again.*

Andy: *I just looked over my shoulder and its huge jaws were just like... it felt feet away from me...*

*I'll try again.*

*They just said it was the most modern mine so imagine what the older ones are like, eh?*
Grigori: *Five thousand people with wheelbarrows!*

## Return

---

### *Transcript.*
### *Taimyrski Mine.*

Grigori: *We're moving up the tunnel now on foot, and we've been told very politely to sod off because the driver of this vehicle has a norm to fulfil and if he doesn't get out a certain amount of ore, his pay will suffer.*
*So we've decided to move away and leave the poor man alone, struggling in the dark there in the narrow tunnel with his huge vehicle and his heap of ore which has to be removed at a certain rate every day to keep his pay at the level that is now… like… I banged my head on the roof of this car again… thank God for the helmets!*

Locked back into our transport we start on the slow-motion roller-coaster ride back up through the mine's secret 'road' network. I scrutinise the lump of rock Sergey has picked up off the floor of the last cavern and presented as a souvenir to me. The size of a cricket ball, it's heavy and appears to be half rock and half metal, an elemental compression of the chemical table, glittering in the beam of my helmet light.

I also reflect on the absence of any other mining activity as we jolt our way through the many corridors. There are apparently 300 kilometres of tunnels in this particular mine, and whatever is going on is obviously taking place in a completely different part of the network. What we've seen, I suspect, has been laid on specifically for us. I'm flattered and frustrated in equal measure.

We finally arrive back at our starting point and again stagger around for a few moments as our bones re-arrange themselves into their previous settings.

On the walk back up to the lift, we try and interview our

guide. It's a haphazard affair because he's far more interested in cracking jokes and recounting what Grigori tells me in a low voice are slightly off-colour anecdotes. The object of his attention is very much the female journalist who takes it all with non-committal smiles.

Between his bursts of repartee he tells us he's been working in this mine for five years and before that in others that sprawl in their own mysterious subterranean pattern beneath the permafrost here. It's a man-made topography of tunnels and networks that follows the fractal distribution of the ore-bodies.

His eyes gleam with conviction when he tells us he wouldn't swap his job for anywhere else in Russia.

'As a miner, I get a unique experience here. There are no other mines like this on the mainland. A lot of people try to leave Norilsk and go to the mainland but my life is here. I'm not interested in leaving.'

The only time he comes to a stop and considers carefully his response is when I ask what metals specifically come from the mine we're in now. I'm sure I catch a brief moment of panic flitting across his face as he eyes me carefully and considers the question for a few moments. His one-word answer is 'poly-metallic' and then he resumes the climb back up the tunnel.

The information, by the way, is no longer a massive secret. Again, the basic facts are available on the company's own website. Taimyrski is described as having a rich ore body, which means platinum, palladium, nickel and copper with small traces of a host of other metals.

But judging by the miner's reaction to what would be a completely innocent question anywhere else in the world, here in Norilsk old habits die hard. It seems our guide is not going to be guilty of disclosing such sensitive information to an outsider, particularly not a Western one holding a microphone.

The words of the Razno trader echo at me across the years. 'That's enough information for you today, my friend.'

### Waiting Rooms

Back in the underground waiting room, we hang around a bit until a loud hissing of air and ensuing metallic clanking herald the arrival of the lift. This time we're the only people in it. Other than the two drivers of the drill and the scoop we've not seen anyone in the three or so hours we've been underground. I briefly wonder whether we're in the Taimyrsky mine at all but rather in some shaft that's been purpose built for our visit. I reassure myself with the thought that not even Norilsk Nickel would go to such lengths to hide itself from us and put my paranoia down to the diesel fumes I've been inhaling over the course of our underground wanderings.

The lift accelerates us up towards the surface and clear air. I've persuaded Grigori to give his running commentary into the mike for a second time to replace the one that was taken from us on our journey beneath the earth. That's how I'm describing it anyway. Grigori's second take is just as good and just as dramatic as his first.

Once we are back on terra firma, I look wistfully through an open door at the top of the lift-shaft at the snow lying on the ground outside. Even here in the Arctic Circle, the temperature change a mile or so underground is astonishing. I feel as if I've lost half my body-weight in sweat, so hot has it been at the bottom of the mine. The icy grip of the wind that blows through the door is for once a welcome relief.

Even more so is the massively powerful shower we get to enjoy back in the changing room. Grigori and I savour the experience of hot running water and take longer than any of the others in soaping ourselves and indulging in the pounding of the pressurised HOT water. I also take a moment's pleasure in noting that The Bear's body is indeed covered with a thick mat of hair – a rare case of first impressions proving correct in this Russian mirror-world.

Reassembled outside with the woman journalist who has been granted her own shower and changing room, we once again swing ourselves into the ubiquitous minibus and make our way back to Norilsk. Grigori and I spend the time checking the recordings we've just made.

We're not displeased in the context of the early mishap of deleting the first batch and almost dropping the equipment into the mud. We assure ourselves that the BBC will definitely have some hi-tech gadgetry to smooth out the distortions created by the heavy underground machinery. Sergey is chatting away with the Norilsk minder, trying to get him to commit to an interview with the top guy here. THE MAN.

Back in town, our two 'journalist' companions are dropped at the same spot as the other day and we are driven over to the company's head office. Although we've seen it on our walks around the town – it's hard to miss sitting as it does at the end of the main street, Leninsky Prospekt – it's the first time we get to enter the hallowed ground.

It's a far grander building than just about anything else in Norilsk and, fittingly, is the only building constructed here on solid rock. The rest of the town is built on the permafrost, or rather it's not, since normal building foundations would crack due to the movement of the ground caused by the annual thaw and refreeze. So, the town is built on piles driven many metres into the ground with a space of around half a storey left between the earth and the bottom level of the buildings.

Not so the Norilsk headquarters though. Oh no!

The doors are impressively massive blocks of oak. Entering them is like stepping into a castle. The inside hallway is cavernous and completely lined in marble. Two flights of stairs lead off grandly in front of us. We're told the place was designed by a St Petersburg architect, someone famous, back in the 1950s.

I glance furtively up the staircase but Norilsk Nickel is not ready just yet to allow us any further into the inner sanctum. It seems the deal is that if we're going to interview the head guy here, we're going to have to submit written questions for approval in very Soviet style. We're shown to a bench running down one side of the foyer and spend the next fifteen or so minutes working out our intended interview under the watchful eyes of the minder.

We hand him our workings like a bunch of schoolboys after finishing a test and he tells us we're to wait on his response back at the hotel. The hotel is literally about five minutes walk away but our minder insists that we take the company minibus.

I resent the compulsory use of the minibus. I feel I'm being slowly sucked deeper and deeper into the company's gravitational pull, into its zone of control.

Grigori and Sergey don't seem to agree. For them, it's just about getting a free lift in a warm vehicle.

Over a late lunch back at the hotel, I tell them I want to interview some more 'normal' citizens. Just stop the occasional passer-by and try some random encounters with the locals.

Neither is very enthused. Sergey points out that he needs to be by the phone in his hotel room so we don't miss the call and our interview with The Man. That would be a mistake, he says. It could be taken as a deliberate snub and Vitaly Bobrov is not a man to insult in any way.

Grigori agrees and says he needs 'a little lie-down' anyway.

I try to sleep. But the unchanged light oozing in through my window and the excitement of the mine visit make it impossible.

I footle around with the recording equipment. I go to the restaurant and have a coffee. I make a recording there. I'm so bored I even try several times to record the sound of the lift, but I can't capture the terror inspired by the grating of the doors and the small bang every time the thing lurches into life.

At around four in the afternoon Sergey bursts into the room before I have time to register his knock. He's received the call. We're to present ourselves back at the headquarters at five o'clock.

---

***Transcript.***
***Andy's Audio Journal.***
***Hotel Room.***
***Afternoon.***
***Waiting to Go and Meet THE MAN.***

Andy: *We are poised to meet one of the top managers here apparently. He's so important that he hasn't given us a time for the interview itself. We have to turn up at the Norilsk Nickel building at five and at some stage he will*

*grant us an audience for about ten or fifteen minutes.*
*It's interesting for me because my attitude to this sort*
*of thing is that I couldn't really give a toss about how*
*important people think they are. If you start going down*
*that route as any sort of journalist, it means you're not*
*going to ask the questions that you want to ask. But I*
*couldn't help but notice that Grigori and Sergey are both*
*a little bit nervous about meeting this man. So God knows*
*what happens to us if we do ask the wrong question! I*
*think it takes quite a lot to make those two nervous. No*
*one's quite explained to me what will happen if he doesn't*
*like us or he doesn't like the interview.*

At five minutes to five we present ourselves suited and booted back at the Norilsk Nickel building. We're told to sit on the bench again, and we spend the next ten minutes or so fidgeting with what is our full range of recording equipment – we've brought a tape recorder as back-up in case the MiniDisc fails as well as an extra mike. We talk in hushed voices. There's something of the cathedral about the entrance hall that commands a subconscious respect. Eventually, our minder comes to fetch us and I notice that he seems as nervous as we are.

We're escorted up to the very top floor of the building and get to sit in a large waiting room which contains some very plush, very impressive-looking, black leather sofas. There's something Kafkaesque about this whole process, a sense of entering one ante-room after another, of passing through levels of security and classification. What monster will the inner chamber hold, I wonder.

Grigori and Sergey talk quietly to our minder. I look at a large map on the wall. It's a schematic of all the mines and refining plants in and around Norilsk. It looks like a representation of some military campaign with black arrows sweeping around in dramatic arcs. I consider that I'm probably breaking some sort of law by even looking at it, even though I can't understand the Cyrillic lettering.

After a few minutes we're joined by two more senior

members of the local public relations team, including the head of the department here, and then are finally ushered through double doors into The Man's room.

## The Man

Wow! Despite myself I'm impressed. The room is huge! Forty feet by forty feet at the very least. On one side in a corner is a gigantic desk – that, I presume, of The Man himself – and on another side of the room is a long mahogany board table with room for about twenty people to sit. The rest of the office is sparsely decorated but what furniture there is looks antique and expensive. My eyes are drawn in particular to a nineteenth-century pendulum clock sitting behind glass and encrusted with finely-worked gold.

But as soon as I catch sight of The Man striding across the office expanses to greet us, everything else fades into insignificance.

To describe someone as larger than life is a bit old hat, I know, but in this case it is literally true. The guy is massive! He's a mountain of a man! The size of a professional wrestler and a big one at that! His head looks like a giant boulder hewn from one of his own mines. His complexion is deeply pitted, but embedded in that rock-head, like precious stones, are two limpidly clear blue eyes. When it's my turn to greet him, my hand disappears into something the size of a ham and I'm grateful he's not one of these men who feel it necessary to demonstrate their muscle-power with an over-firm handshake.

It strikes me, though, that he has no need for such cheap machismo. After all, the sheer presence of him is enough to make you nervous. I'm not easily physically intimidated but you'd have to be unusually cold-blooded not to be overpowered by this guy's aura. I now fully appreciate Sergey and Grigori's anticipatory nervousness about meeting him.

We sit down at the long board table and there are a few moments of pleasantries. He tells us he's been to London but doesn't like it much – too rainy. I tell him via Grigori that our rain is their snow, which produces a round of laughter, suspiciously sycophantic in the case of the three members of the local public relations department.

Grigori goes into a preamble about the purpose of our trip to Norilsk, how we've won this prize to make a documentary for the BBC, how we're trying to capture something of the lives of the ordinary people here, and so on. At the point when he is explaining that we're not completely ignorant about the place and the company, thanks to our work in the metals field, Bobrov interrupts and with a glance at his underlings says something in Russian.

He laughs, followed first by the three press relations stooges and then less wholeheartedly by Grigori and Sergey.

Grigori turns to me to translate. 'I was just explaining that we knew a bit about Norilsk before we came here and he says, 'Are you with the BBC or British Intelligence?''

By the time The Man's punch line has been passed down to me, his eyes are resting on me and there is no longer any laughter in them, adding to my sense of unease.

The format of the interview is that Sergey gets to ask the prepared questions in Russian and Grigori gets to translate Bobrov's answers into English and say them into the microphone. The etiquette is that you do not interrupt The Man while he's speaking and only at the very end of the interview is there room for a couple of non-prepared questions.

This leaves me slightly redundant for much of the duration, although disconcertingly Bobrov seems to address his answers in my direction, making frequent eye contact.

The Soviet-style nature of the interview, with the pre-submitted questions, makes it stilted, and several times I suspect we are getting answers to the questions the company thinks we should have asked. But The Man's personality still resonates throughout.

The two senior public relations officers take studious notes all through the interview.

***Transcript.***
***Inteview with Vitaly Bobrov, head of Norilsk Nickel's***
***Arctic Circle Division.***
***A.K.A. The Man.***

Question: How did you join the company and when?

The Man via Grigori: *It's a very simple story. I cannot tell a super story. My family knew about Norilsk because my uncle worked in Norilsk. He was made a political prisoner here in 1946. He was sent to the beautiful city of Norilsk.*

(Bobrov manages to communicate both passion and irony in the comment. Extraordinarily, he is the first person we've met to mention Norilsk's pre-1950s history.)

*I was at school and I showed a predisposition to technical science – chemistry was my favourite subject – and I also knew that by that stage working in Norilsk enabled people to live a decent life. So by the end of school I had made a decision for myself that I would go to the Moscow Chemical Technology Institute and I would tie my subsequent life and fate with Norilsk.*
*That dream stayed with me after I graduated from the Institute. But my wife, who was a Muscovite and an only child, didn't want to move. According to our tradition, children live with their parents or at least near them.*
*And there was another reason that stopped me realising my dream at that stage. It's difficult to explain to BBC listeners but at that time you had to have a permit from the police to reside in Moscow and that was at a premium of course. Living conditions in Moscow were much better than anywhere else in Russia. The problem was that once you left, you forfeited your permit. You could never get it back.*
*But the dream was still there. I always wanted to come here. I worked for five years in Moscow after I graduated.*

*My daughter was no longer a baby. I decided it was time to go to Norilsk and I came and I was on my own here for a year and then my family followed me. I was already a qualified engineer in Moscow and had reached a certain position, but when I came here I became a simple worker at the smelter for almost a year.*

*That's the normal way with all the top managers of Norilsk Nickel today. We started at the very bottom and then we gradually progressed through the system.*

*That's how my dream came true and I'm here now.*

Question: What changes have taken place in the company since you joined?

The Man via Grigori: *The way people worked here – without being too pompous – it was heroic. Both then and now. Between 1996 and 2000 we were again producing as much as in our best years in the 1980s. And that was after the period of perestroika, when our output fell by twenty to thirty percent.*

*Today one of the main problems is the environment. In the past we used to say, 'Any amount of metal at any price.'*

*People's attitudes and mentality have changed. The question today is how to produce as much metal as possible without fouling up the environment.*

*The whole system of motivating the workforce has undergone a degree of change.*

*The most positive part of that is that we are now a shareholding company. If we'd remained within the state system, our employees' pay would be two or three times less than what they are getting now.*

(This is indeed indisputable. Thanks to the fact that what Norilsk Nickel produces in such prodigious quantities commands high prices on the international market and these prices are denominated in dollars, the company can afford to be generous when it comes to paying its workers in roubles.

The 2001–2004 collective agreement with the Norilsk unions

included a provision that wages rise by twenty-five percent from the base in the year 2000. By the end of 2002, the actual figure was an average increase of a hundred and forty-three percent on the base year. By the end of 2003 – the year of our visit – workers in the Arctic Division are earning almost five times the national average.

After years of feeling financially trapped here in the 1990s – too little money to afford a plane ticket out or to bribe their way to a good apartment somewhere else in lawless Russia – Norilsk's citizens are now among the most generously well-off in the country.

Mind you, as Velery Melnikov has reminded everyone, they are not as well off as the miners working for the world's other big nickel producer, Inco in Canada.)

*Technologically, even in the old times, we used to improve our technology constantly. We started the Nadezhda smelter and it was all the best technology at the time.*
*Today we are planning much further ahead. We have a long-term programme to the year 2015 which enables us to judge the investment policy much better over the long term.*
*We are going to invest between $350 and $400 million dollars every year to upgrade equipment with a resulting improvement in the environmental situation.*

(Our interview with The Ice Queen has obviously been reported upwards. We're getting a lot of stress on the environment from The Man.)

*And we are introducing more equipment to automate and mechanise our labour. We have removed female employees as much as possible from areas where production is harmful to people's health.*

(Take note of the rider in that sentence, 'as much as possible'.)

177

*The whole working schedule has been lightened quite a bit. It's not as much workload as we used to have before. These are the main issues at the moment...*

Question: How has the motivation of the workforce changed?

The Man via Grigori: *In the past there was a system of money rewards. For people who produced more, they got bonuses. Today we are trying to stimulate higher productivity by reducing the numbers of the workforce not only in the main production area but in all auxiliary services as well. We now invest more money in equipment that allows people to work more effectively with less spending of physical force.*

(I'm a little unsure at this stage whether Bobrov has understood the question. He goes on to wax lyrical about the company's investment in super-efficient technology. The implied answer to the question is that there used to be cash bonuses but the workforce is now motivated by fear of losing its job. I'm pretty sure that's not what he wants to say. Oh! Hold on! Here's the bit about the carrot.)

*The key thing is the technological processes within the established operating regime. Now the workforce is encouraged to treat the equipment better and they are rewarded accordingly.*

(The company's rewards system is a curious encapsulation of the rapid zigzag of Russia's recent history. It includes a range of special honours for above-quota achievement among the workforce. The company itself can bestow 'Honorary Plaques' (in three grades), 'Honorary Titles' ('Top Manager', 'Top Specialist' and 'Top Worker'), 'Letters of Award', 'Letters of Gratitude' and, perhaps most enticingly, 'a valuable present'.

The Polar Division around Norilsk gets its very own honours: 'Honorary Employee of the Polar Branch', 'Labour Veteran of the Polar Branch' and 'Staff Member of the Polar Branch'.

Everything's painstakingly itemised in the company's Social Contract with the Workforce[ii]. In the same document Norilsk Nickel says that it 'carefully preserves and respects its historical symbols'. These include The Order of Lenin, The Order of Red Labour Banner and The Order of the October Revolution.

Such symbolic rewards, harking back as they do to the shock-worker star status of the Soviet days, are bestowed by the great and the good. The company's 1999 annual report notes proudly that former president Boris Yeltsin awarded 'medals, honours and honorary titles' to one hundred employees for 'service to the state, significant personal contribution to the production of nonferrous and precious metals and the development of the social sphere'. In the same year his successor Vladimir Putin sent a personal letter of congratulation and thanks to employees of the Olenogorsk Mechanical Plant, a first cousin in the extended Norilsk family.)

Question: What are Norilsk Nickel's social programmes?

The Man via Grigori: *We have a few social programmes and they have been introduced over a number of years now to enable people who have finished their careers here to move to the mainland and establish themselves there. For the first two years after they retire, they get six-fold the state pension and the company pays them to enable them to settle down in other places.*

*We also have a programme, which we call 'mother', which enables parents, mothers especially, to look after their children at home until they're seven. They're paid an average salary as if they are working. After seven years and the child goes to school, then the mother returns to her job.*

*We also have a programme of one-time bonuses for people who have shown themselves especially valuable to the company. That programme embraces a wide range of jobs and people in the company and the point of that is also to enable people, especially those who are pensioned off, to go and settle on the mainland.*

*We have another programme of corporate pensions. A few years before people retire, they work out a kind of programme for themselves concerning the type of business they would like to set up on the mainland when they retire. And during that time, in the few years before they leave the company, the company pays them a certain share of the capital necessary to start up their business.*

*We make a point of having a variety of programmes like that so everybody can choose for themselves what suits them better.*

(Now, the observant reader will note that there's a certain theme running through these social programmes... the helping hand extended to move people out of Norilsk itself once they have come to the end of their useful working lives. Pensioners just add to the company's cost-base by using up power, heating and social services – all areas which are now contracted out to the municipal authorities, but for which Norilsk Nickel itself is still the prime financier. The lifetime achievement award at Norilsk always seems to involve a one-way ticket to the mainland.

Now we're on the subject of depopulation, though, will The Man confirm what Zelenin has said about the long-term future of the town here?)

Question: What is your view of the future of the company's relationship to the city of Norilsk? Will the city ultimately disappear?

The Man via Grigori: *In the last six years the company has halved its workforce but it doesn't mean that most of these people have left Norilsk. They are still living and working here in the city.*

*And if we have 60,000 employees, I cannot imagine how we can work the shift method.*

(This is obviously the company shorthand for what Zelenin

had proposed: using 'shifts' of workers flown in from central Russia for a few months at a time, essentially rotating the entire workforce in and out of the mines and plants.)

*The living conditions are good enough to keep it as it is. So today I cannot see it happening.*

(That's a no then! Or is it quite? What about tomorrow?)

Question: What are relations like with the unions?

The Man via Grigori: *They are perfectly normal relations. Just like any other company.*
*For a long time we had been carrying out a policy of concessions to the unions without thinking of the possible consequences of that policy. As a result, the leadership of the unions has become separate from the company. They are not even employees of the company but they are getting salaries both from the union and from us.*

(Grigori explains by way of background that under original labour laws, a union leader was released from his work duties but was still paid by the company as well as the union. According to Bobrov, there are around 150 people in this position, but I think we all know which one in particular he is probably thinking of most.)

*And people who are being paid but have no duties within the company, they don't feel a responsibility for what is happening in the company. But they have to justify their existence. That's why a certain number of these people create situations. They bring out conflict. They come up with demands for increased pay which are not justified by any economic or any other calculations. And these people refuse to enter a dialogue with the management as to how what they are suggesting can be achieved, and they have only a limited following within the workforce. It is not significant. It is not the majority of the workforce.*

181

*The majority, all they want is to work and earn as much as possible and improve their lives.*
*Because this small number of political leaders don't have support within the workforce, they adopt other methods of influencing the management, like hunger strikes, ultimatums and so on.*
*I don't know any person on earth who would say I don't want to receive more money for my work, but reasonable people sit around the table and try to think how to achieve that. But people who have lost their connection with the production side of things and who have spent ten years at their desks in the union offices, they don't quite see it that way. But we don't really have any conflict with the majority of our workforce and there are no intentions to hold strikes.*

(The last said with some finality and a nod of the boulder-head.)

*There are current problems as anywhere. Sometimes the management has neglected these problems over a period of time and it has irritated some sections of the workforce... problems like showers not working or a building needing a new coat of paint... but we are trying to improve these things and make people's life and work as comfortable as possible.*
*I'm constantly in contact with union leaders at the units of the division. I don't really need the interference of these other union leaders who are not part of the company.*
*I always think it's much simpler to face an employee and look him in the eye and sort out what the problem may be.*

(Yup! I imagine that would resolve just about any problem if this giant of a man gets to look you in the eye. The guys I've seen in the mine and smelter are well-built chaps but The Man is exponentially bigger still. Yet again, I am struck by the sheer physical presence of the general manager. He's got the sort of physique that could send you crashing against a wall if he turned too quickly to talk to you.)

Question: What would you like to tell to ordinary people in the UK about yourself and the company?

The Man via Grigori: *I have great respect for people of all professions and I've never divided them into main professions and auxiliary professions. I treat everybody in the workforce with great responsibility and affection. I respect their loyalty to their work and their attitude to their labour.*
*I was a simple worker myself and I learnt from my supervisors on the production floor. To this day I'm friendly with their families as well, although I was a young and learning worker twenty years ago and a lot of my teachers don't even exist any more. But I still support their families, and their children and their wives. They were my teachers and I treat them with affection and respect.*

(I'm starting to place The Man in the movie role of a Mafioso boss in New York, a boss of bosses, a Don Corleone, the ultimate arbiter of the good and bad in life in this town.

We've come to the end of our pre-arranged questions at this stage and Bobrov, who of course knows this, decides to end the interview on a flourish. He sits back in his chair and says with a broad grin...)

*But the future of the company is quite clear! First in the world! Number one in mining and metal production! And we'll get there!*

(Thanks to a quick prompt from Sergey, I get to ask a question just as the Russians look as if they're about to stand up from the table. It's the one that's been hovering on my lips since The Man's first words.)

Andy: *You said your dream was always to work in Norilsk.*

*It strikes me your dream must have been something of a nightmare in the early 1990s?*

(The Man's huge head is shaking from side to side before the question has even been fully translated, his features changing from good-natured gruffness to concentrated steadfastness.)

The Man via Grigori: *No. No. No nightmare.*
Andy: *Just because I thought the whole economic reality had changed?*
The Man via Grigori: *It was the same all over the Soviet Union, not just in Norilsk.*
Andy: *Were there any doubts in your mind that Norilsk Nickel could actually go out of business?*

(Interestingly, he doesn't wait for this to be translated at all before replying in Russian.)

The Man via Grigori: *No never! It is impossible! Norilsk has unique deposits. It's completely autonomous from all other organisations. This peninsula has gas deposits. There are water resources to turn the electric turbines. We are part of the rest of the country on paper but we are not part of the system. We are completely self-sufficient.*
*And we have very rich ore. That's also our advantage.*
*But the main thing is the people. They're convinced, they're loyal, they're hard-working professionals.*
*I never thought the company would go down. The question was only how long it would take before we got back off our knees, never whether we would cease to exist.*

(The Man nods his boulder-head forcefully and everyone at the table takes it as a signal the interview is now officially over.)

After the briefest of handshakes, we're escorted back downstairs by our minder who tells us he'll be in touch early tomorrow with a view to going to the port of Dudinka.

This time, I decline on our behalf the offer of the minibus return trip. As we walk the five minutes or so back to our hotel, Sergey, who's met Bobrov before, tells us he's surprised at how much the big man has calmed down. He seems positively chilled out these days, according to Sergey.

Apparently The Man has a reputation for flying off the handle, a prospect that is quite frankly terrifying for anyone the size of a normal human. I'd rather poke Tony Soprano in the eye just for the hell of it!

## Disco Queens and Vodka Dreams

Grigori and Sergey appear mightily relieved by how things went, and there's a particularly intense bout of vodka drinking and joking over dinner which we've decided to take next door at the restaurant-cum-nightclub. No singer this time thankfully. Just a DJ offering a mixture of 1970s and 1980s disco greats – the sort of thing you'd expect to hear at a wedding reception party.

Over dinner – a very passable steak in my case, and not reindeer for once – Sergey resumes his favourite dinner conversation of identifying who is and who isn't in some form of the spook game here.

Our new minder is, Sergey says. His bosses even more so, and senior ones at that, he says. I accuse Sergey of just trying to put the wind up Grigori and me. Sergey just laughs and says that before 1989, when Norilsk Nickel was under the administration of the Department of Defence, the first and foremost company department was that of 'security'. 'Department number one!' Sergey says in English.

'Department number one' is now just the local 'public relations' team.

Grigori interrupts Sergey's dissection of the local information network and points across the table at the dance floor in front of us. Three middle-aged women are giving it their all to a version of *Saturday Night Fever*. Now that, Grigori says, is something you never used to see in the old days.

Still frustrated by our increasing ensnarement in the company web in this company town, I suggest we do an impromptu interview with them. Grigori is sceptical but I persuade him to go and get the recording equipment from the hotel anyway.

Sergey goes over to The Three Russian Degrees and uses his trademark disingenuous charm to try and get them to join us and give an interview for the BBC. They graciously accept and bring their drinks – a couple of bottles of vodka in ice buckets – over with them.

There's a flurry of animated conversation in Russian between Grigori and Sergey and our Three Degrees. When I manage to get a word in edgeways with Grigori and ask about the interview, he shakes his head laughing. 'No, we can't broadcast what they're saying – it's all too obscene.'

So we get to socialise instead. I'm peer-group-pressured, very much against my will, into joining in with a round of dancing. My partner is in her late forties or early fifties. She presses herself up against me and rotates me slowly around the centre of the dance floor. Her overwhelmingly powerful perfume cannot completely hide the faint sweet odour of vomit when she talks to me. In Russian. Which ensures complete incomprehension on my part.

More vodka is ordered. The conversation becomes yet more animated. Only having to defend my nether regions against the persistent, predatory hands of my Third Degree is keeping my mind anywhere near a balanced keel. I'm sure it would much rather be spinning around like the disco ball above the dance-floor.

I stagger off to the gents and try splashing my face with cold water, but I know the damage has already been done. The effects of neat vodka build slowly but then take on a frightening acceleration of drunkenness. Before you know it, you're holding on to the psychological sides for dear life.

I return and am shocked to find that my two male companions have legged it. The Degrees manage to make me grasp that Grigori and Sergey have gone to take the recording equipment to the hotel, saying they will return shortly.

Will they hell! I'm appalled by this desertion in the face of the enemy, although the ladies appear to have taken one casualty too. It was the one who was most obviously drunk. I suspect she has passed out in the ladies.

Slightly panicky now, I try and convey, in a rambling series of increasingly desperate communications, my need to depart. I manage to duck a last attempt at a kiss from my dance partner and walk as fast as I can to the exit. I'm weaving like a landlubber on a pitching ship and willing myself not to fall down the grand stairway. Escape is the only thing on my mind.

I emerge into the chill light of early-morning Norilsk. I light up a cigarette of relief and savour it, as only a man who has cheated an unspeakable end can.

The cigarette is a mistake. Or maybe it's the 'fresh' air, even though the adjective is particularly inappropriate in the city of Norilsk. All I know is that it should have taken me three minutes to smoke it and five seconds to turn right and head into the hotel.

Fifteen minutes later I find myself wandering a few streets away, dressed only in the light shirt I wore for dinner.

I look at my watch. I've lost a slice of time in a hole as dark as any Norilsk mine. I stand still and try and get my eyes to work as a team and my brain to get up off the ground where it's fallen asleep.

I've obviously wandered off. Why did I do that? Where was I going? Are The Three Degrees following me?

I can only answer the last of the questions. The streets are completely deserted. As the vodka cocoon gradually lifts from me, I shiver in the freezing wind that is gusting through the grey cityscape. I stagger around for a few minutes before vaguely recognising where I am. It takes me just over five minutes to walk back to the hotel... fast!

Relief when I eventually reach my bed is tempered by a sickening appreciation that I could quite possibly have frozen to death had I not emerged from the depths of my vodka dreams at the time I did.

I would have been just another Siberian statistic. A lot of Russians freeze to death every year. Most of them in exactly such circumstances. Death by misadventure. Death by vodka.

[i]Komsomolski, Mayak, Medvezhi Ruchey, Oktyabrski, Skalisty, Taimyrski, Zapolyarny.

[ii]Concept of Socioeconomic Development of MMC Norilsk Nickel for the period ending 2015. Company document, dated Norilsk, 2004.

# ESCAPE TO SIBERIA
## 'You're lucky you've seen this'

Andy: *Hello, this is Andy. I'm sitting in my room. It's Thursday, 28 May about 10.15 in the morning.*
*We are awaiting Norilsk Nickel to tell us when they're going to pick us up and take us to the port of Dudinka which is about fifty miles away. It did originally look as if a shortage of Norilsk Nickel minibuses meant we would have to take our own taxi there, but apparently this has all been corrected and we're awaiting confirmation of this as I speak.*
*I have quite mixed feelings about this. I personally would have preferred not to be escorted, as it were, to the port but rather to have taken our own taxi so we could stop off and do things on the way. The problem is you can't just turn up at Dudinka and go and see the port. It is part of the company Norilsk Nickel so you do have to have a company official present there. But I was rather hoping that we would not spend the entire journey there in his presence and in the official Norilsk Nickel transport. It does not allow for much... how shall I put it?... ad-libbing of the journey.*

## Wheels within Wheels

I lie on my bed smoking and watch the smoke curl up towards the ceiling. The off-white staining of the paint suggests that a lot of previous guests have spent their time doing exactly this.

Our stay here is becoming inextricably interwoven with the company. It is daily shortening the leash of independent movement. When we're not out with our minder, it seems we're waiting to hear from him. He's starting to become an unwelcome fourth member of the team.

It's another Norilsk blast from the Soviet past, another reminder that Moscow's dash for the future is being weighted down by the state's morbid hand.

I'd like to dismiss Sergey's spotting skills in terms of government agencies as an example of his mischievous sense of humour. But I know in my gut that he's probably right. The first clue was the Soviet-style checkpoint on the way into town. If you're paranoid enough to put a checkpoint manned by armed police in the middle of nowhere, you're probably going to be keeping a very close eye on what is going on inside the city proper.

Lt Ivanov's seamless career path from police officer to company public relations officer, which struck me as odd when I first heard about it, makes a lot of sense if you assume that the public relations department itself is merely an evolution of the original Soviet department number one.

The 'security' function in Norilsk arrived along with the very first batch of prisoners in the 1930s. It wore a uniform and carried a rifle and its first order was for the first workers to build their own barbed wire compound.

The NKVD became the KGB and it never left Norilsk. When the KGB became the FSB in the 1990s, it didn't leave Norilsk. But no company trying to get onto the world stage of big mining companies was going to be taken seriously if it maintained a department called 'security'. Transferring all the loyal security people to a new 'public relations' department has a neat Orwellian logic to it.

And the department does seem massively over-staffed from what I've seen. The longer we're here, the more PR officers come out of the woodwork. Bear in mind that very few journalists of any kind, whether Russian or Western, get to come here, particularly since the city closed itself.

The local media, as far as I can tell, comprise a newspaper, a clutch of magazines, a radio station – and we've already seen how big that is – and a TV company.

And judging by the sort of questions asked about the infamous goose at the press conference, I can't imagine handling them is too challenging – enough for one or two full-time PR people, not the battalions that seem to exist here.

I wonder where The Bear and The Inquisitor fit into this. Different department? Different agency? Different masters?

Is there a daily round-table conference taking place to swap notes and analyse the activities of this dodgy-looking BBC team that's turned up in town?

What do they make of our Interros credentials and the fact our number includes apparently an honorary citizen of Norilsk?

Does the Interros connection make us more or less suspicious in the eyes of the locals?

Jeez… it's enough to make your head spin! Am I getting paranoid? Is it something someone's putting in the vodka? Is it the vodka?

Through the haze of my spreading confusion I get a fleeting but intense sensation of the subtly shifting balances of power that make this place tick.

Norilsk is no more a monolithic mass than is Russia. Its Soviet uniformity belies the overlapping and competing interests that are compressed into this little piece of the Arctic Circle.

First, there is the national interest in a company that accounts for around 1.9 per cent of Russia's annual Gross Domestic Product and 4.3 per cent of its exports and controls some of the country's most valuable mineral assets. Set against it are the commercial interests of the Interros Group, the sprawling mega-company of young technocrats, preaching their new market relations mantra.

But there are other layers of potential conflict as well – this is not a two-dimensional game. The flows of political power around Norilsk are as labyrinthine as the network of tunnels that lie beneath the permafrost.

The bureaucratic status of the city is itself hopelessly muddled. Thanks to some now-forgotten dialectic argument among the Soviet planners of the Union of Socialist Republics, Taimyr is a tiny 'Autonomous Area' with the same federal rights as the Territory of Krasnoyarsk in which it sits, the size of a pinprick in a region that is ten times the size of Great Britain.

Even more confusingly, the city of Norilsk lies within Taimyr but is under the jurisdiction of the Territory of Krasnoyarsk. It is a key financial contributor to both federal authorities.

The city is fractured along these oblique power lines. On one occasion, apparently, three different sets of emergency services bickered for so long about who had jurisdiction over which particular bit of the tundra around Norilsk that a downed helicopter crew had frozen to death by the time a rescue party arrived[i].

At the top level, it has led to bitter feuding between the company, the city and the two regional governments, largely over the split in tax revenue from Norilsk Nickel that bankrolls everyone else. The 2002 election of Alexander Khloponin as governor of the Taimyr Autonomous Area only exacerbated relations with the fiery governor of Krasnoyarsk, former-General Alexander Lebed.

Khloponin, after all, was the previous general director of Norilsk Nickel and very much an Interros man. Lebed was associated with the company's arch rival in the south of the region, the equally huge Krasnoyarsk aluminium smelter which is the largest of its kind anywhere in the world and is owned by another Russian oligarch, Oleg Deripaska.

When Lebed died in a helicopter crash in April 2002, all hell broke loose in political terms as the two giant metals groups fielded rival candidates for the position of governor of Krasnoyarsk. Norilsk's candidate, Alexander Khloponin, won but there remains a deep-seated north-south divide in the giant Siberian territory. So much so that Valery Melnikov, the union firebrand who is standing for mayor of Norilsk, has been painted by the company as a stooge of the Krasnoyarsk aluminium smelter, which in this city is tantamount to saying he molests little children.

But Melnikov also embodies a growing divide between company and city and between company and workforce. As we've already experienced, not everyone here is happy with the new 'market relationships' being imposed from above.

And somewhere right at the core of this power flux is the self-interest of Norilsk itself, a Siberian city as much as a Russian one, an island fortress, separated by a thousand-mile moat of ice and tundra from its Italian-suited masters in Moscow.

These myriad competing interests converge on the common goal of turning this once-secret city into a mining and metals powerhouse that will carry on pumping tax money into the local and national economy.

But none of the sides – and I'm not sure yet how many there are – seems to trust the others. I sense that the arrival of strangers with their unusual background and their BBC letters of introduction has sent ripples through this interwoven structure of power. Sadly, like a minor pawn on a three-dimensional chessboard, the rules of this game are a complete mystery to me.

I take some satisfaction, though, in imagining the amount of paperwork our all-too-brief stay here is going to generate. What conclusions will be drawn, I wonder? I don't think we'll ever hear anything... or I certainly hope we won't... but I sense that our visit will very marginally affect the never-ending shifting of this slow power dance between the forces that run through this strange city.

The stakes are high! The fate of Norilsk, its inhabitants and many thousands of other Russians resides in the fortunes of just one man, the oligarch who sits at the very top of the pyramid. And these are dangerous times for the Russian oligarchs.

Vladimir Guzinsky, the construction and media baron, has fled to Israel via a stint in a Greek prison, where he was held briefly on a Russian extradition warrant. Boris Berezovsky, former owner of an empire that spanned car manufacturing, oil production and media, has been granted political asylum by the UK. And the net is closing in on Russia's wealthiest oligarch, Mikhail Khodorkovsky, head of the giant Yukos oil group.

But Vladimir Potanin is no ordinary oligarch. Ruthless enough to build a commercial empire valued at ten billion dollars, he has also been canny enough to keep it. But then, unlike former theatre director Guzinsky and former mathematician Berezovsky, Potanin has always been something of an insider.

Often described as a blueblood among the oligarchs, Potanin had an impeccable Party upbringing. Born in 1961 he followed in his father's footsteps by entering the Soviet Department of Trade via the Moscow Institute for International Relations – a finishing school for the KGB.

It was the perfect on-the-job-training for setting up a private trade finance bank when Gorbachev freed the economy from the trammels of central control. 'I was maybe a little bit more prepared than my colleagues,' he once admitted with typical under-statement[ii].

Potanin was widely credited with being a major intellectual force behind the controversial backdoor privatisations of the country's biggest companies in the 1990s. He was Russia's deputy prime minister briefly between late 1996 and early 1997, a period which fortuitously coincided with his gaining control of Norilsk Nickel.

But he had sniffed the change of the wind of power in Moscow faster than most others. He had backed Vladimir Putin to win the 2000 presidential elections and then listened when Putin, in his 'private chats' with the oligarchs, had told them to keep out of Kremlin politics and he would keep out of their dubious financial dealings of the last ten years. Guzinsky and Berezovsky hadn't listened.

When Putin told the oligarchs it was their duty to contribute to the economic and social recovery of the country, Potanin had listened carefully. Unlike Khodorkovsky, he hadn't signed an agreement with China to build an oil pipeline there and he hadn't been linked with selling a big stake in his company to the Americans.

'My strong opinion is that Putin is very anxious about the destiny of Russia, really anxious,' Potanin said in 2000[iii]. 'And he wants Russia to be strong. He wants a strong Russia in the international society. He wants his country to be a player in, let's say, the champion's league. He doesn't want to win in small competitions.'

Potanin has produced just such a potential champions-league player in the form of Norilsk Nickel. He seems to have done it with one ear carefully tuned to the wishes of Putin and the darker forces that lurk in the shadows of a man who himself emerged from the ranks of the KGB.

The company regularly wins Russia's top accolades for commercial companies. In 2002 it was 'Company of the Year' and won three separate awards in a competition for the country's most 'socially effective organisations' – for 'the organisation of youth work', 'the welfare of mothers and children' and 'training of personnel'. It has won the Certificate of Honour for the country's best exporter in 1998, 1999 and 2001.

But there is no end to this game between commerce and state. There are only times of uneasy truce in this counter-revolution emanating from the Kremlin. Potanin's future and with it that of Norilsk rests on his ability to keep pleasing Moscow.

The state's refusal to allow Norilsk Nickel to release details of its precious metals production or its reserves may just be a case of old habits dying hard, but from the Kremlin's perspective it is also a very useful way of placing restraints on Potanin's financial freedom of movement.

Mining companies are valued by stock markets on how much they produce every year and how big their underground reserves are. In other words, how many more years will they be able to churn out metals at current rates? Without that information, there can be no independently verifiable valuation of a mining company's worth. The lack of such a valuation makes it very difficult for the company to sell its shares on international stock markets.

As such, state secrecy laws effectively serve to keep Norilsk Nickel Russian. Putin has promised many times to repeal the law but so far 'promises, promises, nothing but promises'.

_____

***Transcript.***
***Andy's Audio Journal.***
***Hotel Room, 1.00 p.m.***
***Waiting to hear from Norilsk Nickel.***

Andy: *It's Andy again. We are still awaiting word from Norilsk about our trip to Dudinka.*
*I was originally told by Grigori we were going to be picked up at one but it's just gone one now. I popped my head round the door of Sergey's room – he's our liaison man as it were – and he said... 'oh well... you know... I'm waiting for them to contact me... it could be ten minutes, twenty minutes, thirty minutes...'*
*There's been quite a lot of this while we've been here. You get the impression that wheels are turning behind the scenes somehow but you have no insight into that. You just wait for them to tell you when they are ready.*

## A Trip to the Seaside

We finally get the call from our minder, whom I have now decided to call Department Number One (D1 for short).

Extremely frustratingly, in the light of the transport options, we get the worst of both worlds. D1 is to accompany us but we have to get a taxi and we get to pay for it. I curse quietly under my breath as we drive off from the hotel, the three of us cramped in the back seat while D1 gets the front seat.

Before long, though, my mood is improving as we motor out towards the airport. The approach into Norilsk with its steady accumulation of dark colours and heavy air is neatly reversed on the drive out. As we travel ever further from the city, the rusting junk drops away, the pipelines thin out, the snow starts to lighten through a spectrum of grey and the sky becomes clearer.

By the time we hit the turn-off to the airport, we're back in the winter moor landscape of dark grass patches appearing through the snow. The squat airport building lies a couple of miles down the left fork. We continue straight on. There is no other choice. This is the full extent of the road system here. One road goes to the airport. The other goes to Dudinka.

It's a two-lane road, running alongside a single line of stubby electricity pylons and a single-track railway line. The line is how the company transports the finished metals to the port of Dudinka.

I'm looking forward to seeing the port. The Russians all seem to think that the Nadezhda smelter has star rating in terms of this country's capacity to overcome the seemingly impossible. But Dudinka does it for me. The port is a Russian triumph of human will over the literally unstoppable forces of nature.

Dudinka sits near the mouth of the River Yenisey. It's fair to say the Yenisey is probably not the best known of rivers, even in most of Russia. But it actually ranks as the world's sixth longest, flowing from the Mongolian mountains to divide Siberia neatly down the middle before joining the Kara Sea, passageway to the Arctic Ocean.

In winter the river's completely frozen. The company uses nuclear icebreakers to lead out convoys with its precious cargo. Norilsk Nickel once floated the idea of buying up a couple of the Russian navy's older nuclear submarines to ship metal to Europe but the plan was quickly shelved in the face of a polite but firm 'no' from the big port authorities in the West.

But it's in spring that the real fun starts. The Yenisey starts to thaw, sending a surge of melt-water and mini icebergs down towards the Kara Sea. Dudinka lies smack in the middle of this Siberian tidal wave and risks flooding annually when the flow reaches its peak, which is right about now in fact.

The annual meltdown also makes operating a heavy-duty goods port something of a nightmare. Unable to stop the approaching calamity, the company simply dismantles the loading facilities and moves them several hundred yards back up the shore. For two to three weeks the docks are submerged beneath the swollen Yenisey. When the spring surge has abated, everything gets rebuilt as it was. It's a hell of a way to run a port, but I like the second-hand thrill of mad defiance being flung in the face of the massive forces of nature in this wilderness.

It's a particularly Russian defiance as well. This is the country that dismantled whole factories in the face of the approaching Nazi army, shipped them across the Urals and rebuilt them brick by brick in Siberia's vast interior.

That's what we're now driving through. The wilderness. The tundra. Or the 'toondra' as the locals pronounce it. The road is a pencil-line of black tarmac etched across an endless landscape of snow, ice and patches of grass. The sky is a light blue. Occasional lakes of melted snow glitter in the sun.

It's been warm all day. Back in the city just about all the ice and snow has melted, apart from where it has been piled up at the corners of street junctions. Here in the car, everyone's wearing sunglasses and I can feel the warming caress of the sun as it catches the back of my neck through the rear window.

After forty minutes or so, approaching the halfway point, we stop by the side of the road and get out to stretch our legs and, in the case of the driver, D1 and myself, have a cigarette.

Suddenly unprotected by our steel casing, we shiver in the constant strong wind that is ripping across the landscape. The sun is shining but the temperature outside the car is about fifteen degrees colder. The cigarettes get drawn more quickly as we all start stamping our feet to keep warm before hastily piling back into our protective shell.

The journey continues, the driver carefully avoiding the many gaping potholes that have sprouted in the road with the biggest annual thaw on the planet. At one stage we come across a four-man crew repairing the worst of them. The emergency procedure is apparently to break bricks in half and then sledgehammer them into the ground. Seems to be effective, though.

After the first minutes of visual exhilaration at leaving the grey cloak of Norilsk, the 'toondra' assumes its own two-tone monotony. All the raw materials of life are here, but for most of the year they sit hardly functioning in a frozen desert that stretches thousands of miles in just about every direction.

Only in full summer – June and July – does the 'toondra' briefly explode with life and the burst of colour is accompanied by an annual plague of mosquitoes that roam the vast distances in grey clouds. Their approaching noise is said to be loud enough to drown out men's voices.

The tundra must rank with the world's most hostile regions. Some of the people we've met here seem to really like it, but for me it contains a lurking sense of animosity towards the human race.

The drive lasts nearly an hour and a half.

As we approach Dudinka, we take a left turning into a maze of rail-track sidings, freight cars and loading cranes. We soon get lost in this sudden proliferation of motoring choice and D1 is reduced to asking a couple of local youths where the main port authority building is.

After a bit more meandering we finally pull up in front of a modern, eight-storey building. It's located right at the side of the river. Sergey and D1 disappear inside to see if we can get an interview with the port manager. Grigori and I wander over and climb a small embankment to look out over the mighty Yenisey.

---

*Transcript.*
*Grigori and Andy on banks of the Yenisey.*
*Dudinka.*

Andy: *Well, we've just arrived at the port of Dudinka, which we've just found out is 335 years old which is quite surprising, and which also claims to be the northernmost town... in... the northernmost town in...*

Grigori: *... in Russia.*

Andy: *This provoked a bit of a conversation as to whether it's Russia or the world. I have no idea.*

*First impressions of Dudinka? The first thing you see is a forest of cranes as you approach the town. What it reminds me of... Grigori, do you remember those pictures taken when they first discovered oil in America and they had those bobbing oil-rigs? The cranes look a little bit like that to me.*

Grigori: *Except they're not bobbing. Their heads are*

199

*hanging down and they look like a bunch of very sad storks.*

Andy: *But anyway, now we're standing on the banks of the River Yenisey. It is actually the warmest I've experienced it here so far.*

Grigori: *Yes... the sun is very hot. We're protected from the wind here and the sun is hot and there is quite an extensive patch of clear water in front of us. The rest is still covered in ice and the ice breaking is expected any day now, so I thought that our arrival might cause it to start.*

*Apparently once it starts, the ice goes past Dudinka very quickly. Usually it is gone within two days and most people in Norilsk have actually never seen the ice breaking because you have to be here. I've been told some people come with tents and they spend a few days here sleeping in their tents, hoping to be here when the ice starts breaking.*

*We saw a helicopter hovering over the river. They are watching very closely for signs.*

Andy: *How wide do you think this river is? I was just trying to estimate it but it's quite difficult because if you look over there... look... it could be almost a mile across.*

Grigori: *Yes... it is probably about a mile here.*

Andy: *It's put me in particularly chipper mood in fact. It's fantastic to be in front of such a great natural sight.*

*I think I'm going mad up here... do you know what? I just had a sudden desire to go swimming. You might have to restrain me at this stage. Too many days in Norilsk, I think, that's my problem.*

Grigori: *Okay, it's time I dragged Andy into the port authority building where the deputy head of the port is awaiting us.*

In fact, the port authority deputy manager is walking over to us from the building in the company of D1 and Sergey. He is a bulky man in his forties with heavy jowls. But his eyes twinkle with good humour and he exudes the exultation of a man who is doing the job he most wants to be doing in the world. It's a rare thing, but refreshing when you come across someone who is that lucky and knows it. He tells us he only came to work here for two years and that was eighteen years ago, which pretty much says it all.

As we're all introduced, he asks jokingly whether we've been looking at his port. It's currently submerged beneath the bit of embankment we've just been standing on, he tells us.

Damn! How had we not thought to look? Both Grigori and I had been so lost in the magnificence of the bloated river that we'd forgotten the fact that the loading berths were lying just feet beneath the surface in front of us.

Our first stab at an interview is soon interrupted by the guy's secretary coming running out with a sheaf of papers in her hand. They go into brief consultation off to one side and he then signs the proffered documents. He walks the few paces back to us and our waiting microphone.

---

*Transcript.*
*Interview with Dudinka Deputy Port Head,*
*Viktor Viskonov.*

Andy: *So, now we've found out the port infrastructure is in fact beneath the water and the ice, what I don't quite understand … not being a technician… what is down there and how does it survive being under water?*

Viskinov via Grigori: *The berths are down there. All the infrastructure of the buildings. The rails that the cranes move on. Everything is under that ice and water. Underground communications, electricity cables, everything is down there, everything is under water.*

Andy: *And is there ever damage to that stuff once the waters recede?*

Viskinov via Grigori: *Not yet, but there are already quite large bits of ice there. When they start moving, everything will be at risk of damage.*

Andy: *How long does it take you to prepare, to move the cranes back and prepare for this event every year?*

Viskinov via Grigori: *It takes a month but it doesn't mean we stop work. We're still loading ships while preparing for the ice to break. And it also takes us a month to rebuild what is destroyed and start loading ships again.*

Andy: *So the stop to the shipping system is two or three months?*

Viskinov via Grigori: *Maximum of ten days there is no loading.*

(After years of experience the port workers at Dudinka have fine-tuned the movement of part of the docks and their subsequent reconstruction to coincide with the period of maximum flooding and resulting danger from fast-moving icebergs.

Behind us the big dockside cranes are huddled in silence, their motionless heads drooping in mock sadness at this unaccustomed bout of inactivity. Normally they are scattered up and down the five miles of dockside. Each one is railed back to a winching machine, which hoists it up the steep embankment. It is then transferred to another line of rail and shunted into a protective area near the port authority building.

The movements are carefully sequenced to maximise the amount of loading and unloading time before the port lapses into total inactivity.)

Andy: *So timing is everything. Presumably you must be monitoring all the time.*

Viskinov via Grigori: *It is a science to get it right time-wise. Yeah, we keep monitoring the ice. We fly helicopters up the river and we establish when it is likely to start breaking.*

(A helicopter has indeed been flying around ever since we arrived. It hovers for periods out in the middle of the river, then turns and speeds over to another stretch, where it hovers again. It looks like a giant mosquito, taking steps in some elaborate dance intended to awake its countless millions of dormant friends out in the tundra.)

Viskinov via Grigori: *The water level now is about eight*

*metres above the berths, and from where we are standing
it is twenty metres to the bottom of the river. Sometimes it
flows over here, the embankment where we're standing,
when it's at full flood.*

*In 1988 we had a very serious flood here. The water came
as far as this embankment and there is a building half-
demolished over there. It was destroyed by the flood.*

Andy: *I presume you've been doing this for decades. Has it
changed at all over that time?*

Viskinov via Grigori: *It hasn't changed much. The berths
are the same and the rails are the same but the equipment
of course is more modern now.*

Andy: *But you've had to do this every year since forever?*

Viskinov via Grigori: *Yeah, since the port started in 1944.
We are preparing to celebrate the sixtieth anniversary next
year.*

(Around ten years closer to reality than the city of Norilsk
itself, then!)

*By Sunday the water will come up quite close to where we
are standing. It will rise by another five or six metres.*

(The moment the flood passes, they will begin reconstructing
the port again. River ships from Krasnoyarsk, more than a
thousand miles to the south, are following behind the ice.

As well as being the sole route for shipping the metal out,
Dudinka is the main route for supplies into the city, at least
when the Yenisey is open to traffic.

The sea navigation season reopens in the middle of
June, when the berths are ready for the bigger Arctic Ocean
carriers.)

Andy: *What happens in winter?*

Viskinov via Grigori: *There are two unique features about
this port. One is that it is flooded and destroyed every
year and the other one is it's the only port in these kinds
of conditions that can load ships in winter. We use ice-*

*breakers to bring ships in here.*

Andy: *The whole thing is frozen?*

Viskinov via Grigori: *The whole thing is frozen except for a path for ships. They come from the sea with those nuclear ice-breakers and load and unload in winter.*

*We are really getting sick of having to rebuild this port every year.*

(This accompanied by a shrug of the shoulders and a roll of the eyes.)

*But we commissioned an Austrian company to build two cranes for us... those two cranes to the left of us. They are on wheels with rubber tyres. They don't need any rails so we just drive them away when the ice breaks and as soon as the ice has gone we just drive them down again. They can also operate at up to -50°C. There are no cranes like that anywhere else in the world.*

*Most of the old cranes... -40°C is their lowest operating temperature. Soon all these old cranes will be gone and we will only have cranes like the new ones and at least we will not have to rebuild the rail approach and the rails for the cranes to operate, which will make it much easier and faster.*

Andy: *Is there any other place in the world where they have these problems?*

Viskinov via Grigori: *No, there is nothing like this in the whole world.*

Andy: *Good, that's what I thought.*

Viskinov via Grigori: *You're lucky you've seen this.*

He beckons us inside the building and we turn the microphone off to follow him. We enter a low-tech office building and take a centrally located staircase to climb a couple of floors before entering what I take to be his office. It is spacious but the desk, table, chairs and filing cabinets give it a very purposeful functionality.

On the wall is a picture of the same building submerged

to the top two floors in flood water. The great flood of 1988 is obviously a significant collective local memory. The port manager becomes animated when he talks about it, often breaking into a broad smile as he recounts a string of flood anecdotes.

From what I can tell, it seems the flood of '88 may not have been a totally natural phenomenon. Apparently frustrated by the slow pace of the thaw on the river that year, someone had taken the executive decision to drop two and a half tons of dynamite on the ice upstream to speed things along.

The guy's chuckling away at the memory as Grigori translates: 'He says it was a particularly impressive bang when it went off.'

Visnikov produces a picture album and flicks through some of his favourite snaps of the port: the three local fishermen who were caught out by the speed of the thaw one year and found themselves floating on a bit of ice out into the Kara Sea; the indigenous native racing towards a waiting helicopter as a wall of ice hovers precariously over a ramshackle wooden house.

Visnikov's favourite, I suspect, is the nuclear-powered cargo ship. Twelve storeys high, apparently. There are several shots of him being shown around the massive bays and shaking hands with the crew.

I ask Grigori to ask him whether he gets bored in summer, when Dudinka is just a normal port that can get on with the business of loading and unloading boats without ice and floods.

Viskinov via Grigori: *When I have the time, I just disappear up the Yenisey and do a lot of fishing. That's my recreation. We have a lot of gyms and swimming pools and restaurants and I don't get bored. We even have masseuses.*

Judging by the big smile which breaks across Viskinov's face at this point, I suspect Grigori's been careful as to how he's translated that last word.

The secretary's back with another sheaf of papers – she's

been hovering for the last couple of minutes, reluctant to interrupt her boss. The phone rings and Vishnikov goes over to his desk to answer. Simultaneously, the flustered-looking secretary pounces and starts to lay out documents in front of him even as he talks in quick staccato Russian to whoever is at the other end of the line.

It's clear that this guy has a port to run, *ferchrissakes*, and we're now holding things up. Without any prompting we pack away our recording equipment, get a smiling nod from still-glued-to-the-phone Visnikov as we thank him, and go back down to the entrance and the waiting taxi.

It's three thirty and none of us have eaten – lunchtime was spent in our hotel rooms waiting for the word to go from D1. The concept of room service is not one that has made it as far as Hotel Norilsk.

We decide to go into the centre of Dudinka and grab a quick snack before returning to Norilsk over the tundra wastes.

Maybe it's the euphoria of leaving the greyness of Norilsk itself, maybe it's the clear blue skies, maybe it's the seagulls shrieking overhead – the first signs of natural wildlife we've seen in our stay here – but Dudinka has a jaunty seaside feel to it. The buildings are painted in strong vibrant colours – royal blues, reds and dark greens – and the centre is decidedly more bustling than that of its landlocked neighbour.

By this stage of our trip, my mind is getting used to filtering out the numbing uniformity of the Soviet architecture and the maze of giant pipes running down the sides of the streets. Actually, Dudinka has even more of these than Norilsk itself, although the haphazard lagging is reminiscent of the copper smelter. Holes have been stuffed with bits of cloth or have had pieces of wood nailed across them, but a myriad small jets of steam still quietly hiss and whistle in the background.

We find a small snack-shop on the first floor of a building looking out over the main crossroads of the town. The fare is surprisingly recognisable – toasted sandwiches, cakes and patisserie. We are the only men in the place. The other six or seven tables are occupied by young mums chatting over an afternoon cappuccino and pairs of older women bristling with shopping bags.

They are the lucky ones. As we sip our own cappuccinos, I gaze down on an impromptu market at one of the junctures of the crossroads. Three ancient-looking women, their heads wrapped in shawls and their small bodies encased in layers of warm clothing, are selling sunflower seeds from the tops of battered old ironing boards.

## We are the Past

They are a strong reminder that even here, a town also under the control of the new model technocratic army of Interros, there are many losers in Russia's fourteen-year old revolution.

Russia's pensioners, the generation that had only lived under the smothering ideology of The Party, were the least prepared for the shock economic therapy practised on the country in the years after the Berlin Wall came down in 1989.

They'd watched the world as they knew it collapse in smouldering ruins to be replaced in the early 1990s with financial uncertainty – the indebted government struggled to keep basic pensions payments up to date – and violence, as criminal gangs fought it out in the streets of Moscow and St Petersburg.

Any lucky enough to have built up any savings saw them effectively wiped out in the 1998 financial crisis which resulted in a seventy percent devaluation of the rouble and a sustained period of hyperinflation.

They are there also in modern Moscow's metro system and subways, selling bunches of lavender, a doleful reminder of the humiliated Soviet system.

In Moscow, Grigori had taken me to have dinner with some of his friends 'from the old days'. Dinner was a typical Russian buffet – plates of cold meats, smoked fish, salads, gherkins and regular rounds of vodka. Uly, the man who told us the anecdote about the co-worker and the statue of Lenin, was a big man whose robust appetite, lively story-telling and occasional roars of laughter belied his seventy-three years.

His recent life history was all too typical of Russia's lost generation. He'd been a technical manager at a Soviet factory for which being a fully paid-up member of the Party was an essential pre-requisite. As such, he was on a promise of a spacious retirement apartment and a good-level state pension.

By the time of our visit, he'd seen his pension lose most of its purchasing value, his savings lost in the near-collapse of the banking system in 1998 and he was now sharing a small two-bedroom flat with his wife, daughter and great-grand-daughter. The missing generational link – his grand-daughter – had disappeared into a shadowy world of drugs and parties, leaving her baby girl behind to be brought up by her own mother, Uri's daughter.

To supplement his eroded pension, Uri was working as a sub-contractor in a furniture-fittings factory, although in Russia's free-wheeling capitalism the factory's production apparently switched at bewildering speed depending on what its 'mafia' owners thought would make most money.

It's not what he thought his retirement would be, he told us with a rueful smile. Still, he had a friend, aged eighty, who was holding down eight different jobs to make ends meet, so it could be worse!

And one Soviet legacy was still helping the family survive – the dacha in the countryside. Nikita Khrushchev, leader of the Soviet Union in the 1950s and early 1960s, had determined that every family should be allocated a plot of land outside the cities so they could supplement the chaotic Soviet food distribution system by growing their own produce. The only rule was that you weren't allowed to build any stone structure on the land, only wooden, to avoid any taint of property ownership.

Uly waxed lyrical about the apples he got from his dacha. He traded what he didn't need for other produce from other pensioners' dachas, forming a low-level grey economy of their own. Khrushchev, I feel, would have been proud of his legacy.

I was impressed by Uly's stoicism in the face of these late-life setbacks but he was one of those guys resourceful enough to survive under just about any system, I reckon. Did he think that Russia now was the best of all possible worlds or the worst of all possible worlds, I asked him.

Ninety-nine percent the best, he replied. His generation was the past anyway – the future belonged to the children and it was going to be a better future than anything his generation had known.

It was a magnanimous view from someone who had reached retirement only to lose just about everything and who was now facing the prospect of working until the end of his life to support three generations of family.

It was not one totally shared by the other members of his family. Neither his wife nor his daughter could quite hide a certain bitterness that lent their faces a hard quality whenever they were in their natural set.

Now, as I look down at the three tiny figures selling their sunflower seeds at a corner of a crossroads in Dudinka, I wonder doubtfully whether they would share Uly's magnanimity about Russia's recent history. For them, life is a struggle for basic survival in a country with a long, long history of basic survival.

### Return to Darkness

We leave the snack bar and get back into our taxi for the return journey across the void in which Dudinka and Norilsk sit like ink-spots on a giant sheet of white paper.

The sun's still warm and all of us, D1 included, lapse into the universal state of car-sleep – moments of snoozing punctuated by shuddering wakefulness. It's only when we're around half way back that the party re-animates itself.

A short distance further on the conversation comes to a halt as Grigori, who's sitting in the middle at the back, dramatically points ahead through the front windscreen and half gasps: 'Look!'

There on the horizon is a huge dark storm-cloud of greyness eating into the pale-blue sky – a nuclear-sized mushroom of pollutants from the world's single biggest concentration of metals-making facilities.

By the time we drive back past the airport, the cloud has eaten us whole again. The sun is gone and the sky is now the colour of a rainy overcast day in London. Just as they miraculously disappeared on our journey out, pipes now sprout out of the ground in ever-growing numbers to greet our return. The empty white landscape accumulates rusting structures, half-built buildings, half-demolished buildings, power pylons and railway lines like the scribbles of an increasingly demented cartoonist. By the time we get to the city there is no white backdrop any more, just a million shades of black, grey and brown.

We're deposited back at our hotel and bid farewell to D1. I am pleased to see the back of him. He hasn't been very good company, a dour, serious individual who has given the strong impression that his trip with us amounted to some sort of punishment duty.

This is our last evening in Norilsk and we decide to try out a different restaurant, one that's been recommended by D1 and the taxi-driver. We walk for about fifteen minutes through the oppressive gloom. The snow has just about all melted now and huge pools of black liquid flood the streets. Sometimes they are so big that we have to walk a whole block to get around them.

When we get to the restaurant, we are greeted with a hand-written sign in Cyrillic bearing the very Soviet throwback message: 'Closed today for sanitation.'

Sergey's unperturbed. He knows another one he's been to before, he says. No, he doesn't know its name. No, he can't quite remember which street it's on. But we'll find it. Slightly naively, Grigori and I decide it's at least a plan of action.

And so follows a long, meandering walk around the edges of Norilsk, a near total circuit of the city, punctuated by Sergey asking various people for directions, setting off purposefully for a few minutes before admitting to being lost again. Grigori has told me Sergey has twice been to the North Pole, once by parachuting out of a plane and once on skis. How he managed the latter is something of a mystery to me on the evidence of our current zigzagging through the concrete grid of the city centre.

At one point we turn the corner – 'just round here,' Sergey says – to see the street stop abruptly a hundred yards or so in front of us at a giant slagheap. A column supporting the statue of Lenin stands right at the end, staring out defiantly at the emptiness beyond.

Another time, we enter a street so grim in its demeanour that it stands out even in this city. It stretches ahead of us like a canyon between uniformly-sized grey administrative blocks. There's been no attempt to brighten any of them with the light orange or green paints that you see elsewhere in the city. The fact that we are the only pedestrians in the whole street lends it a dream-like quality, a backdrop to a black-and-white horror film.

Maybe it's the rise in temperature today, but there's been a noticeable deterioration in air quality. The air itself seems to have a palpable presence, resisting our passage, so thick is it with particles from the metals factories. It stings the eyes and makes us cough. The smell of sulphur and its unnameable metallic undercoating is close to overwhelming.

There are far less people out on the streets than is normal at this hour of the day. Some of the women pedestrians walk with handkerchiefs pressed over mouth and nose to keep out the noxious miasma.

And yet I thoroughly enjoy our circuit of the city. It seems a fitting thing to do on our last evening. I still marvel at Norilsk's utilitarian grimness and its Soviet defiance of the forces of nature. I like the pride of the Norilskites. I like the fact they know they're somehow special for living here. Without meaning to, I realise I have become fond of this city.

Finally, finally, we end up in Maxim's restaurant, which for any reader actually planning a trip to Norilsk and for those of you who can get the required special permit I would recommend as the best restaurant I've eaten in here so far. Absolutely excellent food, charming maitre d' and by Russian standards relatively low-key on the multimedia theme, confined as it is to one large screen showing a football match. The place is full, with a well-heeled young crowd of diners.

Not the restaurant for which Sergey had been aiming at any stage, though, I note.

*Transcript.*
*Andy's Audio Journal.*
*Hotel Room.*
*Last Morning.*

Andy: *Just one other thing, a little travel tip here. I made a point much earlier on about the correct way of walking on the pavement, i.e. equidistant between the buildings – to avoid falling stalactites, and the road – to avoid being sprayed with puddles.*

*By yesterday evening… it had been a relatively warm day, I think it got up to four degrees above freezing… virtually all the snow and ice had melted. So, a quick correction. Under such conditions walk very close to the buildings because there aren't going to be any stalactites falling on your head to worry about whereas most of the roads are filled with huge craters of black sludge… or water… or whatever it may be. All the cars look as if they've been in cross country rallies. Quite often the water's up to and beyond the sills of the doors. So, a huge problem of being sprayed with this horrible brackish water as they pass.*

*So, a little update there. When it gets warm, stick to the buildings. You'll be safe and you'll avoid being deluged by the most horrendous black sludge you can imagine.*

*Had a particularly bad evening for insomnia. I thought I would have got used to it by now… this twenty-four-hour daylight… but if anything it's got worse. Were I to stay here any more I think I would just pile all the furniture against the window. Last night, for example, our last night here, I went to bed about quarter past one and woke up at quarter past two, convinced it was nine o'clock in the morning and I had already missed the taxi for the plane. Just a nightmare!*

*Probably preferable to coming here in twenty-four-hour darkness… although possibly jury out on that one… I think I would at least sleep quite well.*

[i]New Times (Moscow) 05/02/2002
[ii]PBS Interview, 10/6/2000
[iii]PBS Interview, 10/6/2000

# THE LEVIATHAN AWAKES
## Coming in from the Cold

Andy: *Just wanted to tie up a few themes which have recurred through this audio journal.*
*Funnily enough, when I was recording the last piece there was a knock on the door and Sergey's voice. He was with The Bear, the guy with the dubious photographer's credentials. He'd come to say good-bye, and I have to say, for just a few seconds, I thought... Oh God! This is it! They've actually come to confiscate the tapes because of that interview with the contractors. But no! Charming man that he is, he just wanted to say good-bye.*
*The drive back out to the airport is uneventful. The main hall is buzzing with activity. The woman in front of us at the check-in counter is having a furious argument with an airline official. She's waving a small dog in his face. Grigori tells me she is refusing to have the animal put in the hold. Another airport official comes over and takes her to one side whilst making soothing noises.*

Once checked onto the flight, we dutifully return our special permits to the police, although I cause Grigori a temporary panic by failing to remember where I put the original copy which had been handed over by D1 a couple of days earlier. I understand Grigori's concern about being confronted by

215

the local cops after doing something as naughty as losing our special permits, but I can't get worked up about it myself. 'What are they going to do? Keep us here?' I ask him as I search through all the pockets of my luggage until I find the guilty document scrunched up in a ball.

By the time we are taxiing out onto the runway, a full winter blizzard has descended, the wind blowing curtains of snow across the airport. It is hard to see even the terminal building from the plane. Looks like the big thaw of the day before was not quite the onset of spring.

I spend the four-hour flight in a deep sleep, drained by the intensity of our visit and by the constant daylight that tortured my nights in Norilsk.

I only wake when we are already circling Moscow, locked in a holding pattern that swings us over one corner of the huge city before pulling us back out over the forests that circle it.

I notice that every time the aircraft banks all the passengers strain against their seatbelts and crane their necks to look out the window. Unconvinced that Moscow is actually THAT interesting a city from the air, it takes me a while to appreciate that what the assembled two hundred or so Norilskites are responding to is not the city but the green forests that surround it.

It's a kaleidoscope of green, a luxuriance of greenness, the sort of multi-hued green that only a big forest approaching full bloom can produce. I find myself responding to it too, pulled along by the magnetic sway of the rest of the passengers. Some of these people, maybe most of these people, haven't seen such greenness for months. There is no greenery at all in Norilsk itself, or at least not outside people's apartments.

There's not a lot of greenery in the tundra for that matter. Many browns, yes, but not much green. Even the forest we drove through on the way to Talnakh had been so dark, its colours seemed to have been drained out of it.

I can sense the collective disappointment that this visual feast has to end when we eventually begin our steep descent to the airport.

But the greenness is still there on the road into Moscow. I

stare out of the bus window at it. I inhale deeply. I'm not sure how Moscow stands in the traffic pollution stakes – poorly, I suspect – but the first breath of air on exiting the airport was like a blast of pure oxygen. It smelled clean and sweet with a background scent of forest.

I realise with a shock how much my nose and lungs have acclimatised to the cloak of fumes hanging over Norilsk. How I've got used to rinsing out my nose after every walk around the city to clear the dark soot ringing my nostrils. How I've learnt to live with the omnipresent background smell of sulphur, sometimes merely a trace on a clear day, sometimes a sickly, gluey intrusion as on our last day.

Seeing Moscow again is seeing it with new eyes. Where everything had seemed grey to me when I first arrived, this time round my eyes only pick out the bright colours of the trees lining the streets, the pedestrians walking along the pavements and the lurid advertising boards.

Tramping back through the maze of footpaths and driveways to Sergey's flat, I luxuriate in the lilac trees that line the roads, the smell of the air on a hot spring day and the chatter of the birds.

'I think I've died and gone to heaven,' I say to the two others. Grigori just grins at me and nods in silent agreement.

The apartment blocks here no longer look decrepit to my eyes. The roads are clear of black pools of sludge and no one's been dumping rusting metal all over the place. It feels good to be home.

### Ink-Souls

*Transcript.*
*Andy and Grigori at Norilsk Nickel's headquarters.*
*Moscow.*

Grigori: *Okay, it's the 30th of May. We're back in Moscow and we're standing in front of Norilsk Nickel's head office in Moscow. It's in the very heart of the city, right next to the mayor's office. The Moscow Mayor Luzhkov is next door.*

*Apparently in the same building there are offices of all the representatives of local government where Norilsk is – the Taimyr and Krasnoyarsk regions – so it's all a very compact seat of power here and very easy to manipulate and extend their long arms.*

*Andy, what do you think of it?*

Andy: *Um… actually I'm not a big fan of it. It looks a very modern structure. It is an octagonal building about ten storeys high, either in marble or fake marble, I wouldn't want to conjecture which one of the two.*

Grigori: *Right now, knowing Norilsk Nickel, I would expect it to be real marble.*

Andy: *And it's got an extension coming out which is a fake Roman building, isn't it?*

Grigori: *It's pseudo classical style with columns and a big entrance like a Roman temple.*

Andy: *Yes. I think I would emphasise the word pseudo there, actually. Just one other thing which Grigori hasn't mentioned but which he's just explained to me is that it's round the back of the Moscow mayoral office, which was, however, a key Soviet building as well.*

Grigori: *Yes, it was the Moscow Soviet. Before that it was actually built to house the Moscow governor-general before the revolution.*

Andy: *I can't help but notice on the mayoral building that no one can really be bothered to take the Soviet artwork off. I mean, what's that about? Just can't get round to it?*

Grigori: *Yes, there's bits of Lenin everywhere.*

Andy: *You'd think people might find that a little bit out of date now, a bit embarrassing, no?*

Grigori: *I think they just don't want to waste the money removing Lenin from the walls.*

Andy: *Anyway, highly symbolic, I feel, that in one of the seats of power in Moscow, guess who's lurking just around the back? It's our good old friends Norilsk Nickel.*

We're here to meet one of the senior guys in the Moscow public relations department, someone whom Grigori has spoken to many times but never met, he tells me.

As we wait in the gleaming foyer with its leafy atrium, I look at the plaques on the wall next to the security desk. I can just about make out the company's name in Cyrillic script by now but I can't discern it here at all.

I'm not completely sure that we are technically in the Moscow headquarters of Norilsk Nickel, whatever Grigori says. It feels more like an office block for civil servants and technocrats, one of those peculiarly Russian places that exist between the visible and invisible power structures of the country.

At one stage Grigori catches my arm and nods in the direction of an expensively-blue-suited guy wandering slightly aimlessly across the foyer. 'The governor of Kraznoyarsk,' Grigori says under his breath with a significant look in his eyes.

As Khloponin strolls out the front glass doors, my eyes turn back to the security barrier excluding us from the inner sanctum and I wonder who else is working in this glass tower. Johnson Khagazheev for sure, Grigori has told me. The old comrade is still holding out against meeting us, having added a completely new list of conditions for an interview. I'm reconciling myself to understanding that we are not going to meet him. I suspect that even were we to wait for many years, we would never get to interview The Legend.

I am somehow not completely surprised that power over the destiny of a huge part of Russia lies in this insulated modern office block. Here they all are, these players in their slow waltzing political struggles – the governor of Taimyr, the governor of Krasnoyarsk, and their largest taxpayer, Norilsk Nickel, nestling close to the heart of what is the ultimate source of national power – Moscow.

It all seems very cosy for secret meetings in smoke-filled rooms and backdoor deals between arms of the government. As Grigori rightly points out, these people have long arms, long enough to stretch 2,000 miles to one of Russia's remotest cities up in the Arctic Circle.

Just the same as it ever was. Norilsk was born here in the inner sanctum of Stalin's Soviet Union and to a greater or lesser extent its fate is still being determined here. The only time it enjoyed any real independence from Moscow, the chaos years of the early 1990s, it nearly died without the centre's warm embrace.

Norilsk may be an extreme example but most of Siberia is a creation of Moscow and its 'ink-souls', as the Siberians have always referred to the suited bureaucrats of the capital or St Petersburg.

Russia has a population of around 144 million people. Just over 25 million of them live in Siberia's industrial cities, many working in climactic and environmental extremes comparable to Norilsk.

They are there because the Soviet leadership dreamed for half a century of populating this last uncharted wilderness. It was a mechanistically practical solution to developing the region's huge resources of natural reserves. It was a defiantly rationalist desire to demonstrate that the superior Soviet system could control even this inhospitable frontier land. It was a paranoid military strategy to create a core 'Russia' that would survive invasion by an enemy force, a lesson learnt from the Great Patriotic War of 1941–1945.

Over 300 factories were dismantled and relocated from western Russia to Siberia during the War. The workers employed there were relocated as well. Just as the millions of gulag prisoners were sent there. When the Soviet Union couldn't send people to Siberia, it called on volunteers from its young party cadres to go there to 'conquer new lands' and help build Russia into a super-power that would eclipse the inferior capitalist system.

But man, whether Soviet or Russian, is losing the battle against Siberia. The wilderness may yet prove to be the winner of this atavistic struggle for supremacy. Following the collapse of the Soviet system and its replacement with the whirlwind economic events of the 1990s, people in Siberia started moving back across the Urals as local industries and the towns around them died. The whole of Russia is suffering an acute bout of population decline but the problems are most severe in Siberia, particularly the North and East, the most climactically challenging regions.

The young leave for the better job prospects of cities such as Moscow and St Petersburg. Those pensioners who can afford it leave to spend their last days in the sun, not the chill pre-death grip of the Siberian winds. Some, like Mrs Norilsk and her husband, just plan to leave because where they live is 'a shit-hole'.

This exodus is accelerating but not as fast as either Norilsk Nickel, or indeed Russia, would like. Siberia remains a huge drain on Russia's finances. The big cities are too isolated from each other to create any sense of independent market dynamism. They remain inextricably attached to the umbilical cord of subsidy tied back to Moscow.

Norilsk Nickel is at the heart of a similar subsidy web. It has effective responsibility for an area that in Western European terms is equivalent to a medium-sized country. In 2002 the company paid out just over a third of its profits in taxes to the federal, regional and city budgets and provided a host of indirect subsidies through channelling funds into local medical, health and educational facilities.

The new vision of the Moscow ink-souls is to 'liquidate' the city, to use the unfortunate word that was born of Zelenin's Russian and Grigori's translation. No more migrants are going to get in, and the company will keep gently nudging people to leave once they are no longer capable of adding to the productivity of the mines.

Norilsk will become something close to a pure mining city with no 'surplus' citizens. If that sounds extreme, the template already exists on the other side of the globe. Canada combines huge mineral resources with extremes of temperature and environment. It too has large swathes of inhospitable tundra stretching up to the Arctic Circle. But it long ago evolved methods of running its far northern industries on a seasonal basis with the workforce shrinking in winter and blooming again in summer. Its northern territories have less than one percent of the country's total population. Everyone else lives in the warmer southern belt running along the top of the United States.

But I've got a strong feeling that not everyone in Norilsk

is going to go quietly. For every person we met who talked about leaving, we met another one who wanted to stay put – dreams of the tundra, dreams of 'soulfulness', a collective pride in this isolated island fortress, a sense that the city can find some middle ground between its Soviet past and its capitalist future, a path that no longer seems possible in the rest of the country.

My all-too-brief visit has left me with a strong sense of the simmering Siberian resentment against all the years of manipulation from Moscow, against the long arms that reach so many miles across the wasteland.

As I look again at the plaques on the wall – still suckered into believing I can decipher the Cyrillic alphabet with its semblance of half-recognisability – I wonder whether there's an office here too for the Norilsk mayor. Valery Melnikov, I suspect, would sweep into Moscow like a blast of icy Siberian wind.

## Long Arms

After making the marbled entrance hall look untidy for ten minutes or so we are joined by Grigori's contact.

He is in his early fifties with intelligent pale-blue eyes and an inquisitive face. He's dressed in expensive-looking separate jacket and trousers and has the cultured demeanour of a senior master at a posh English public school. His English is as close to fluent as it's possible to get.

He takes us around the corner to a tearoom that is dripping with gold mirrors and velvet chairs and is populated with the haut monde of Moscow. The waiters wear black bow ties and starched white aprons.

Over coffee he tells us about his struggle to drag the company up to Western levels of public relations. How previous attempts to open up Norilsk to the media have backfired with the publication in both the British and American press of big 'exclusives' about the place with headlines such as 'Hell on Earth' and 'Gulag City'. How the locals are a bit reluctant to fully embrace the glasnost being propagated by Moscow. The latter seems something of an understatement to me but I keep my thoughts to myself.

He seems at first slightly taken aback and then genuinely pleased when we tell him we really enjoyed our stay and had got some fascinating interviews. I can tell it's not a reaction he is used to.

Grigori and he chat away about the past and mutual friends before he brings the coffee meeting to a polite close. He pays the extortionately high bill for which I'm very grateful. We've carefully nurtured our limited budget but we're down to the very last of our £4,000 and in no position to pay for what I reckon are the most expensive coffees I've ever drunk from what I can glimpse of the bill as it's passed over to the waiter.

On this charming man's shoulders rests a considerable burden. Giving Norilsk Nickel an acceptable face to the West has become a matter of considerable urgency. A few months before our trip to its Arctic heart in May 2003 the company embarked on an aggressive expansion phase that would end up stupefying the rest of the mining world.

Its first corporate foray was to snap up Russia's biggest and most profitable gold producer, Polyus, in October 2002. The deal looked logical. For Norilsk Nickel it added another string to an already strong bow of metals production. To make it even easier, the gold from Polyus is refined at the same plant in Krasnoyarsk as Norilsk uses for its own platinum and palladium production. As icing on the cake for the Interros Group, Polyus had also already introduced the sort of innovative work practices that are of interest to Norilsk Nickel. It was one of the very few Siberian companies to have introduced a three-month-on/three-month-off shift system at its remote Olympiada mine in the south of Krasnoyarsk Territory.

New York and London stock market analysts nodded approvingly at what was seen as the first signs of consolidation in Russia's fragmented gold mining industry. They applauded Norilsk Nickel for paying what was the equivalent of $14 per ounce of gold produced, when the international gold price was way above $300.

But the same analysts were left speechless when Norilsk said a month later it intended to buy control of a company in the United States, particularly when that company is the only American producer of platinum and palladium and the major supplier of the metals to the huge automotive manufacturers of Detroit.

Stillwater Mining is as American as apple-pie, with two big mines in the forested mountains of Montana.

Adding to the Russian company's chutzpah was the fact it intended to make a large part of its payment in the form of physical metal – 877,000 ounces of stockpiled palladium to be precise. That may not sound a whole lot outside the precious metals markets, but it was about a fifth of what the whole world used the previous year¹ and was valued at US$157 million. Norilsk said it would also pay $100 million in cash. What it wanted in return was a majority stake in and de facto control of Stillwater Mining.

The idea that the United States would happily give up control of its only source of two key industrial metals to a Russian upstart with a shadowy ownership structure and a decidedly non-politically-correct history seemed a complete non-starter.

But in December 2002, one month after the deal was announced, the US Treasury Department, which has to approve foreign purchases of strategic assets, gave it the nod.

The Stock Exchange Commission then also approved it, finding Norilsk Nickel's accountancy practices good enough to buy a company that had its shares traded on the New York Stock Exchange. The fact that Norilsk wasn't able to provide any detailed production or ore reserve figures because of the state secrecy laws back in Russia didn't seem to faze anyone. Estimates from one of the big global banks were used instead.

In June, one month after our visit, the US Federal Trade Commission, which concerns itself with possible monopolies, also gave the deal the thumbs-up, and the former gulag bought up a prime bit of real estate in the heart of America and stretched its long arms further to control more than half of the world's yearly production of palladium and a good chunk of its platinum to boot.

It was a truly breathtaking coup and a subject that still

provokes heated debate and convoluted conspiracy theories on a host of American websites.

Stillwater is not only the sole domestic source for the current 'green' catalytic converter technology used by the auto industry, there's a good chance it will be the sole future source as well.

President Bush has fought back against criticism for not signing up to the Kyoto Agreement on reducing greenhouse gases with an avowed vision of 'a hydrogen economy' – one that will see hydrogen gradually replace oil as the energy that powers the country's cars and homes. That needs fuel cells which combine hydrogen and oxygen to generate electric power with much lower emissions than a standard internal combustion engine.

In February 2003 Bush gave a speech[ii] in which he said that 'hydrogen fuel cells represent one of the most encouraging innovative technologies of our era'.

He went on. 'If you're interested in our environment and if you're interested in doing what's right for the American people, if you're tired of the same old endless struggles that seem to produce nothing but noise and high bills, let us promote hydrogen fuel cells as a way to advance into the twenty-first century. If we develop hydrogen power to its full potential, we can reduce our demand for oil by over eleven million barrels per day by the year 2040. That would be a fantastic legacy to leave for future generations of Americans.'

There's only one issue for future generations of Americans. Fuel cells use… guess what? Why, platinum of course! And guess who now controls the only domestic source of platinum in the United States?

In fact, Norilsk Nickel is at the cutting edge of research into fuel cell technology and has signed an agreement with the Russian Academy of Science to pool their resources in developing technology based around the dual use of platinum and palladium. The tie-up between commercial and academic worlds was hailed by Norilsk general director Mikhail Prokhorov as 'a unique opportunity for our country to once again be counted among the leading economically developed world powers'.

In every vehicle that today rolls off the assembly lines of General Motors is a catalytic converter made from the metals from Stillwater and it looks as if in twenty or thirty years' time every vehicle will be using some form of fuel cell made from the same metals, or it will do if Norilsk Nickel has anything to do with it.

Norilsk Nickel used some strong arguments to make its case for taking over Stillwater Mining. The American company was teetering on the brink of financial collapse thanks to a collapse in the price of palladium. The market had slumped from over $1,000 an ounce in 2001 to below $230 at the end of 2002. That was because the big car companies were desperately trying to reduce the amount of the metal they used in each catalytic converter, having been burnt by the steep price rises of the 1990s.

It was an ironic twist of fate that the previous years of high and volatile prices had, of course, been in large part a result of the shenanigans surrounding Russia's exports of its precious metals.

But what Russia had messed up, Russia could fix. Norilsk Nickel's investment in Stillwater Mining would not only save an American company from financial collapse but the 877,000 ounces of metal could be used to guarantee supplies to the American automotive industry, it argued.

Norilsk Nickel talked about 'reinvigorating' Stillwater through the deal, about ensuring 'the availability of a reliable ongoing supply of palladium to manufacturers' and about allowing palladium users worldwide to 'continue to advance important research on additional uses of palladium'[iii]. I think it's fair to say the last reference is to the hydrogen fuel cell.

The fact that Norilsk Nickel quickly found some very influential new American friends to explain the advantages of it buying Stillwater probably helped as well.

It hired the lobbying firm Baker Botts to represent its interests in Washington. Baker Botts is headed by a man called James Baker, or more accurately James Addison Baker III, and if the name rings a faint bell, he was US Secretary of State under the administration of George Bush Senior.

Whether Baker Botts or Norilsk Nickel came up with the lobbying strategy, the Russian newcomer was highly sensitive to American interests in its selection of independent representatives for the board of Stillwater Mining.

Its five proposed directors included Craig Fuller, the former Chief of Staff to then Vice President George H.W. Bush, and former Senator Donald Riegle, who had served as Chairman of the Senate Banking Committee.

The curious Russian–American mining marriage was discussed at the very highest level and is widely reported to have been part of the agenda between President Bush and President Putin when they met in St Petersburg in June 2003, just days before final clearance was given for Norilsk Nickel to move on Stillwater. The joint statement from the two men referred to the need to 'continue our bilateral co-operation in the area of the economy and other fields'[iv].

Its first international prize will make Norilsk Nickel hungrier. Two months after our visit it will buy up another big gold mine – Matrosov – in the remote Magadan region in north-east Siberia. In September its arms will encircle another Russian gold company – Lenzoloto – in Siberia's Irkutsk region. Lenzoloto is itself a holding company controlling several local gold mines. Crucially, its location is expected to give it a big advantage when Russia's largest undeveloped gold deposit – the fabled Sukhoi Log field – goes under the auction hammer.

Its domestic shopping spree will propel Norilsk Nickel into the top ten of the world's largest producers of the yellow metal. The former prison camp will join the exclusive club of big South African and North American gold companies. A few months later still, in March 2004, not even a year after our visit to Norilsk, the Russian upstart kicked over the club's drinks table and announced it had just bought a twenty percent stake in one of the establishment's oldest members – the South African granddaddy of the gold world, Gold Fields Ltd.

It's not bad progress for a company that was close to the brink of its own collapse just ten years or so ago. Vladimir Potanin's Interros Group seems to have pulled off something close to a miracle with Norilsk Nickel. It has delivered Vladimir

Putin his dream of becoming a championship league player on the international stage and it has done so in double-quick time.

## On Our Knees

'I never thought the company would go down. The question was only how long it would take before we got back off our knees, never whether we would cease to exist.'

Remember The Man's answer to my question about the early 1990s, the period of national financial disaster? Now swap the word 'company' with 'country' and you start to appreciate the true value to Moscow of the Interros Group's turnaround of Norilsk Nickel.

Russia was on its knees in the early 1990s, spiralling downwards into a vortex of violent change. Liberation from years of totalitarianism came hand in hand with disintegration and collapse. The country spent most of the decade in the economic equivalent of intensive care. People lost their jobs without knowing the meaning of the words 'job insecurity'. People lost their savings. Pensioners lost their pensions.

Fear of the informer was replaced by fear of the Georgian gangster and Chechen terrorist.

The military might of the Soviet army, paraded year after year across Red Square in Moscow, was shown up for what it was – a hollowed-out façade of power – by the lost war in Afghanistan and the shambles of a coup attempt.

A generation of Russians saw what they had taken to be reality dissolve in front of their eyes, just as fast as the rouble was disappearing down the plughole of the global currency markets. The once great power that had defeated the Nazis was reduced to the role of impoverished country cousin on the world stage.

It was just one big national humiliation to crown all the small personal humiliations endured by most of the country's population.

In Norilsk Nickel, Potanin and his team have shown how a Soviet relic can be transformed into a new Russian powerhouse.

And they've done and are still doing it, in a very Russian way using some archetypal national characters. Vitaly Bobrov, head of the Arctic Division, is the incarnation of Russia's potential for ferocious willpower and authority. If this man told me to go and attack the Germany army on the opposite bank of the Volga armed only with a penknife because there aren't enough rifles to go round, I'd probably do it. The Legend may yet elude us, but The Man strikes me as being a chip off the same block.

Then there is Dmitry Zelenin, the youthful prodigy chess-player, always planning his next move, applying to Norilsk Nickel the same scientific principles he had used on mathematical problems back at the Moscow Technical Institute.

Somewhere just out of sight behind Zelenin is Vladimir Potanin, a man from Russia's shadow-world, who emerged from the elite ranks of the Party to become deputy prime minister and the head of what just might be the country's most powerful company. A nationalist, who has shown Moscow that Siberia may still hold the key to fulfilling Russia's dreams of regaining its national prestige, without resorting to tanks and missile launchers either.

Beneath Siberia lies the mineral wealth that may get Russia back off its knees. And not just the metals that run through the rock a mile under the Arctic permafrost. Russia is the world's second largest producer of natural gas and, probably even more surprising for most readers, the second largest producer of oil after Saudi Arabia.

In a world where reserves of both are finite and shrinking – you burn it, you lose it – who's got the oil and gas becomes an increasingly pressing geopolitical concern.

And Russia's got a lot of it. The speed with which Norilsk Nickel has emerged from the tundra to build a strategic position in the platinum and palladium markets is mildly shocking. The fact that Russia supplies a quarter of all the oil and gas needs of the European Union should probably be more so, particularly since its reserves are going to outlast ours by some margin.

We are becoming ever more dependent on Russia's natural resources. After forgetting about the country cousin with his begging bowl, we may soon have to heed a bit more closely what our eastern neighbour says.

It's quite possible that Russia may yet again become just as dominant an influence over the next generation's lives as it was for mine, living under the shadow of the Cold War.

The ongoing tussle between the free market principles of the Interros Group and the interventionist tendencies of the State is part of a broader civil war over Russia's future and how it's going to use that economic influence over us. I'm personally rooting that Interros' 'market relationships' ideology will win out over the other side's, even if I'm not exactly sure what the other side's ideology is.

For the moment at least, the concept of Russia emerging as a new, resource-based superpower is still half born, another fantasy taking gradual shape in the Siberian dreamlands.

On our last day in Moscow we go for a walk in the park with the ruined palace of Catherine the Great over the road from Sergey's apartment.

It's a hot day. The grassy banks and shaded copses are full of families picnicking, couples strolling and people walking their dogs.

We go and sit in a big open-air restaurant and have beers and sashlik in a throng of exuberant, laughing Russians. 'All very social,' Grigori says proudly.

I know he's personally been transformed by his trip here. After cajoling and pleading for many months to leave his home city back in the early 1990s, he seems genuinely pleased to find it in such good nick and in such rude health.

Moscow's got back up off its knees again. People we've met here seem to have accepted the horror years of the early 1990s as just another part of the long Russian ordeal against hardship. Now, the shops are full, there's plenty of work and for the first time in many generations you can make plans for your kids without reference to your score-sheet with the Party hierarchy.

Norilsk is a long way away. And so too are the political machinations that play themselves out there. All that is 'mafia', the term the Muscovites seem to use to describe any obscure source of power, whether it be the fearsome Armenian street-market gang-masters or the super-rich oligarchs who whisk by in their blacked-out limousines between the super-expensive restaurants and clubs that have sprung up to cocoon them from curious eyes. It's all mafia stuff, as far as everyone else is concerned. Even Grigori and Sergey use the term between long discussions on the latest twists and turns of the continuous Moscow power play.

But if the 'mafia' can keep on generating jobs and increasing Russia's prestige, then that'll do just fine. After all, life's good when the meat section of the supermarket has meat in it.

### Potemkin's Village

I like the story of Potemkin's Village. I'd heard the expression several times but never knew where it came from until I started researching for my trip to Russia.

The story goes that Grigori Potemkin was foreign minister, commander-in-chief and lover of Catherine the Great. He led the military campaign that resulted in the annexation of Crimea and organised a lavish thousand-mile trip down the Dnieper River for Catherine and her court to marvel at this addition to the Russian empire.

The Queen duly saw mile after mile of pristine villages and happy waving peasants and valued Potemkin even more highly.

But it was all a sham. Potemkin had constructed hollow wooden façades of villages all along the river banks of the royal party's journey. The 'happy villagers' were soldiers who were carted overnight to the next 'village' downstream to repeat their performance of feudal contentedness.

Thus was born the term 'Potemkin Village', now meaning a façade, either physical or figurative, concealing a less desirable reality.

The whole story is apparently a load of baloney but I like it even more for that. It makes it even more Russian. It's all about false projections and skewed reflections. Much of my time in Russia appears to have been the same. 'Don't judge a book by its cover' is the pithier English equivalent of Russia's Potemkin Village. And I have learnt many times in the last two weeks the wisdom of that particular adage. It's just that it's so damn difficult not to judge Russia by its cover.

Moscow is not a pretty city by any stretch of the imagination but I learnt to view its surface grey uniformity as an old mask that hides a rejuvenating face.

It prepared me, as Grigori had rightly predicted, to see Norilsk 'as a Russian'. Even after the Moscow acclimatisation I was blown away by the visual horror of our first journey into Norilsk. As was Grigori, it has to be said. The sheer Soviet-ness of the city itself simply adds a time distortion to what is already a sensory distortion.

Only when we started walking through the sets of anonymous padded doors did we get to see there was a warmer, more colourful human heart. The friendliness of the people, even those whom I suspect were not quite what they seemed, constantly surprised me. I started to get an inkling of what Simona had meant with her 'soulfulness' and the 'special relations between people here'.

But Russia is never going to let the visitor get away with a one-dimensional ride. Behind the walls of a count's residence we found a scene straight out of a James Bond film. In the middle of nowhere, which is where Norilsk literally is, we found an armed checkpoint with Russian police stopping traffic in the swirling snow. For every Uly, laughing uproariously as he tells his anecdotes from the old days, there is an Inquisitor, The Bear's 'friend', who looks so stern and takes his ten-pin bowling far more seriously than is normal.

Russia seems to delight in being so annoyingly enigmatic. There's almost a deliberate teasing of expectations, not dissimilar to the damn Cyrillic script with the letters that look like their counterparts in English but turn out to be something completely different.

But I know that I've filled out my own hollow construct of what Russia is like, even if I'm not sure how the parts fit together or whether some of them might be more façades.

I'm not claiming to be an expert on 'Russia' after such a short stay. I appreciate that the two places I've visited are among the wealthiest in the country. Lots of smiling, waving peasants! But the important thing is that I truly appreciate that now. My 'Russia' was in fact the 'Soviet Union'. I had just never got that pre-1989 map out of my head.

But 'Russia' is no longer Azerbaijan, Armenia, Ukraine, Uzbekistan. Nor does 'Russia' do much justice to 'Russia' either, just as 'America' doesn't capture the diversity of the Americans' self-descriptive 'United States'.

The official name is the Russian Federation and it has twenty-one autonomous republics and sixty-eight autonomous territories. It has many nationalities, each with its own tradition and history. It is split east from west by the Urals, a tectonic rift separating Europe from Asia and 'Russia' from Siberia. It's still learning how to fit all the parts back together in a new design.

I'm not embarrassed by my one-dimensional view of the country. I don't think it was my fault. It wasn't that I wasn't curious. It's just that prior to 1989 the Soviet Union wasn't exactly forthcoming.

Cities like Norilsk didn't officially exist back then. There were a lot of blanks on the map. Or maybe in Norilsk's case that should be even more than there still are.

Norilsk is the last place on earth I thought I'd ever get to visit. Which is why it was my choice as a Journey of a Lifetime. Until I actually got to Norilsk I hadn't fully understood just how much I was driven by the youthful desire to go there because I wasn't supposed to go there.

It was a secret city and it is now a secretive city. No one can just go there as if it were any other city. Only the gatekeepers can let you in. Just as only the gatekeepers could let you out in its first incarnation.

Once there you realise there are inner gates and compounds in this Arctic City. Once again, only the gatekeepers have the keys to let you in. Doors behind doors. Wheels within wheels.

We entered this alien city. We traipsed around its grim streets. We inhaled its stinking breath. Our eyes adjusted to its continuous murky twilight. We waited incarcerated in our cheap hotel rooms while the gatekeepers judged how much further we would be allowed to travel.

And all the time I was there I was as thrilled as if I'd just climbed Everest. I marvelled at the Soviet severity of its dark concrete lines. I was awed by the sci-fi sprawl of the mines, metals plants, writhing pipes and mysterious pools of black liquid. I chuckled when the full force of the Arctic wind struck me in the face as we rounded a street corner. I savoured the touch of the company's tentacles gradually encircling us, pulling us in towards it.

I was thrilled because I knew I shouldn't really have been there. Not so long ago I'd have been classified as an enemy. Not so long ago I don't think I would even have got into Russia, let alone one of its little secret hidey-holes. As for sharing coffee and camembert with these strangers from behind the Iron Curtain...!

I shouldn't have been there because there was nothing in my life for me ever to expect to be there. By my mid-thirties, as I was falling into the middle-England cocoon of contented affluent inertia, I had let youthful dreams of discovering hidden cities in strange climes slide away quietly with the passage of the years.

I've changed since then. I have strange dreams still. This one came true.

---

**Transcript.**
**Andy's Audio Journal.**
**Kitchen in Sergey's Moscow apartment.**

Andy: *Oh yes. One last thing. Here we are back in Moscow and a huge sense of déjà vu because... guess what?... we are STILL waiting to see the elusive Mr Khagazheev, the general manager of Norilsk Nickel in Soviet times, The Legend who build Nadezhda, blah, blah, blah.*
*I have to say that at this stage I am pretty convinced we are not going to see him and to some extent I think that's*

*quite fitting.*

*It would almost have been disappointing had we been able to access all the people that we wanted to see. It wouldn't somehow have been quite in keeping with the city of Norilsk and its history.*

*I've ended up quite admiring him for his ability to hold out against really quite extensive pressure applied in various Machiavellian ways by Sergey and his mates.*

*I quite admire him being the unreconstructed Soviet man that he is. Grigori's got very annoyed with him and feels that he's been playing games with us and all that, and he's been cursing him most of the day. Me? Well, I'll take my hat off to him and why not? I'm almost pleased that we never got to see him in the end.*

Johnson Khagazheev officially informs us one day before we are due to fly back to London that he will not be able to grant an interview to the BBC.

[i]Johnson Matthey. Platinum Review 2003

[ii]White House press release, February 2003. 'Remarks by the President on Energy Independence' given at the National Building Museum, Washington D.C.

[iii]From the company's website. 'About our investment in Stillwater Mining Company'

[iv]White House press release, 1 June 2003. 'President Bush, Russian President Putin Sign Treaty of Moscow.'

# POSTSCRIPT

# POSTSCRIPT

On re-reading some of the original transcripts from our time in Norilsk, I am surprised by how paranoid I became about the company in such a short period of time. I wonder whether it was down to the undoubted alien feel of the place or the fact that I found it so hard to sleep properly in the twenty-four-hour daylight.

But in researching this book I came across the following reference in the company's charter of what constitutes its areas of business (see Appendix III). 'Work related to the use of information constituting a state secret, protection of information containing a state secret, and/or providing services to protect a state secret.'

And now I'm not sure again.

Since our visit in 2003 and the publication of this book in 2006, the company itself and some of the key characters in this book have taken further big turns in the course of their lives.

## Norilsk Nickel

Norilsk's move to buy a twenty per cent stake in Gold Fields Ltd provoked something of an unseemly corporate fisticuffs between several gold producers for control of the company. In the end the South African giant managed to fend off various unwelcome advances, most of them instigated by its new shareholders. By the middle of 2005 some sort of tentative peace deal had been negotiated. Ian Cockerill, the chief executive officer of Gold Fields, told the press that Norilsk is 'very much at the centre of some of the strategic thinking of Gold Fields and we look forward to their contribution in that process.' As a peace token Gold Fields offered Norilsk two seats on its board.

Norilsk Nickel evidently had other plans though, transferring all of its gold investments into a new company called Polyus Gold. This then sold the Gold Fields stake in March 2006 for a cool $2 billion, netting close to $1 billion from the investment just as Norilsk was preparing to spin its new daughter off into a separate company. The result was that Polyus was poised at the time of writing to step onto the international stage of major league gold producers with plentiful cash in hand to continue its own aggressive expansion policy in other directions.

It looks like the Interros Group has given Putin not one but two championship league players.

Norilsk Nickel and the Interros Group, meanwhile, have formed a joint venture entity called Smart Hydrogen to pioneer the coming hydrogen revolution, powered of course by the palladium and platinum it produces in such abundant quantities. The new creation's first move in April 2006 was to grab a thirty-five per cent stake in Plug Power, a US company at the cutting edge of fuel cell technology.

The Siberian Dream is evidently alive and kicking.

### Dmitry Zelenin

Apparently fulfilling Grigori's forecasts, Dmitry Zelenin was elected governor of the Tver Region of Russia in December 2003.

Tver will be a challenge even greater than Norilsk. One of the largest regions in European Russia with a population of 1.7 million, it lies between Moscow and St Petersburg and is something of a basket case even by modern Russian standards. With no natural resources to speak of, some forty-four per cent of its population lives below the poverty line and the mortality rate is currently running at three times the birth rate.

*The Diplomat* magazine nicely summed up the issues facing Zelenin. 'If Tver can become a success story, then lessons learned here can be exported to other regions. But if Tver continues to stagnate, Russia's other resource-poor regions can take cold comfort.'

Zelenin has taken the unprecedented step of inviting the United Nations to help him revive the region. From UNICEF to the United Nations Development Program, the international agency has responded, claiming Tver will be a focal point for its efforts across Russia.

There are plans to turn the road linking Moscow and St Petersburg into a 'Russian Heritage Highway', showcasing the travels of Russia's famous nineteenth-century writer Alexander Pushkin. The former head of tourism for the state of Nevada in America has been hired to advise Tver on the project.

## Vitaly Bobrov

At the beginning of 2004 Vitaly Bobrov left his position as head of the Polar Division of Norilsk Nickel to become vice governor of the Krasnoyarsk Area Administration, working under his former Norilsk boss, Alexander Khloponin. He is now responsible for the fuel and power sectors, the alcohol market, financial reorganization of bankrupt companies, telecommunications and 'the co-ordination of Northern life', meaning primarily Norilsk itself.

He gave an interview to the Norilsk Nickel house magazine about his new job. Jokingly he told the interviewer he has not yet used the fireplace in his official residence on the bank of the Yenisey, preferring to go and sit outside on his favourite 'bench with a fir-tree'.

## Valery Melnikov

Melnikov was allowed to stand again for new mayoral elections in October. The local elections committee was left with little choice when the other three candidates withdrew their nominations, apparently in solidarity with him against the blatant political interference in the May elections.

The authorities reacted by fielding their own candidate, none other than our good friend Johnson Khagazheev, in the hope that The Legend could still command enough affection with the population to defeat the troublesome Melnikov.

The strategy didn't work. Melnikov received fifty-one per cent of the vote with Khagazheev trailing in second position with thirty-four per cent. The committee waited until the stroke of midnight before reluctantly declaring Melnikov the winner. Even then it said it would be investigating him further for a breach of campaigning rules and tried to get the election annulled. It didn't succeed.

After his brief foray into the world of politics Khagazheev resumed working for Norilsk Nickel. In March 2004 he was put in charge of the company's non-core activities and became vice president of the company.

## The Lesser White Fronted Goose
The famous goose has become the symbol of Norilsk Nickel's ecological programme and is the centrepiece of the company's new 'green' logo.

# APPENDIX I

## The Interros Group

On its website Interros describes itself as 'one of the biggest private investment companies in Russia' with assets under management valued at $10 billion and employing over 190,000 people.

The business empire of one man, oligarch Vladimir Potanin, it grew out of a foreign trade company established in 1990.

In 1992, a bank, MFK, was acquired after an evaluation of 'the development prospects of the financial market during the transition period'. The foreign trade activities were spun off into a new company, The United Export and Import Bank, UNEXIMBANK for short.

In the mid-1990s, UNEXIMBANK acquired stakes in several huge Soviet behemoths through the loans-for-shares schemes.

The Interros company itself was set up in 1998 to assume responsibility for the bank's sprawling industrial holdings. Its functions included 'corporate restructuring, anti-crisis management, investment strategy development, financial control and personnel training'.

Having survived Russia's second economic spasm in 1998, when the rouble was devalued by some seventy per cent, Interros dumped most of its assets except Norilsk Nickel and began acquiring new ones. The indebted UNEXIMBANK was transformed into a new bank, Rosbank, which through further acquisitions has grown into one of Russia's biggest banks.

Its arms spread throughout Russian society.

In 2001, the Agros group was set up to consolidate Interros' growing agricultural business. Agros is one of Russia's biggest suppliers of grain, cereals, pasta and poultry.

In 2002, the Silovye Machiniy (Power Machines) group was created from the merger of Interros' extensive interests in turbine manufacture and power plant construction. It is now Russia's biggest supplier of power-generation equipment and exports to eighty-nine countries.

Later the same year, the disarmingly innocuous sounding Open Investments company was formed through the concentration of Interros' extensive property interests. The company is focused on residential property in and around Moscow, commercial properties and retail parks.

Through its Prof-Media arm, Interros controls well-known Russian newspapers such as *Izvestiya* and *The Moscow Times* and a host of glossy magazines, making it the biggest publisher in the Russian language. It owns radio stations in Moscow and St Petersburg and has recently been building cinema multiplexes in the country's big cities.

The Novogor company runs public utilities, most noticeably the water and sewage infrastructure of the city of Perm (population: 1.1 million).

The Roza Khutor subsidiary is building an Olympic-quality ski resort in the far south of the country near the Black Sea holiday location of Sochi.

For good measure, the chairman of the board of trustees of Russia's famous Hermitage museum is Potanin.

Potanin, a former deputy prime minister of Russia and a blueblood among the country's oligarchs, is president of the Interros Group.

Like Potanin, Andrei Bougrov, managing director of Interros, graduated from the elite former Communist Party finishing school, the Moscow State Institute of International Relations. He worked at the Soviet Union's permanent mission to the UN, was Russia's representative at the World Bank and is currently a member of the country's Council on Foreign and Defence Policy.

Potanin's brief curriculum vitae on the Interros website notes he is fluent in English and French. Bougrov is fluent in English and Arabic, the latter and his schooling giving some hint as to why he is on the country's Defence Policy Council.

Serguey Barbashev is deputy general director of Interros. Born in 1961, the same year as Potanin, he served in the Soviet army until 1984 and then in the Ministry of Interior armed forces until 1991, in the process graduating through the Moscow Higher School of Militia.

The impeccable credentials of the three most senior officers of Interros give them an unusually high degree of insight into the obscure workings of Russia's power structures and may go some way to explaining why Potanin remains a powerhouse in the country's economy, unlike fellow oligarch Roman Abramovich, who has redirected his interests to Chelsea Football Club, and Mikhail Khodorkovsky, who was arrested late in 2003 on charges of fraud and tax evasion (see Chapter Eight).

# APPENDIX II

## Metals from Norilsk

### Nickel

Physical and chemical characteristics:
Latin name Niccolum (Ni)
Chemical element of Group VIII in Mendeleev's periodic Table
Atomic number 28
Atomic weight 58.71
Density 8.90 g/cmi
Melting point 1,453°C
Very resistant to the effects of air and water

History: Nickel was discovered in 1751. As recently as 100 years ago, it was still considered to be a worthless variety of copper. The name of the metal comes from the German name given to an evil spirit who was reputed to interfere with the work of copper and silver miners.

Uses: Around sixty-five per cent of nickel is used as an alloy in the production of stainless steel. Stainless steel has many industrial and construction applications but is most commonly associated with home products such as pots, pans and kitchen sinks. Another twenty per cent of nickel is used in the production of 'special' steels and 'super' alloys with a wide range of specialised applications in the aerospace and military industries. Around nine per cent is used in plating and another six per cent in other applications, particularly coins.

Norilsk: Norilsk Nickel produced 239,000 tonnes of nickel in 2003, making it the world's largest producer and giving it an estimated twenty per cent share of global production.

## Copper

Physical and chemical characteristics:
Latin name Cuprum (Cu)
Chemical element of Group VIII in Mendeleev's Periodic Table
Atomic number 29
Atomic Weight 63.546
Density 8.96 g/cmi
Melting point 1,083°C

History: Copper is one of the metals first used by man in the form of its alloy with tin – bronze. Its name derives from the Latin for Cyprus, where the Romans mined much of their copper needs. Brass, an alloy of copper and zinc, came into general use later and both alloys have remained ubiquitous in human life every since.

Uses: Copper is still used in a host of consumer goods from decorative brass to keys to coins. It also remains a material of choice for many plumbing applications. But its electrical conductivity qualities has seen demand surge with the onset of the electronic revolution of the late twentieth century and it is now one of the most-in-demand metals, used in everything from power transmission cables to telephone lines to silicon chips.

Norilsk: Norilsk Nickel produced 450,000 tonnes of copper in 2003, meaning it accounted for 3.3 per cent of total world production.

## Cobalt

Physical and chemical characteristics:
Latin name: Cobaltum (Co)
Chemical element of Group VIII in Mendeleev's Periodic Table
Atomic number 27
Atomic weight 58.9
Density 8.85 r/cm3
Melting point 1,493°C

History: Cobalt was used in the colouring of ceramics in ancient times but its modern name derives from Medieval

German. It was applied to 'gnomes' living in the Schneeberg mountains in Germany and, like nickel, blamed for problems in the mining of silver. Until the twentieth century, the only application for cobalt was in the colouring of paints.

Uses: As well as still being used as colouring for glass and ceramics, cobalt has a wide range of uses in modern industry. It is a major component of 'super' alloys used in jet engines and turbines, high-speed steels such as those for cutting instruments, and magnetic steels. It has long been a subject of research in weapons programmes, although no country has publicly admitted to developing the 'cobalt bomb', often dubbed 'the doomsday weapon'.

Norilsk: Norilsk Nickel does not include its cobalt production in its annual report but is estimated by the Cobalt Development Institute to have produced just over 4,500 tonnes in 2003, giving it just over ten per cent of global output.

## Platinum

Physical and chemical characteristics:
Latin name Platinum (Pt)
Chemical element of Group VIII in Mendeleev's Periodic Table
Atomic number 78
Atomic weight 195.08
Density 21.45 g/sm3
Melting point 1,769°C

History: Platinum was used, often together with gold, by the ancient Egyptians and by the pre-Inca South Americans but its modern history dates from the Conquistadors' invasion of South America. They gave it the derogatory name 'platina', meaning 'little silver' and initially discarded it as worthless. However, its popularity grew among alchemists in the eighteenth century, and in 1751 Swedish scientist Theophil Sheffer categorised it as belonging to the precious metals family. With this seal of approval it was swiftly adopted by Europe's royal families. In 1795 it was used as the basis for the metric system introduced by the French in the wake of the Revolution because of its durability.

Uses: Jewellery now accounts for around thirty-eight per cent of platinum use, marginally overshadowed by its forty per cent use in catalytic converters. These convert the noxious fumes from the vehicle engine into less harmful carbon dioxide, nitrogen and water vapour. Over eighty-five per cent of all the vehicles produced around the world each year are now fitted with catalytic converters. Platinum is also a key component in computer hard disks and is essential in the manufacture of pacemakers.

Norilsk: Norilsk Nickel is still not allowed to divulge details of its platinum production since the information is classified by Russia as a state secret. However, the authority on the subject is the Johnson Matthey Group which estimates that in 2003 the company supplied over one million ounces of the metal, giving it an implied seventeen per cent share of the world market. Including Stillwater Mining in the United States, in which Norilsk bought a controlling stake early in 2003, the figure rises to around nineteen per cent.

## Palladium

Physical and chemical characteristics:
Latin name Palladium (Pd)
Chemical element of Group VIII in Mendeleev's Periodic Table
Atomic number 46
Atomic Weight 106.42
Density 12.02 g/cm
Melting point 1,554°C

History: Palladium was isolated as a metal in 1803 by the British scientist William Hyde-Woollaston who named it after Pallas, the asteroid that had been discovered the year before. For many years it was the poor sister of platinum and only started to be used for dentistry in the 1930s. But in the 1970s its use rocketed with the invention of the catalytic converter in cars.

Uses: The automotive sector now accounts for over half of all palladium used. It is also used in tiny quantities in circuit boards for computers and in mobile phones. It remains a mainstay of the dentistry profession and is often alloyed with platinum for jewellery.

Norilsk: As with platinum, Russian secrecy laws do not allow Norilsk Nickel to disclose how much palladium it produces. But the authority on the subject is the Johnson Matthey Group which estimates that Norilsk accounted for 2,950,000 ounces of supply in 2003, giving it an implied global market share of forty-six per cent. The figure rises to above fifty per cent of world production if Stillwater Mining in the US is included. Norilsk bought a majority stake in Stillwater in the first half of 2003.

## Rhodium

Physical and chemical characteristics:
Latin name Rhodium (Rh)
Chemical element of Group VIII in Mendeleev's Periodic Table
Atomic number 45
Atomic weight 102.9055
Density 12.41 g/cmi
Melting point 1,963°C

History: Rhodium was discovered by the British scientist William Hyde-Woollaston in 1804, one year after he discovered palladium. Rhodium gets its name from the Greek 'rhodon', which means 'rose', on account of the pinkish red colour of its salts.

Uses: Rhodium is used in alloys with platinum and palladium in catalytic converters in vehicles. It has a range of other eclectic uses, from headlight reflectors to airplane sparkplugs.

Norilsk: Like the rest of the platinum group metals produced by Norilsk Nickel, the company is prohibited from divulging its production by Russian state secrecy laws. However, Johnson Matthey estimates Norilsk Nickel supplied 140,000 ounces in 2003, equivalent to just over nineteen per cent of global production.

## Iridium

Physical and chemical characteristics:
Latin name Iridium (Ir)
Chemical element of Group VIII in Mendeleev's Periodic Table
Atomic number 77
Atomic weight 192.22, a platinum group metal
Density 22.65 g/cmi
Melting point 2,447°C

History: Iridium is a platinum group metal, produced only as a by-product. William Hyde-Woollaston was evidently bored with finding new metals by 1804 so he handed over the baton to his commercial partner, Smithson Tennant, a fellow Cambridge scientist, who discovered iridium later that year. He named it iridium after the Latin for rainbow, 'iris', due to its multi-coloured compounds. It is the second densest metal after osmium. It is also extremely rare. Total world production is less than a tonne every year.

Uses: Its first use was a hardening element in fountain pen tips. As a component of alloys it is now used to make crucibles and other very high-temperature apparatus for the laboratory.

## Ruthenium

Physical and chemical characteristics:
Latin name Ruthenium (Ru)
Chemical element of Group VIII Mendeleev's Periodic Table
Atomic number 44
Atomic weight 101.07
Density of 12.37 g/sm3
Melting point 2,250°C

History: Ruthenium is another of the platinum group metals. It was named after the Latin for Russia, 'ruthenia', because it was first identified by two Swedish scientists from a platinum ore sourced from Russia's Ural region. In 1844, Russian professor Karl Karlovich Klaus obtained a pure sample from the oxide, and ruthenium became the last of the platinum group metals to be isolated.

Uses: Ruthenium is used as a hardening agent for platinum and palladium alloys. The addition of 0.1 per cent ruthenium to titanium increases its corrosion resistance by a hundred times. Specialist applications in industrial applications and for chemical reactions.

## Gold

Physical and chemical characteristics:
Latin name Aurum (Au)
Chemical element of Group I in Mendeleev's Periodic Table
Atomic number 79
Atomic weight 196.9665
Density 19.32 g/cm3
Melting point 1,064.4°C
A precious yellow metal, malleable

History: The Latin word 'aurum' means 'glowing dawn', which is apt because its lustre has attracted men from the very earliest times. The fact that it does not react with either oxygen or water gives it an immutable quality which has made it the key form of currency in trade for most of mankind's history.

Uses: Gold has a number of commonly known uses, particularly jewellery and dentistry. It also has applications in industry, but the simple fact is that most of the gold ever mined lies in bank vaults around the world as a store of wealth held by governments and individuals.

Norilsk: Norilsk Nickel was a relatively small producer of gold, which was a by-product of mining other metals, until it bought Polyus, Russia's biggest gold mining company, in November 2002. Its production shot up from 132,000 ounces in 2001 to 968,000 ounces in 2003. Through a series of further acquisitions among the country's fragmented mining community, it could rank itself among the world's biggest ten producers by the end of 2003.

## Silver

Physical and chemical characteristics:
Latin name Argentum (Ag)
Chemical element of Group I in Mendeleev's Periodic Table
Nuclear number 47
Nuclear weight 107,8682
Density of 10,5 g/sm3
Melting Point 961.9°C

History: Silver, like its classier big sister gold, has been known since ancient times. Like gold, it has been used for jewellery and as coinage throughout man's history. It preceded gold as the standard on which 'money' was valued for Europe between the sixteenth and nineteenth centuries.

Uses: As with gold, silver is used extensively in jewellery and dentistry and remains the favoured store of wealth in countries such as India and China. Its key commercial use remains photography although its role in traditional film is under attack from the recent boom in digital photography.

Norilsk: Norilsk Nickel is a relatively small producer of silver, even its Polyus subsidiary being overshadowed by the much bigger new Russian producer, Polymetal.

# APPENDIX III

## The Business of Norilsk Nickel

The following is an excerpt from the company charter of Norilsk Nickel, approved by the board of directors in 2002. The charter is available at the company's website.

The list rewards a close read in terms of the scope of the company's activities.

## 2. BUSINESS OF THE COMPANY

<u>2.1</u> The main goal of the Company is to make profit.

<u>2.2</u> The main types of Company business are as follows:
• Exploration, investigation and exploitation of mineral deposits;
• Building, operation and repair of objects located on the surface and in underground mines and structures, designed for exploration, investigation and operation of mineral deposits, extraction and refining of ores and other minerals;
• Development of design and technical documentation related to operating mining works and objects;
• Operation and repair of equipment, driving machinery and communication equipment, transportation means and equipment ensuring safety of production and personnel;
• Blasting works;
• Operation of permanent warehouses storing explosives and of distribution chambers;
• Ore enrichment, transportation of ore concentrate using waterways, operation of hydro-technical structures;
• Sale of metals obtained through ore processing;
• Sale of ore and ore concentrates;
• Metallurgical processing of ore, ore concentrate,

secondary non-ferrous and precious metals, production of products from non-ferrous and precious metals, production of sulphur, vitriolic acid;

• Production, transfer, distribution and sale of electrical and heat energy;

• Storage of petroleum and refined petroleum products;

• Operation of surface and underground water supply, systems of industrial-drinking water supply and water circulation;

• Production and sale of technical and technological oxygen;

• Operation and maintenance of telephone and radio relay communication systems;

• Maintenance and operation of petroleum bulk plants, petroleum stations, including mobile filling stations;

• Assembly, adjustment and operation of energy supplying electro-thermal and energy equipment and devices for the consumers;

• Transportation, forwarding and other activities related to sea, domestic waterways and air transportation;

• Passenger and cargo transportation using automobile and railroad networks;

• Construction, reconstruction, repair works, maintenance of automobiles and railroads and roadway structures;

• Works and services in the area of nature preservation;

• Fire safety activities;

• Work related to the use of information constituting a state secret, protection of information containing a state secret, and/or providing services to protect a state secret;

• Development of town-planning documents;

• Architectural activities;

• Sanatorium and resort services, health and medical services;

• Planning and survey work, including work related to the use of land;

• Topographic & geodesic and cartographic work during construction activities;

• Engineering & survey work in connection with

construction, design and assembly of buildings and structures with levels I & II of responsibility;

•Operation of engineering systems in towns and populated areas;

•Manufacture of construction materials, structures and objects;

•Educational services in the area of middle, high and post-vocational professional and appropriate additional education;

•Refining of precious metals;

•Buying from the public of jewelry and other consumer items made of precious metals and stones, and buying scrap of such metals;

•Processing of scrap and waste of precious metals into final products;

•Geological and survey work, drawing up and publishing of geological maps, including digital and electronic maps;

•Geophysical (including gravimetric) works for the study of earth's subsoil;

•Drilling of holes for water, and geological and exploratory holes for hard and other minerals;

Production, distillery, storage, wholesale and retail sale of ready alcoholic goods;

•Operational and exploration drilling of holes;

•Extraction and transportation of natural gas and gas condensate;

•Processing of gas and gas condensate;

•Export and import activities, in the procedure established by the legislation of the Russian Federation;

•Investment of Company's working capital and raised funds including currency resources into joint ventures with Russian and foreign organizations, companies and citizens, including the creation of subsidiary and dependent enterprises in both Russia and abroad;

•Construction of oil & gas mainlines;

•Design of factories and objects for oil and gas industry;

•Operation of oil & gas mainlines;

- Construction of factories and objects of the gas industry;
- Operation of factories and objects of the gas industry;
- Repair and assembly of oil and gas drilling equipment;
- Preparation of staff (main professions) for potentially dangerous industrial factories and objects;
- Assembly of equipment at factories for explosive and fire hazardous materials;
- Repair of equipment at factories for explosive and fire hazardous materials.

# About Eye Books

Eye Books is a dynamic, young publishing company that likes to break the rules. Our independence allows us to publish books which challenge the way people see things. It also means that we can offer new authors a platform from which they can shine their light and encourage others to do the same.

To date we have published 60 books that cover a number of genres including Travel, Biography, Adventure, Reference and History. Many of our books are experience driven. All of them are inspirational and life affirming.

Frigid Women, for example, tells the story of the world-record-creating first all-female expedition to the North Pole. Sue Riches, a fifty-year-old mother of three who had recently recovered from a mastectomy, and her daughter Victoria are the authors – neither had ever written a book before. Sue Riches is now a writer and highly-sought-after motivational speaker.

We also publish thematic anthologies, such as The Tales from Heaven and Hell series, for those who prefer the short story format. Here everyone has the chance to get their stories published and win prizes such as flights to any destination in the world.

And here's what makes us really different: As well as publishing books, Eye Books has set up a club for like-minded people and is in the process of developing a number of initiatives and services for its community of members. After all, the more you put into life, the more you get out of it.

Please visit www.eye-books.com for further information.

# Eye Club Membership

Each month, we receive hundreds of enquiries from people who have read our books, discovered our website or entered our competitions. All these people have certain things in common: a desire to achieve, to extend the boundaries of everyday life and to learn from others' experiences.

Eye Books has, therefore, set up a club to unite these like-minded people. It is a community where members can exchange ideas, contact authors, discuss travel, both future and past, as well as receive information and offers from Eye Books.

Membership is free.

# Benefits of the Eye Club

As a member of the Eye Club:

• You are offered the invaluable opportunity to contact our authors directly.
• You will receive a regular newsletter, information on new book releases and company developments as well as discounts on new and past titles.
• You can attend special member events such as book launches, author talks and signings.
• Receive discounts on a variety of travel-related products and services from Eye Books' partners.
• You can enjoy entry into Eye Books competitions including the ever popular Heaven and Hell series and our monthly book competition.
To register your membership, simply visit our website and register on our club pages: www.eye-books.com.

# 2006 Titles

Fateful Beauty – The Story of Frances Coke 1602-1642
– Natalie Hodgson
Fateful Beauty is the true story of a young woman who, at the age of 15, was forced to marry a mentally unstable man in order to fulfil the wishes of her ambitious father. It is well researched and gives a vivid picture of life at this time - political intrigue, life at court, civil war, and family and personal trauma.
ISBN 1 903070 406. £12.99.

On the Wall with Hadrian – Bob Bibby
Newly opened Hadrian's Wall path, 84 miles (135km), stretches from coast to coast and inspired travel writer Bob Bibby to don his boots and traverse the scenic and historical route. The book gives insight into Hadrian, his people and his times along with an up-to-date guide on where to visit, stay, eat and drink.
ISBN 9781903070499. £9.99.

The Good Life Gets Better– Dorian Amos
The sequel to the bestselling book about leaving the UK for a new life in the Yukon, Dorian and his growing family get gold fever, start to stake land and prospect for gold. Follow them along the learning curve about where to look for gold and how to live in this harsh climate. It shows that with good humour and resilience life can only get better.
ISBN 9781903070482. £9.99.

Changing the World. One step at a time –
Michael Meegan
Many people say they want to make a difference but don't
know how. This offers examples of real people making
real differences. It reminds us to see the joy and love in
every moment of every day. And that making a difference
is something everyone can do.
ISBN 978 1903070 444 £9.99

Prickly Pears of Palestine – Hilda Reilly
The Palestinian/Israeli conflict is one of the most widely
reported and long standing struggles in the world yet
misunderstood by many. Author Hilda Reilly spent time
living and working in the region to put some human
flesh on these bare stereotypical bones and try and make
the situation comprehensible for the bewildered news
consumer.
ISBN 9781903070529. £9.99.

# Also by Eye Books

**Zohra's Ladder – Pamela Windo**
A wondrous collection of stories of Moroccan life
that offer a privileged immersion into a world of deep
sensuality.
ISBN 1 903070 406. £9.99.

**Great Sects – Adam Hume Kelly**
Essential insights into sects for the intellectually curious
– from Kabbalah to Dreamtime, Druidry to Opus Dei.
ISBN: 1903070 473. £9.99.

**Blood Sweat & Charity – Nick Stanhope**
The guide to charity challenges.
ISBN: 1 903070 414. £12.99.

**Death – The Great Mystery of Life – Herbie Brennan**
A compulsive study, its effect is strangely liberating and
life enhancing.
ISBN: 1 903070 422. Price £9.99.

**Riding the Outlaw Trail – Simon Casson**
An equine expedition retracing the footsteps of those
legendary real-life bandits, Butch Cassidy and the
Sundance Kid.
ISBN: 1 903070 228. Price £9.99.

**Green Oranges on Lion Mountain – Emily Joy**
A VSO posting in Sierra Leone where adventure and
romance were on the agenda; rebel forces and threat of
civil war were not.
ISBN: 1 903070 295. Price £9.99.

**Desert Governess – Phyllis Ellis**
A former Benny Hill Show actress becomes a governess
to the Saudi Arabian Royal Family.
ISBN: 1 903070 015. Price £9.99.

**Last of the Nomads – W. J. Peasley**
The story of the last of the desert nomads to live
permanently in the traditional way in Western Australia.
ISBN: 1 903070 325. Price £9.99.

**All Will Be Well – Michael Meegan**
A book about how love and compassion when given out
to others can lead to contentment.
ISBN: 1 903070 279. Price £9.99.

**First Contact – Mark Anstice**
A 21st-century discovery of cannibals.
Comes with (free) DVD which won the Banff Film
Festival, and features Bruce Parry of *Tribes*
ISBN: 1 903070 260. Price £9.99.

**Further Travellers' Tales From Heaven and Hell – Various**
This is the third book in the series of real travellers tales.
ISBN: 1 903070 112. Price £9.99.

**Special Offa – Bob Bibby**
A walk along Offa's Dyke.
ISBN: 1 903070 287. Price £9.99.

**The Good Life – Dorian Amos**
A move from the UK to start a new life in the wilderness
of The Yukon.
ISBN: 1 903070 309. Price £9.99.

**Baghdad Business School – Heyrick Bond Gunning**
The realities of a business start-up in a war zone.
ISBN: 1 903070 333. Price £9.99.

**The Accidental Optimist's Guide to Life – Emily Joy**
Having just returned from Sierra Leone, a busy GP with a
growing family ponders the meaning of life.
ISBN: 1 903070 430. Price £9.99.

**The Con Artist Handbook – Joel Levy**
Get wise as this blows the lid on the secrets of the
successful con artist and his con games.
ISBN: 1 903070 341. Price £9.99.

The Forensics Handbook – Pete Moore
The most up-to-date log of forensic techniques available.
ISBN: 1 903070 35X. Price £9.99.

My Journey With A Remarkable Tree – Ken Finn
A journey following an illegally logged tree from a spirit
forest to the furniture corner of a garden centre.
ISBN: 1 903070 384. Price £9.99.

Seeking Sanctuary – Hilda Reilly
Western Muslim converts living in Sudan.
ISBN: 1 903070 392. Price £9.99.

Lost Lands Forgotten Stories – Alexandra Pratt
The retracing of an astonishing 600 mile river journey in
1905 in 2005.
ISBN: 1 903070 368. Price £9.99.

Jasmine and Arnica – Nicola Naylor
A blind woman's journey around India.
ISBN: 1 903070 171. Price £9.99.

Touching Tibet – Niema Ash
A journey into the heart of this intriguing forbidden land.
ISBN: 1 903070 18X. Price £9.99.

Behind the Veil – Lydia Laube
A shocking account of a nurse's Arabian nightmare.
ISBN: 1 903070 198. Price £9.99.

Walking Away – Charlotte Metcalf
A well-known film maker's African journal.
ISBN: 1 903070 201. Price £9.99.

Travels in Outback Australia – Andrew Stevenson
In search of the original Australians – the Aboriginal
People.
ISBN: 1 903070 147. Price £9.99.

The European Job – Jonathan Booth
10,000 miles around Europe in a 25-year-old classic car.
ISBN: 1 903070 252. Price £9.99.

Around the World with 1000 Birds – Russell Boyman
An extraordinary answer to a mid-life crisis.
ISBN: 1 903070 163. Price £9.99.

Cry from the Highest Mountain – Tess Burrows
A climb to the point furthest from the centre of the earth.
ISBN: 1 903070 120. Price £9.99.

Triumph Round the World – Robbie Marshall
He gave up his world for the freedom of the road.
ISBN: 1 903070 08 2. Price £7.99.

Fever Trees of Borneo – Mark Eveleigh
A daring expedition through uncharted jungle.
ISBN: 0 953057 56 9. Price £7.99.

Discovery Road – Tim Garrett and Andy Brown
Their mission was to mountain bike around the world.
ISBN: 0 953057 53 4. Price £7.99.

Frigid Women – Sue and Victoria Riches
The first all-female expedition to the North Pole.
ISBN: 0 953057 52 6. Price £7.99.

Jungle Beat – Roy Follows
Fighting terrorists in Malaya.
ISBN: 0 953057 57 7. Price £7.99.

Slow Winter – Alex Hickman
A personal quest against the backdrop of the war-torn
Balkans.
ISBN: 0 953057 58 5. Price £7.99.

Tea for Two – Polly Benge
She cycled around India to test her love.
ISBN: 0 953057 59 3. Price £7.99.

Traveller's Tales from Heaven and Hell – Various
A collection of short stories drawn from a nationwide
competition.
ISBN:  0 953057 51 8. Price £6.99.

More Traveller's Tales from Heaven and Hell – Various
A second collection of short stories.
ISBN: 1 903070 02 3. Price £6.99.

A Trail of Visions: Route 1 – Vicki Couchman
A stunning photographic essay.
ISBN: 1 871349 338. Price £14.99.

A Trail of Visions: Route 2 – Vicki Couchman
A second stunning photographic essay.
ISBN: 0 953057 50 X. Price £16.99.